Forest Communities, Community Forests

Forest Communities, Community Forests

EDITED BY JONATHAN KUSEL AND ELISA ADLER

ROWMAN & LITTLEFIELD PUBLISHERS, INC.
Lanham • Boulder • New York • Oxford

ROWMAN & LITTLEFIELD PUBLISHERS, INC.

Published in the United States of America
by Rowman & Littlefield Publishers, Inc.
A Member of the Rowman & Littlefield Publishing Group
4501 Forbes Boulevard, Suite 200, Lanham, Maryland 20706
www.rowmanlittlefield.com

PO Box 317
Oxford
OX2 9RU, UK

British Library Cataloguing in Publication Information Available

Library of Congress Cataloging-in-Publication Data

Forest communities, community forests / edited by Jonathan Kusel and Elisa Adler.
    p. cm.
   Includes bibliographical references and index.
   ISBN 0-7425-2584-8 (alk. paper) — ISBN 0-7425-2585-6 (pbk. : alk. paper)
   1. Community forests—United States—Case studies. 2. Forest management—United
States—Citizen participation—Case studies. I. Kusel, Jonathan. II. Adler, Elisa.
   SD565.F538 2003
   333.75'0973—dc21   2003001920

Printed in the United States of America

♾️™ The paper used in this publication meets the minimum requirements of American
National Standard for Information Sciences—Permanence of Paper for Printed Library
Materials, ANSI/NISO Z39.48-1992.

Contents

Foreword

Finding a Cafeteria of Possibility in an Array of Community Forestry Case Studies

My chance to review these twelve excellent case studies happens at a most opportune time. Current efforts in the United States to reduce public participation in decisions about public forests returns us to the practices of favoring a few at the expense of communities and the environment. I strongly suspect that many traditional foresters in and out of public agencies support this reduction in public participation as a return to the authority of professional foresters. In Nepal, a nearly two-decades-long push to return many important management plans and decisions about public forests to community groups is now having the forest service there seeking "to take back" these lands. It is interesting that many of these lands sought by the agency were lands decimated under their prior control and were re-greened under village and community management. Over the past two years, I had a John Eadie Fellowship from the Scottish Forestry Trust to examine public participation in forest matters in Scotland, England, and Wales that permitted me to see and experience the great flourishing of community-based forest management happening in city, suburb, and country, most of which was being ignored (except for proclamations that "forestry is for people") by the traditional forestry training and educational establishment in Britain.

These case studies reflect one trend in forestry as it is actually practiced and one that greatly contrasts with forestry as it is researched and taught in North America and around the world. Indeed, the general closing or loss of traditional forestry programs, such as those at Duke, Oxford, and elsewhere, suggests a profession in decline. In many universities, the profession is simply being absorbed into vague programs, such as bioscience, global environmental policy, environmental science, or schools of the environment (an emergent tendency at the oldest continuous forestry program in the United States: Yale University). In developing regions of the Southern Hemisphere, similar trends are playing out, and the global challenge is to provide a revitalized forestry that captures broader and more idealistic ecological hopes and public service attitudes. This twenty-first-century approach is not unlike the 1960s and 1970s hopes of Jack Westoby and some of his UN Food and Agricultural Organization (FAO) colleagues. Westoby and his small band of supporters wanted to move forestry from being an enemy of the people to being a supporter for achieving broad human aspirations, particularly those of the poor.

Further, the shift in scientific and public expectations about forestry has been away from the traditional desire for maximizing timber or biomass productivity and toward an emphasis on maximizing the production of biodiversity and sustaining ecosystem health. Let me underline the significance of this worldwide shift in emphasis—it is a move from prime attention on a few tree species of high commercial value to an ecosystem approach that covers the entire forest system and its potential for producing multiple goods, benefits, and services, many of which have no direct market price or value. It is strongly dependent on a significant sense of (and often an actual) community ownership, involvement and participation in policy, and planning and management of their nearby forest ecosystem.

These trends do not mean that those foresters who continue to maximize biomass production are not important. With a growing human population and its habitat being more and more in urbanized areas, the need for woody fiber and the finished products it can provide assures a steady and increasing demand for wood. However, the changing technologies of wood chemistry and adhesives and genetics mean that nearly any woody vegetation, from hemp to hazel, is a potential source of useful biomass. This is likely to mean less need for traditional field silviculturalists, except those who can translate their skills to increasing the production of biodiversity in forested ecosystems. The challenge to academics and researchers is to retain biomass technical improvements and to complement these traditional commercial activities with an emergent set of community–forest ecosystem management practices that emphasize native and multipurpose trees, woodlands, and forest ecosystems that provide a wide and ever expanding array of goods, benefits, and services. The interesting fact is that throughout the world the early exploration of this renewed diversity is already being done by the many rural, suburban, and urban community/neighborhood woodland groups. So the populace, a few pioneering professionals in the field, and a scattering of academics are helping to advance forestry attitudes and practices not seen since the fourteenth century. This set of case studies is another stage in developing a full-fledged, systematic, science-based community forestry profession.

What these case studies emphasize and support with their insights is the need for a new kind of forestry that treats human social systems as part of the whole. What is needed is the capture of these community forestry learning curves and their conversion into a more systematic (even scientific) form so that the curve is accelerated and more widely available for training and application to a renewed forestry for the twenty-first century. In short, a modern forestry cannot emerge simply by extending those practices and forms of knowledge that have served commercial forestry. We require a new forestry, and most of this is being empirically and pragmatically tried out at the local level. Except for short-term training programs, such as the Regional Community Forestry Training Center, which is loosely affiliated with the Kasetsart Forestry Faculty, there are no major forestry degree–granting, graduate research–producing institutions staffed with full-time ladder faculty that are fully involved in research and teaching on community forestry. My suggestion is not for the replacement or destruction of the present system of commercial forestry research and training practices but rather for the creation of an entirely new parallel research and training system that gives legitimacy and substance and that advances sustained learning for community forestry practices that have been emerging over the past forty years.

In short, I see a much broader impact of these studies than the editors and authors of this volume intended. Along with the work of Mark Poffenberger and his colleagues; Marilyn Hoskins and her colleagues at the FAO, Rome; a couple of decades of work by South and Southeast Asia FAO forestry programs; the Community Forestry reports from Kasetsart; and so forth, we have a body of sustained and continuing work. It is time to bring this substantial corpus of work out of the realm of "gray" or "fugitive" sources and make it the core literature of a truly new and revitalized professional forestry discipline. This means a body of theory that cumulates and directs findings, a standard set of methods, and the usual canons of scientific proof that identify the universals and separates them from what is locally unique. Let us admit that the case studies here probably give too much emphasis to places with large hunks of federal or other publicly owned land. So the struggle can often be put into the context of small communities attempting to gain the attention of large bureaucracies in order to have their voice heard. Yet this is not typical of most of the world. Take the northeastern United States. Maine, often thought to be a wild forestland, has only 4 percent of its land in public ownership. In contrast, my native state of Oregon has a federal ownership of over half its land, equaling a total land area that is larger than all the land in Maine, Vermont, and New Hampshire. So there may be problems in the lands west of the Mississippi, but they do not start with internationally owned, absentee corporations that see the value in the land for uses other than timber production. So the folks in New Mexico (see chapter 4) think they have big problems when "away" wilderness folk "lock" up their land. They should try dealing with a South African corporation whose board of directors is far away and nearly unreachable in a legal sense or, later, with Plum Creek from Montana, who shares the vision that Maine looks a lot better as developable real estate than as multiple-use timberland.

So there are conditions of uniqueness in each of our cases. Yet despite the uniqueness of each case, I find certain recurring tendencies and lessons that could raise our understanding above the special distinctions, and I see a similarity and a set of systematic guidelines for future practices that incorporate or resolve these similar and recurring patterns and processes in community management. Some central tendencies to consider and to research in rural and urban community forestry development—or some lessons outside the comfort zone—follow.

1. Emphasize functions being sought rather than focusing only on the tree, the woodland, or the forest. If you become caught in the object rather than the process of achieving desired goals, community managers will drift into their own form of "trained incapacity" as do commercial forestry organizations. That is, you will always be looking for something to do with your trees rather than looking for the best means to solve your problem—people leaving, abuse of cultural heritage, low service and income bases, unemployment, or hinterland isolation. The tree and woodland may be a means to solving the problem, but it should not be the sole factor when one can look outside the forest and maybe find a whole range of more workable solutions. See, for example, chapters 2 and 3.

2. Do not buy in to the idea that systems are moving toward some socioecological climax or steady state. With changing systems, human or biophysical, there is a need for flexibility, adaptability, diversity, and resiliency in development strategies. Our reality is one of dynamic response to constant internal and external perturbations. There is not a nice, smooth curve and a gentle landing that holds forever.

3. Do not focus only on your particular bit of forestland. Fit that land into a watershed, catchment basin, transportation corridor, and so on. In short, think of the property as an element within an ecosystem. This will compel better anticipation of changes affecting the property. Further, it will give a larger focus and relieve the trained incapacity to develop strategies only in terms of what can be done with trees and woodlands. All the case studies offer some variant on this idea, as do the community forests studied in Britain and Asia.

4. A community forest group may be a not-for-profit organization, but it should not be seen in this light. All commercial opportunities must be considered. An excellent model for this are the national parks of the People's Republic of China, where in even the most sacred national parks (for example, Sun Yat Sen Mausoleum in Nanjing) no possible vehicle for income gain goes untried.

5. Our analytic approaches could be improved if we start by trying to recognize the greater degree of unity in problems and opportunities for mutual learning by seeing some sort of continuum of density of habitation or clustering of work opportunities. Intellectuals like nice taxonomies with their confident bins in which to tidy up an untidy world. We hear a great deal of talk about rural community development as if it were a species apart from urban community development. Yet one suspects that there is a great deal more romanticism than empiricism in these distinctions.

6. Real rural or urban community development requires connecting primary production to its processing and its consumers. Growing, harvesting, and processing should be part of a total development effort. The value-added industries, along with some tourism-serving and other service activities, can give a more balanced jobs basket so that when one element is down, others are there to fill in. Chapters 6, 9, 10, 11, and 14 address this issue in diverse ways.

7. To talk of an effective and efficient participation in natural resource decisions does not mean to follow some arbitrary scale of involvement that may satisfy some intellectual sense of order. It means the ability to say no or yes or to tell policy or management persons to do these other actions rather than the ones that are proposed and to have the legal authority, either individually or in concert with others, to enforce these choices. This usually means something akin to ownership rights and responsibilities or voting rights and responsibilities. These are vested, enforceable rights backed by the power of the state. Though other forms of participation granted by some corporation or agency are nice, they are still gifts, not rights and responsibilities. Indeed, I suspect that these other forms of participation function more like "infomercials." Rather than honest, open, and legitimate purveyors of real information with real choices and consequences, they are nothing more than advertising or public relations efforts.

8. Most volunteer and other community efforts reflect the drive and energy of a few persons. Often the interest of the "wider" public is well reflected; they just do not show up to meetings until something really bothers them. There needs to be attempts to keep all stakeholders informed, but do not despair if everyone is not as active as the core. In addition, recognize that this core is composed of ordinary human beings who, in the course of life, become tired or burned out or simply move away. There is a need for designing a way to institutionalize their "charisma" and their leadership so that there is real continuity of the effort. Ultimately, all community groups need some professional infrastructure if the good works are to be sustained. See chapters 5, 6, and 8 for support and discussion of this issue.

9. As Jack Westoby notes, forestry is more a political science than a pure biological science (all the cases in this volume give evidence of such a tendency).

Of course, it works with biophysical realities and objects. However, decisions as to the when, where, who, what, how often, and why of our forestry actions are essentially political decisions. Some social classes or interest groups gain from those decisions, and others will lose. To save a grove of older trees or a habitat favored by certain bird species by prohibiting motorized access may be a good biological decision but is often a class and/or generational form of discrimination and hence political. Our decisions are never simply about biology but most often about human behavior. A less frequent retreat into "science" and a more open recognition of the reality of scientific forestry as composed more of political science than biophysical science gives a greater humility. It also gives greater openness to wider participation and greater attention to seeking diversity on a wider range of activities and calls for the creation of real mechanisms that give legitimacy to the voiceless. Over generations and times and issues, there will remain the need for discussion, argument, adjustment, compromise, and even agreement—but the discussion goes on about what the purposes of our forest are. And that very reason that has us talking together about the importance of our forest is one of the more valuable purposes of our forest.

So our twelve cases raise a good many more questions and possibilities than may have been intended. Truly, the future of a vital and effective forestry for the future—and one that seeks to answer the big questions raised by Westoby and others—is in our hands.

William R. Burch Jr.
Hixon Professor of Natural Resource Management
School of Forestry and Environmental Studies
Yale University
New Haven, Connecticut, U.S.A.

Note

I would like to thank David Rook and the Board of Directors of the Scottish Forestry Trust for the support of the John Eadie Fellowship and the many enthusiastic community foresters in Britain who helped me to more clearly understand the great shift that is happening in forestry around the world and even in my own backyard.

Acknowledgments

This book was made possible by a Ford Foundation grant in support of the Seventh American Forest Congress Communities Committee and its Research Subcommittee and is based in part on work supported by the Pacific West Community Forestry Center. The Communities Committee is one of the most notable outcomes of the Seventh Congress and may well be its enduring legacy. We are grateful also for a grant from the William and Flora Hewlett Foundation to Forest Community Research that enabled completion of this project.

Warm appreciation is reserved for the case study authors. They endeavored long and hard in developing each of the cases, none receiving compensation commensurate with the task or the patience required of this effort.

Thanks to Joyce Cunningham of Forest Community Research for her commitment and for her attention to detail with the layout and production of the manuscript. Beth Rose Middleton of Forest Community Research and John Bennett provided support that helped bring the project to completion.

Warmest appreciation of all is reserved for the many in the communities and others involved in the community-based work who took the time to tell their stories and share their experiences. On behalf of all of the authors and the Communities Committee, thank you!

Jonathan Kusel

Introduction

Jonathan Kusel

The Seventh American Congress and the Communities Committee

In February 1996, the Seventh American Forest Congress convened in Washington, D.C. Like its predecessors, this Congress brought together government policymakers and representatives from conservation organizations and businesses to discuss the status and the future of the nation's forests.[1] American Forest Congresses had convened six other times since 1882, usually at ten- or twenty-year intervals, with varying degrees of pomp and circumstance—tree plantings, appearances by presidents, and even a televised debate—but always with the goal of providing a valuable forum for professional resource managers, policymakers, and scientists. With over 1,300 attendees, the Seventh Congress was the most diverse Congress yet. It included not only those people whose professional lives were focused on forest management but also members of urban and rural forest communities from across the country.

In regional roundtable meetings leading up to the Congress, community members joined conservationists, scientists, businesspeople, and government representatives in discussions about the state of American forests and American forestry. The conclusion of these discussions was stark and urgent: Current forestry practices were no longer working—if they had ever worked at all. Open discussion with the American people was needed to develop new ideas and plans. John C. Gordon, Pinchot Professor for forestry at Yale University and a participant in the roundtable meeting that called for the Congress to convene, summarized the feelings of roundtable participants:

> After a decade of gridlock, it's time to engage the American people in a dialogue about our nation's forests. We have a plethora of often conflicting

laws, court decisions, and directives. What the Seventh American Forest Congress seeks is a cohesive policy that is environmentally sound and economically viable.[2]

The official objective of the Seventh Congress was to develop "a shared vision, a set of principles and recommendations that will ultimately result in policies for our nation's forests that reflect the American people's vision and are ecologically sound, economically viable, and socially responsible." The Congress's theme, printed boldly on Congress materials and featured in the title of its newsletter, was "Many Voices—A Common Vision."

From its inception, the Congress emphasized the importance of shared values and public opinion. It recognized the public's contribution as essential, not only in the meetings of the Congress itself but also in ongoing forestry practices in both rural and urban communities across the country.

To assess the state of public participation in forest communities around the country, to recognize the increasing role of communities and their importance in good forest stewardship, and to ensure that public participation in forestry issues continued after the Congress sessions themselves had concluded, the Congress established a Communities Committee. This committee's mission was "to focus attention on the interdependence between America's forests and the vitality of rural and urban committees." In addition, the committee was to promote the following:

- Improvements in political and economic structures to ensure local community well-being and the long-term sustainability of forested ecosystems
- An increasing stewardship role of local communities in the maintenance and restoration of ecosystem integrity and biodiversity
- Participation by ethnically and socially diverse members of urban and rural communities in decision making and sharing benefits of forests
- The innovation and use of collaborative processes, tools, and technologies
- Recognition of rights and responsibilities of diverse forest landowners[3]

To gain a better understanding of how community involvement in forestry was working and what could be learned from past work, the Communities Committee decided to collect case studies of community-based forestry projects from around the country. The twelve case studies in this volume are the result of the work of a number of researchers, many of whom are involved directly with the Communities Committee, and reflect the varied dimensions of community-based forestry that continues to expand across the country.

Case Studies of Forest Community Projects

The premise of these case studies is that healthy ecosystems depend on healthy communities and vice versa. An impoverished and fractious community is less able to steward the natural resources around it. Forestry policies that focus exclusively on biological and ecological goals and that ignore the economic and social capabilities of forest communities jeopardize the long-term health of the ecosystems they are working to sustain. Conversely, an economically and socially healthy community will be better able to manage itself and steward the resources around it. A secure, rather than impoverished, community is more likely to focus on long-term investment and system health. Understanding this reciprocal relationship between communities and ecosystems is the first step toward genuinely integrating humans and human communities with natural ecosystems in forest policies and practices.

But discovering and understanding the issues facing each forest community—its social structure, its capacity, and its history in general and with forest agencies and businesses in particular—is a daunting task for government officials and resources managers, especially those physically remote or disconnected from these communities. Addressing the needs of local communities and understanding their reciprocal relationship with the forest require the participation of communities themselves.

How do communities participate in policy development and forest management? Do they join existing institutions or develop new ones? How do other organizations, such as local U.S. Forest Service offices, timber companies, and conservation organizations, need to change their own expectations and practices in light of the community's more significant role? These are some of the questions addressed in these case studies. The answers have varied from community to community, and so have the results.

In compiling these case studies, the Research Subcommittee of the Communities Committee sought to represent the broadest possible variety of forest communities. The case studies feature communities across the country and include examples of rural and urban forestry. Not surprisingly, many of the case studies focus on communities whose well-being is tied directly to resource-extraction activities, such as timber harvesting. However, resource extraction is not the only source of well-being for these communities. For example, in the communities described in the Merrimack watershed (chapter 12), resource extraction plays only a small role.

The primary purpose of the case studies is to examine the link between community well-being and forest ecosystem health in both urban and rural communities and in different regions of the country. This research elevates community

The case study team strove to compile detailed, realistic case studies that acknowledged the difficulties, the barriers, and even the failures of community projects. To learn from these case studies, the forest community nationwide needs to see clearly what has worked and what has not. Accuracy, rather than enthusiasm, is called for.

Accordingly, the case studies identify some of the barriers to and incentives for community forestry and the different ways in which these barriers and incentives have been addressed. They also identify important process issues, such as initiatives or events that served as catalysts in initiating community forestry efforts, and include overcoming specific barriers. The cases include projects initiated and undertaken primarily by agencies and/or industry as well as community-driven and collaborative efforts, providing another opportunity for examining a wide variety of barriers and incentives. Finally, the case studies address the connections between specific projects and community sectors not directly involved in them. What are the repercussions of a project for community members who choose not to participate in it, for neighboring communities, and for a region at large? The case studies attempt to assess the effects of these projects wherever they may occur.

The case studies presented in this volume are introduced with an editors' summary. The cases are organized by themes that are dominant in American community forestry today. In part I, "Investing in Natural Capital, Investing in Community," practitioners from New York, the Hoopa Tribe in California, and Aitken County, Minnesota, work to reverse patterns of decline and underinvestment in the land and in their communities while identifying and developing mechanisms to secure investment that will jointly advance ecosystem and community health.

In part II, "From Process to Practice," residents from Catron County, New Mexico; the Applegate Partnership in Oregon; Coos County, New Hampshire; the Upper Swan Valley of Montana; and Baltimore, Maryland, organize to tackle paralyzing policy gridlock and social conflict. Their focus on developing good processes fosters new practices benefiting both their communities and their forests.

In part III, "Stewarding the Land," residents of southwestern Colorado; Michigan's western Upper Peninsula; a four-county area in southwestern Washington; and the Merrimack River watershed of New Hampshire focus on making a difference on the ground and in people's minds. Their work on improving the forest works on the "heart" as well, thereby addressing community health as well as ecological health.

It is the hope of all the researchers on this project that these case studies will convey the importance of community-based forestry and contribute to the understanding and development, and ultimately the success, of new community-based initiatives in the United States.

Notes

1. For a history of the first six American Forest Congresses, see Arthur V. Smyth, "A Brief History of the American Forest Congresses," (pamphlet).

2. Smyth.

3. Seventh American Forest Congress Communities Committee (1997). This one-page document presents the committee's mission statement and statement of principles.

Part I

INVESTING IN NATURAL CAPITAL, INVESTING IN COMMUNITY

CHAPTER 1

Linking Water Quality and Community Well-Being in a Forested Watershed

Gerald J. Gray

Faced with a $5 billion to $8 billion bill for the construction of filtration systems to ensure that its residents have clean drinking water, New York City decided instead to invest in land and landowners in a five-county area in the Catskill and Delaware watersheds. With increasing non–point source pollution threatening its water supply, New York City proposed first to acquire additional land and to tighten land use regulations. When upstate counties made clear that this approach would lead to development-induced fragmentation and additional degradation of land and water, New York City started negotiating.

The landmark New York City Watershed Agreement is a novel and bold experiment tying New York City residents to upstream farmers, woodland owners, and communities. The agreement implicitly recognizes that city residents benefit from ecosystem services, such as water filtration provided by headwater forests, and products, such as clean water, both undervalued and, more often than not, treated as free goods. As a result, the Watershed Agreement links the city to upstream residents who, in turn, are linked to the city through their management practices in the watershed.

A premise of the Watershed Agreement is that low-density land use will increase forest filtration and that improved agricultural practices on the region's five hundred dairy and livestock farms will reduce agricultural waste. Both low-density-use and improved agricultural practices will be accomplished through voluntary, incentive-based programs encouraged by an investment of over half a billion dollars.

Perhaps the greatest challenge of the Watershed Agreement will be reconciling a healthy ecosystem with healthy and vital communities. For New York City, a healthy environment is measured by clean water as the city attempts to stave off expensive filtration equipment. Reflecting perhaps its older regulatory approach, New York City's "low-density" use is akin to more restrictive land uses that emphasize open space and recreation. For upstaters, their focus is more on healthy communities and a "working landscape" in which they are allowed to continue their traditional working of the land. Upstaters do not mind being the catchment basin for New York City's water supply, but they want the basin to be a "working" one.

In 1996, New York City and thirty-five rural communities in the Catskill and Delaware watersheds struck an agreement aimed at protecting the quality of the city's drinking water and the economic vitality of the watershed communities. The agreement is hailed as historic for its broad scope, long-term vision, and unique partnership approach and at the same time is seen as a grand experiment.

In response to legislation concerning non–point source pollution and safe drinking water, the federal Environmental Protection Agency (EPA) in 1989 established a "surface water treatment rule" requiring cities to filter drinking water unless their water systems could meet a stringent set of criteria. New York City had already been ordered to complete by 1997 a Croton watershed filtration system, which provides 10 percent of the city's water supply, because of degradation caused by development. The city estimated that a filtration system for the Catskill and Delaware watersheds—which provides 90 percent of the city's water supply—would cost $5 billion to $8 billion to install and $200 million to $500 million for annual maintenance (Coombe 1994). To avoid these heavy costs, the city decided to explore alternative actions in the watersheds, and it was this search for alternatives that set into motion the proposals and negotiations that led to the Watershed Agreement.

This case study discusses how the people involved in the search overcame long-standing political and institutional barriers to reach agreement, describes key features of the agreement, and reflects on how the agreement might be characterized as a community-based approach to natural resource management. It considers how the well-being of people in New York City, the health of the forested ecosystems in the Catskill and Delaware watersheds, and the vitality of the rural watershed communities are connected and how city and rural residents are part of a watershed community. The case study also considers how the agreement is being implemented largely by the people in the watersheds with resources and oversight from New York City. It discusses the institutions and activities planned in the watersheds to meet the goals of the agreement—protecting water quality through a natural systems approach that maintains rural land use patterns and ways of life.

The Watersheds

The Catskill and Delaware watersheds cover 1,580 square miles some 125 miles northwest of New York City (Watershed Forest Ad Hoc Task Force 1996) and include portions of five counties: Delaware, Greene, Schoharie, Sullivan, and Ulster. They provide more than a billion gallons of water each day to New York City's nine million residents, water that has been called the "champagne" of metropolitan waters for its high quality. Nearly 70,000 people reside in the rural watersheds, and thousands of tourists visit each year for recreation, such as hiking, hunting, and fishing.

Forests cover about 75 percent of the steep mountain slopes and deep, V-shaped valleys that form the watersheds and have shaped the history of the communities there (Watershed Forest Ad Hoc Task Force 1996). The region has been "balkanized," with many of the valleys taking on different characteristics as communities cleared forests for farming and forest products industries but found local experience taking various paths (Karl Connell, personal communication). In some areas, soils proved too poor for farming, and farms were sold or abandoned. In many areas, the original dense hemlock forests were cut over or high graded for forest products by the late nineteenth century. As these forests regenerated, mostly as northern hardwoods, forest-based recreation began to play a greater role in many local economies, while farming and forest products industries continued to be important.

Eighty-five percent of the forestland in the watersheds is classified as "timberland" capable of producing commercial forest products. More than 90 percent of this timberland, however, is owned by farmers and nonindustrial private forest landowners who own and manage their lands for a wide variety of reasons. Increasingly, forestlands are owned for recreation and open space, often as properties for second homes owned by people living in New York or other nearby cities. The forest industry owns only about 1 percent of the watershed forests.

The natural beauty of the region and its proximity to New York City and other eastern cities has attracted strong interest in the Catskill and Delaware watersheds as a place to recreate. Hunting and fishing clubs began to appear in the early 1900s, and their members became involved in the conservation movement. These people were concerned about protecting the natural resources and rural character of the watersheds and were often opposed to the economic development plans of state agencies that seemed to promote bringing more people into the region (Karl Connell, personal communication). Today, the beauty of its mountain forests and streams and the pastoral character of its farms and small communities are widely appreciated in the city, as the adverse environmental effects of development on the Croton watershed have been seen. The desire to protect the open-space and working-landscape character of the Catskill and Delaware watersheds complements the need to protect water quality through a natural systems approach.

Watershed Communities and City Relations

The State of New York granted New York City the right to oversee and regulate upstate watersheds in 1906. When the city built the Catskill system of reservoirs in the early part of the twentieth century (1920–1930), relations between the city and rural watershed communities began to deteriorate. The city acquired lands for reservoirs wherever it chose through the power of eminent domain and often paid below-market values, sometimes forcing entire hamlets and surrounding farms to move from valleys to hillsides. With the addition of the Delaware system of reservoirs (1950–1960), antagonism toward the city intensified in the rural watershed communities (Coombe 1994). Exacerbating the hard feelings toward the city, delays in the city's compensation payments forced landowners and businesses into debt, and promises to maintain bridges and roads around the reservoirs were often broken as city budgets tightened in the 1970s and 1980s.

Many watershed residents also believe that the city has not been paying its fair share of property taxes. After building the Delaware system reservoirs in the 1960s, New York City owned 1,584 square miles in the Catskill and Delaware watershed. At that time, the city's property tax liability amounted to one-third of the tax revenues in Delaware County. By 1990, the city's share of the county's property tax revenues had declined to about 15 percent despite increases in property values. Rural watershed communities periodically attempted to raise tax assessments on the city's lands, but the city's attorneys found ways to avoid paying the increases (Ray and Heidlebaugh 1996).

The historic relationship of "domestic colonialism" created a deep distrust, even hatred, of the city by residents of the watershed communities. As the region's rural economy declined and farms went out of business in the 1980s and 1990s, the city became a target for blame. As an illustration of the region's economy, Delaware County had a median household income of $24,000 in 1989, less than three-quarters of the state median of $33,000. Watershed residents witnessed their communities change as more and more farms were sold to city residents, many of whom remained absentee landowners or used farms as second homes. Other natural resource activities, such as forest product harvesting and blue-stone mining, declined, and seasonal tourism became an increasingly important part of local economies. These changes increased the antagonism toward the city as watershed residents sought to preserve rural ways of life.

The New York City Watershed Agreement

As New York City sought to develop a plan to address non–point source pollution in the Catskill and Delaware watersheds and to avoid the high costs of a filtration system, the stage was set for confrontation. In 1990, the City Department of Environmental Protection (DEP) released a draft proposal based on watershed protection measures such as strict regulation of land use activities, aggressive enforcement powers, and increased land acquisition by the city. The draft sent watershed communities into open and vehement opposition, as they saw regulations as a threat to local economies and culture. In a stinging analysis of the proposed regulations, Ken Markert, director of the Delaware County Planning Department, characterized the measures as unjust and unworkable and said that the impacts on farming would cause sellouts to developers—precisely the opposite effect the city wanted (Ray and Heidlebaugh 1996).

The strong response from the watershed communities and receptive city leadership led to a process of intensive negotiation that ultimately resulted in an innovative agreement, shifting more power to the rural watershed communities through voluntary, incentive-based mechanisms while meeting the city's objectives. The 1996 agreement was substantial enough for the EPA to extend a filtration waiver it initially granted in 1993, allowing the city to expand activities from ten pilot farms to other farms, forestlands, and watershed communities (Krudner 1997). After reviewing the first five years of progress under the agreement, the EPA granted another five-year waiver in 2002 (*The Watershed Advocate* 2002).

Perspectives on the Agreement

In large part, the agreement was driven by a sense of crisis among both city officials and residents of the watershed communities engendered by the EPA's non–point source pollution regulations. Faced with $5 billion to $8 billion installation costs for a filtration system and the political backlash of transferring those costs to residents and other water consumers, city officials saw the need for alternative, lower-cost measures to protect water quality in the watersheds. Watershed communities felt that both their current ways of life and their future hopes were threatened by proposals from a city that had historically exploited them. Agreement emerged between the city and watershed communities through a process that transformed crisis into opportunity.

There has been, and continues to be, significant skepticism about whether the agreement can achieve its objectives and be sustainable. Some people question whether the land acquisition program, along with voluntary improvements in management practices and infrastructure, will be sufficient for maintaining water quality. Others question whether the political and institutional complexity of the agreement, which requires significant coordination and funding commitments by various agencies and levels of government, will lead to a breakdown. Environmental organizations have been the strongest skeptics, but even DEP and EPA officials, generally accustomed to regulatory programs, have questioned the agreement's workability (Nancy Wolf, personal communication).

A similar skepticism or pragmatic concern about the fragility of the agreement exists among residents in the rural watershed communities. Despite enthusiasm for the agreement and hope that it will allow watershed communities to maintain their current character, some people consider the agreement a "house of cards" that can collapse at any moment, particularly because the power of the purse is in the city and the regulatory cultures of the DEP and the EPA can resurface (Karl Connell, personal communication).

Within the DEP and the watershed communities, however, are leaders who believe that the agreement will protect not only water quality but also a range of other environmental values, land uses, and economic activities historically suited to the watersheds. Carolyn Summers, director of natural resources in the water quality control division of the DEP, describes the comprehensive watershed protection program as a means of avoiding the high-cost, capital-intensive technology of the filtration system by using lower-cost, natural system technologies that attain broader social, environmental, and quality-of-life goals (Summers 1995). Noting that more than 75 percent of the Catskill and Delaware watersheds is forested and that "the natural filtration and nutrient uptake functions of these privately owned forests are essentially provided free of charge," she calls for a strategy to provide incentives for private landowners to maintain forested landscapes.

Participation in the Agreement

Participation in the agreement has been broad but strategic. The processes through which the agreement was formulated were facilitated by city officials in ways that sometimes strategically excluded groups as they sought to overcome historic barriers of distrust and build bridges of understanding among critical stakeholders. These processes can be considered from three perspectives: those between the city and rural watershed communities, those within the city, and those in the watersheds.

Between the city and rural watershed communities, the story is one of overcoming a history of distrust and anger, changing the culture within the DEP, and having the city people go to the rural watersheds to sit with farmers, landowners, and town representatives, listen to their concerns, attempt to build under-

Whole-Farm Planning

Nearly five hundred dairy and livestock farms in the Catskill and Delaware watersheds make up a vital part of the region's economy. These farmers expressed immediate concern about the City Department of Environmental Protection's (DEP's) 1990 proposed watershed regulations that led to intensive, yearlong negotiations with the city and, ultimately, recommendations to establish a two-phase whole-farm planning program based on principles of voluntary participation, financial incentives, local leadership, and best scientific understanding of pollution prevention. Phase 1 tested and demonstrated whole-farm planning on ten farms between 1992 and 1994 through a $4 million investment by the city. This phase included diagnosis of pollution sources and water quality priorities on each demonstration farm by watershed planning teams, team visits with farmers to review technical and financial options for improving the environmental and economic health of the farm, plan development, and implementation of management actions. With successful implementation of phase 1, the city in late 1994 committed $35 million to phase 2, which sought to enroll at least 85 percent of all farms in the Catskill and Delaware watersheds by 1997. Whole-farm planning is designed to reduce risks to water quality from barnyard runoff, drainage from cropland or fields receiving applications of manure fertilizers, and the loss of soil through erosion. It focuses on sources of agricultural pollutants and factors influencing their transport to farm streams. Priority pollutants targeted by the program are parasitic protozoa, Cryptosporidium, and Giardia, followed by nutrients, pesticides, sediment, fuel, and other toxic chemicals.

standing, and seek solutions. Cornell University played a significant role in helping the city rebuild farmers' trust and define changes in management practices (that is, whole-farm planning) that farmers were willing to test on a voluntary basis and that had the potential of meeting water quality goals.

The agreement between the city and rural watershed communities is widely attributed to effective leadership by key city officials and representatives of the watershed communities. The DEP's commissioner, Albert Appleton, had experience as a farmer and credibility with the environmental community, and this enabled him to play a unique role in changing the DEP's culture, overcoming skepticism in the department and environmental community, and rebuilding trust with the people and communities in the watersheds. Richard Coombe, a farmer and former state legislator from the watersheds, played critical roles first in bringing farmers and later the forestry community to the table to seek an accord (Charles Johnston and Nancy Wolf, personal communication).

Dennis Rapp, deputy commissioner of the Department of Agriculture and Marketing, was recognized for setting up and facilitating the process that brought the city and watershed communities to agreement (Ray and Heidle-baugh 1996). The process involved the creation of a one-year task force composed of two subgroups: a technical advisory group and a policymaking group. The technical advisory group, which became very large, served strictly in an advisory role. A key strategy in Rapp's process was to focus initial meetings on technical information as a means of building common understanding and trust among city officials and watershed participants before the policy group discussed issues and terms of an agreement. Another important facilitation strategy was to structure the negotiation as a mediation that involved keeping the policy group small and the negotiated issues as simple as possible. To do this, Rapp recruited fourteen participants who represented key stakeholders and were willing to negotiate in good faith and constructed the negotiation as a two-sided conflict between the watershed communities and the city. The process limited the number of stakeholders to avoid confusion and excluded stakeholders, such as environmental groups and lawyers, to avoid intransigence or interference in the process.

Within the city, public participation in the agreement's development was narrower than in the watersheds. Discussions involved primarily an array of government officials from federal, state, and city agencies overseeing water quality, and most of the activity involved high-level decision makers. Limited numbers of interest groups engaged in the processes and discussions leading to the agreement. Public awareness of the agreement was limited generally to periodic media coverage. Connections between efforts in the city and efforts in the rural watersheds to ensure water quality were seldom made. Efforts to conserve water or to improve the infrastructure for water quality protection in the city were not linked to improved farm management or other water quality protection activities in the rural watersheds. One exception was a campaign offering minority groups in the city an opportunity to adopt water-efficient toilets. Environmental groups and city officials worked with church leaders to inform residents of the connection between their water conservation efforts and the efforts of rural watershed communities to protect water quality (Nancy Wolf, personal communication). People involved in the agreement recognize the need and opportunity for more education in the city, to reach the broader public, and to target specific audiences, such as absentee watershed landowners and people who vacation and recreate in the watersheds.

One aspect of the process to reach the agreement was that meetings and negotiations nearly always took place in the rural watershed communities. City officials went to the rural communities as a means of reaching out to build understanding and trust. People from the watershed communities seldom ventured into the city for meetings (Alan Rosa, personal communication). Beyond the need for city officials to demonstrate a willingness to overcome historic distrust, this dynamic reflects a cultural characteristic of people in the rural watersheds.

Accustomed to life in small farming communities, many of these people were uncomfortable venturing into the big city or at least preferred meetings and negotiations in the familiar surroundings of the rural watershed communities (Nancy Wolf, personal communication).

One implication of the agreement's being limited generally to high-level city, state, and federal agency officials with watershed participants is that lower-level agency officials, responsible for implementing programs, had little opportunity to contribute and limited understanding of agreement provisions. Some program managers were unclear about how to interpret certain provisions or what they meant for program implementation (Peter Innes, personal communication).

In part because of strong community leadership, the processes to involve key stakeholders and inform residents in the rural watershed communities were more inclusive and extensive than similar processes in the city. In addition to focused discussions with farmers, watershed communities, and forest landowners, numerous public meetings were convened throughout the watersheds. The focused and iterative manner in which the agreement was developed, building on the success of the city's agreement with the farmers to pilot test whole-farm planning (followed by the report of the Watershed Forest Ad Hoc Task Force and the agreement with the watershed communities), also suggests processes of learning and trust building that are important underpinnings of the agreement.

Structure of the Agreement

Key agreement negotiations revolved around the watershed farmers' and communities' three critical concerns and define the agreement's central themes: 1) full funding of the program elements by the city or sources outside the watershed, 2) local program administration, and 3) a voluntary, incentive-based approach rather than a mandatory, regulatory approach (Ray and Heidlebaugh 1996). Although the city had tremendous power based on its legal authority and finances, city officials recognized the validity of these concerns and acknowledged a different but significant power in the watershed communities. The structure and terms of the agreement were built along the recognition of this power dynamic. With respect to the agreement with farmers, a recent EPA report states,

> The program assumed that, in a populated rural landscape, well-managed agriculture was the best protection for water quality. Further, compulsion was unlikely to succeed with fiercely independent farmers, and the program had to be a voluntary one based on providing incentives to farmers to participate. (Krudner 1997, 8)

The design of the agreement is broad and comprehensive, covering a diverse array of objectives dealing with land acquisition, natural resource protection and management, environmental regulation, improved infrastructure, local administration, financial incentives, and community development. Agreement provisions integrate the activities and roles of different agencies and institutions rather than define discrete and separate niches.

The agreement is made up of four key parts: a land acquisition program, new watershed regulations, watershed protection and partnership programs, and a watershed protection and partnership council. Following is a description of these parts of the agreement as presented in a 1996 public review draft.

LAND ACQUISITION PROGRAM

The land acquisition program allows the city to acquire environmentally sensitive, undeveloped land from willing sellers through the purchase of fee title or conservation easements. The city will not acquire property through its power of eminent domain; rather, it will pay fair market value and property taxes after the land is purchased. The program also includes a community review process for property the city intends to purchase. It contains key process elements to allay watershed community fears: willing sellers, fair market value, property taxes, and community review. Only experience through program implementation will show whether these process elements are sufficient to maintain trust between the rural watershed communities and the city. After the first five years of program implementation, the DEP has acquired 19,573 acres, and the Watershed Agricultural Council has acquired conservation easements on an additional 2,250 acres (Victor Brunette, personal communication).

NEW WATERSHED REGULATIONS

New watershed regulations were crafted to ensure protection of the city's water supply while minimizing the adverse impacts of the regulations on the economic and social well-being of the watershed communities. The regulations work in conjunction with existing federal and state regulations and provide additional protections tailored to the existing farms, forests, and communities in the Catskill and Delaware watersheds, which the agreement refers to as a "living watershed." They focus on reducing contaminants from current sources, such as septic tanks and roads, and preventing the introduction of contaminants from new sources, such as land clearing and road and building construction associated with new development. Key elements of the regulations call for a study of the

Key Features of the
Land Acquisition Program

The New York State Department of Environmental Conservation will issue a ten-year water supply permit to the city, renewable for an additional five years. The city has committed $250 million in the Catskill and Delaware watersheds. After five years, the EPA and New York State Department of Health will confer on the sufficiency of this investment; if necessary, the city will invest an additional $50 million in the program.

The Catskill and Delaware watersheds have been divided into five priority areas based on the natural features and proximity to reservoirs, reservoir intakes, and the city's distribution system. The city has developed an acquisition schedule and will focus on its highest-priority areas first. It will contact the owners of 355,050 acres of land in the watersheds out of a total of 550,000 acres in the priority areas. If an owner wishes to sell and accepts the city's offer, the city must purchase the property. Any village or town may exclude certain lands from acquisition by the city.

The program includes a local consultation process for towns and villages to review and comment on any proposed acquisitions, except agricultural easements, which are given special consideration. The city will provide up to $20,000 to each town or village to assist in the review. The city will respond to concerns raised by the town or village within thirty days. Any disputes between the communities and city will be referred to the New York State Department of Environmental Conservation for resolution.

The program recognizes the importance of an initiative to acquire agricultural easements in the Catskill and Delaware watersheds to further protect environmentally sensitive lands and provide economic incentives to farmers. This initiative will be carried out in partnership with the Watershed Agricultural Council.

The city will grant a conservation easement on all property it acquires in fee to the State Department of Environmental Conservation to ensure that the property is undeveloped and held in perpetuity to protect the watershed and drinking water supply. All conservation easements acquired by the city will also be held in perpetuity to protect the watershed and drinking water supply.

sufficiency of one-hundred-foot buffers for septic systems near watercourses and wetlands, establish a working group to analyze the state's regulations regarding pesticides and fertilizers, and encourage the preparation of a comprehensive strategy involving city, county, and local officials when developing new wastewater treatment facilities.

The regulations provide exemptions "for certain activities in designated areas where existing communities are concentrated." Exemptions are intended to allow for continued economic development in the rural communities while protecting water quality through increased regulation.

WATERSHED PROTECTION AND PARTNERSHIP PROGRAMS

The protection and partnership programs are a diverse array of activities that help implement the land acquisition program and watershed regulations while strengthening the partnership between the city and watershed communities. The range of activities presented in the sidebar "Key Features of the Protection and

Key Features of the Protection and Partnership Programs

The city will provide $500,000 for a forestry management program to promote forestry practices that protect the city's water supply from runoff and other pollution. The Forestry Ad Hoc Task Force, the Watershed Agricultural Council, and the city will develop recommendations, and the Watershed Agricultural Council will administer the program.

The city will provide $2 million for a public education program on the city's water supply system and the critical role of watershed residents as stewards of water quality. Up to $1 million of this funding can be used for exhibits on the watershed and the city's water supply at a museum in the Catskills. The Catskill Watershed Corporation (CWC) will manage the program and establish an advisory group of educators.

The city will provide $500,000 for a comprehensive study on community economic development goals and objectives "to meet the economic, social, and environmental goals of the watershed communities that are consistent with the City's water quality objectives and the Watershed regulations." The CWC will manage the study.

The city will provide $59.9 million for the Catskill Fund for the Future over a period of six years for loans and grants for "responsible, environmentally sensitive economic development projects which encourage environmentally sound development." The CWC will make final decisions on which projects to fund, but the New York State Environmental Facilities Corporation will administer the funds.

The city will provide $3 million for localities to retain professionals to assist in the administration of real property taxes paid by the city on city-owned property. The CWC will manage these funds.

The city will provide $1.075 million to fund the operation of the Watershed Protection and Partnership Council. The state will establish and maintain the council.

The city will provide $1.535 million to the Coalition of Watershed Towns for reimbursing costs associated with reviewing and responding to the city's watershed protection programs.

As good-neighbor payments, the city will provide $9.765 million to the municipalities that sign the Watershed Agreement to establish a better working relationship with communities to protect water quality. These funds can be used for public works or improvements that benefit the public and will be managed by the Coalition of Watershed Towns or the CWC.

Partnership Programs" suggests an effort by the city and watershed communities to integrate environmental, social, and economic objectives and demonstrate the city's financial commitment to the watershed communities' well-being.

A key provision of the programs is the establishment of the Catskill Watershed Corporation (CWC) as an independent, locally based and administered, not-for-profit organization to help create a working partnership between the city and watershed communities and to implement many of the partnership programs. The CWC consists of fifteen members: six from Delaware County, two from Ulster County, two from Greene County, one from Schoharie County, one from Sullivan County, two appointed by the governor (one of whom will be chosen from a list of three possible members submitted by the environmental community), and an appointee of the city mayor.

WATERSHED PROTECTION AND PARTNERSHIP COUNCIL

The agreement establishes a nonregulatory Watershed Protection and Partnership Council "to provide a permanent, regional forum to aid in long-term watershed protection and enhancement of the economic vitality of the rural watershed communities." It has broad-based representation and several committees. The CWC is responsible for carrying out many of the partnership programs and serves as a forum for discussion in the Catskill and Delaware watersheds.

The functions of the Partnership Council include serving as a forum for discussions and developing recommendations relating to watershed protection and environmentally responsible economic development, reviewing and assessing watershed protection efforts, soliciting input from all interested parties regarding the watershed and drinking water supply, and dispute resolution.

The Partnership Council has twenty-seven members, sixteen of whom serve on an Executive Committee, which is a mixture of state, city, and watershed representatives and a representative from the EPA. Of the sixteen, the CWC appoints three members for Catskill and Delaware watershed counties, the governor appoints someone to represent the "watershed business community," the mayor of New York City appoints someone to represent water consumers, the environmental community appoints its own representative, and the chair of the Watershed Agricultural Council is a nonvoting member.

Financial Commitments

New York City, the State of New York, and the federal government have committed a total of $1.4 billion over periods ranging from seven to fifteen years for most provisions. The city has committed $666 million to land acquisition and partnership programs and $550 million to infrastructure and water quality improvements, the state has committed $53 million to foster partnership initiatives and help implementation, and the federal government has committed up to $105 million under the Safe Drinking Water Act Amendments of 1996.

The funding amounts and allocations are sundry and diverse, but all the program elements are connected to the water quality and community development goals of the agreement. The breadth of the allocations may be one of the agreement's unique strengths, but it also presents a challenge in terms of monitoring performance.

Although the watershed communities did not make direct financial commitments to the agreement, the commitment of time by local community officials, farmers, and landowners has been an important contribution. In addition, technical assistance from local Soil and Water Conservation Districts, the Cornell Cooperative Extension, and the U.S. Department of Agriculture (USDA) Natural Resources Conservation Service has been essential in designing and building awareness of local best management practices and whole-farm planning. These groups also played a key role in public outreach about the agreement. Individual farmers who willingly engaged in the first pilot projects also contributed to the agreement with their time and resources.

The USDA Forest Service has provided substantial technical and financial support for implementing forestry activities outlined through the agreement. Through 2002, the Forest Service has provided more than $3 million to the Watershed Agricultural Council for programs to assist forest landowners with land management practices, to acquire conservation easements, and to support grants to wood products businesses helping to strengthen rural community economies (USDA Forest Service 2002).

Decision Making

The Watershed Agreement represents a partnership approach among federal, state, city, and local watershed institutions to deal with issues related to the quality of the city's drinking water supply and the economic and social well-being of the rural watershed communities. The agencies that are party to the agreement maintained their legal authorities for developing and enforcing environmental laws and regulations but created a set of processes and innovative institutions for involving watershed communities in decisions and dispute resolution efforts. These arrangements reflect the extent to which the city has been able to share power with the rural watershed communities.

The Watershed Protection and Partnership Council is the primary institution through which parties to the agreement share power. Established as "a permanent, regional forum," the council represents "a broad-based, diverse group of interests that share the common goals of protecting and enhancing the environmental integrity of the watershed as well as the social and economic vitality of the watershed communities." It is a forum for discussion and future action recommendations for all parties to the agreement.

The agreement also recognizes the importance of the council's dispute resolution authority as a means of preventing differences "from festering and spilling over to the courts." All parties have agreed to present disagreements to the council before resorting to litigation. It remains to be seen, however, how well parties to the agreement hold up under pressures from other groups concerned about the agreement.

Two new institutions play key roles in representing the rural watershed communities in decision making through the Watershed Protection and Partnership Council. The CWC will oversee significant funds, such as the $60 million Catskill Fund for the Future. Its structure as an independent, locally based, not-for-profit organization gives it flexibility and legitimacy to act in the interest of the partnership between the city and rural watershed communities. The Watershed Agricultural Council has gained substantial recognition through its effective negotiations for farmers and, more recently, its work with forestry interests. Its membership in the Partnership Council, though nonvoting, gives it the opportunity to have an influential voice for agricultural and forestry interests.

The structure of the Watershed Agreement is complex, creative, and political. It creates new institutions to involve the rural watershed communities in a meaningful way in ongoing decision making and program implementation. Although the process to reach agreement has to a large degree been driven by the city, the agreement itself is structured as a partnership between the city and watershed communities and provides a direct means for community participation in decision making and a voluntary, incentive-based framework for watershed resident participation in the implementation of program activities.

Linking Community Well-Being and Healthy Forests

> To ensure that New Yorkers will continue to enjoy high quality, affordable drinking water, a comprehensive, long-range watershed protection and water quality enhancement program has been developed to protect the economic vitality of the Watershed communities and the public drinking water supply into the 21st century. (New York City Watershed Agreement, 1996)

The Watershed Agreement explicitly links environmental quality, as indicated by clean water, and community well-being, as indicated by economic vitality, by presenting them as compatible objectives of a watershed protection and water quality enhancement program. Maintaining clean water, however, appears to be the primary objective of city officials as they try to avoid the heavy financial and political costs of constructing a multi-billion-dollar water filtration plant. In contrast, economic viability appears to be the primary objective in the rural watershed communities. The mission statement of the Watershed Forest Ad Hoc Task Force (hereafter Forest Task Force) suggests this focus: "To improve both the short and long-term economic viability of forest landownerships and the forest products industry to the benefit of local communities in the New York City water supply watersheds in ways compatible with water quality protection and sustainable forest management." Although both the Watershed Agreement and the Forest Task Force report link environmental quality and community well-being, they reflect different priorities in the City and rural watershed communities.

Both city officials and the Forest Task Force acknowledge the value of watershed forests as a natural filtration system for water quality and as an opportunity to maintain open-space farm and forestland uses on 90 percent of the Catskill and Delaware watershed area. The difference in city and Forest Task Force priorities, however, suggests that the city and rural watershed communities may not see the relationships between environmental quality, forest health, and community well-being in quite the same way. With respect to forest management, for example, it appears that the city's emphasis may be on acquiring priority forestlands and protecting them through restricted management policies that focus on open space and recreation. The watershed communities, on the other hand, appear to be seeking ways to demonstrate the viability of protecting water quality through a "working forest" approach that includes active forest management and timber harvesting. A key issue is whether "working forests" that apply environmentally sensitive management practices can provide the same or even greater water quality benefits as "natural forests" that apply custodial management (Richard Coombe and Charles Johnston, personal communication). Information on this issue will be critical in reaching common ground between the city and the rural watershed communities on what types of management practices will be allowed on city-owned and -acquired forestlands.

More than 80 percent of the forestland in the watersheds is privately owned, which presents an ownership pattern unlike many other metropolitan water supply areas. Seattle, by contrast, owns 92 percent of the forestland draining into its water supply area (Revkin 1997). The Forest Task Force report suggests that the objective of the watershed protection plan should be to maintain forestlands in current ownerships and provide incentives for improved forest management. Its recommendations focus on ways to provide technical and financial assistance as well as tax relief and incentives to private forest landowners. It also recommends strategies for a more attractive business climate for forest products industries. Two key challenges with these strategies are 1) developing public support for "working forests" to help sustain vital rural communities in the watersheds and 2) reaching the significant number of absentee forest landowners and encouraging them to participate in program activities.

The following description of Watershed Agricultural Council programs by the DEP recognizes a clear linkage between ecosystem health and community well-being in the rural watersheds (Department of Environmental Protection publication, n.d.): "At the foundation of these proposed programs and the existing Watershed Agricultural Program is the assumption that supporting the long-term, low density, natural resource based land use patterns of the watershed for water quality protective purposes requires projects and investments to stabilize and develop the economic climate for agriculture and forestry."

The assumption that investments in agriculture and forestry are needed to sustain preferred land uses for water quality protection is the basis for the city's commitment to establish the Catskill Fund for the Future, a fund for economic development in the watershed. Part of the fund is dedicated to "a study to establish a strategy for economic development which will include agriculture and forestry as major segments of the watershed economy." Among the projects that can be undertaken now is "a direct marketing of watershed farm and forest products locally and within the New York City market." Between 2000 and 2002, the USDA Forest Service provided $2 million to the Watershed Agricultural Center for grants to Catskills-based wood products businesses. These grants were for investments in new technologies and innovative marketing campaigns to ensure that forestry remains a viable enterprise, helping to protect water quality and bolster economic vitality.

The potential for "green marketing"—linking sustainable forest products from the watersheds to market niches in the city—is an important opportunity. One example is the potential marketing appeal of linking the reconstruction of the Coney Island Boardwalk to sustainably managed wood products from the Catskill and Delaware watershed and, in so doing, connecting city consumers with forests and communities in the watersheds. However, discussions of this sort that link the markets and economic activities of the city and watershed communities have been limited to this point.

The rural watershed communities are at an early stage in discussions about what they will do with the significant infusion of funding they anticipate for community and economic development. Agriculture and forestry interests are strategizing about how to gain a fair share of this funding, and being preferred land uses in the watersheds, there is enthusiasm about their chances for funding.

Tensions between the city and watershed communities persist about how much timber harvesting as opposed to custodial timber management should be conducted in the watershed forests, and these tensions revolve around water quality. Monitoring activities are being developed to assess the impacts of these and other activities on water quality. Issues related to the current and potential future contributions of different types of forest management to watershed community well-being have been given less attention and are indeed the missing pieces in the Watershed Agreement and Forest Task Force report, which lack a concerted effort to assess and monitor the effects of forest management and production activities on community well-being (Alan White and Ira Stern, personal communication). Generally, there has been relatively little focus on developing information about the current social and economic situation in the watershed communities and how proposed economic development activities are linked to broader goals of sustainability and improving community well-being.

Problems and Barriers

The greatest barriers that had to be overcome in developing the agreement were distrust and resentment directed toward New York City by people in the watershed communities for the way private lands had been taken by eminent domain to create the reservoirs and for the way lands in city ownership were being managed. These sentiments were exacerbated by the feeling that the city was not contributing its fair share in taxes to the rural watershed communities.

Fear of "Crotonization" (named after the city's Croton watershed, which had already experienced the adverse environmental, social, and economic impacts of development pressures) seemed to be a common thread among participants in the agreement. Watershed residents are concerned, however, that the city and environmental groups might go too far in efforts to restrict development in their efforts to maintain the natural, open-space qualities of the region. Through the agreement, the watershed communities have retained substantial flexibility in determining appropriate development in key zones, particularly those near existing towns. This issue of "too much protection" will be one of the most challenging for the city and rural watershed communities as they implement the agreement and explore how to integrate environmental and economic objectives.

Another key issue is how lands acquired by the city will be managed— whether the city will permit forest product harvesting to sustain and develop new industries or whether it will put lands in a custodial or preserve status, such as forever wild, which limits management to maintaining open-space and recreation opportunities. The types of economic activities permitted on these lands and the effect that the acquisition program will actually have on the tax base for watershed communities are important related questions.

Another barrier is uncertainty about how the environmental community will respond to ongoing activities allowed in the agreement. A number of environmental groups have maintained distance from the agreement, expressing skepticism and concern about its ability to protect environmental quality. Some officials in federal, state, and city government have expressed doubt about the ability of the city to maintain its political will and follow through with agreement commitments. If it should begin to appear ineffective or unworkable, the agreement carries political risk for some of those who backed it.

A technical barrier exists around the city's and the EPA's ability to effectively monitor the agreement's impacts on water quality based on changes in agricultural and forestry practices and communities' infrastructural enhancements. The city has restructured its DEP to assess the types of changes needed in the watershed. It has increased the number of officials in the rural watersheds to identify priority infrastructure changes in communities and to enforce new regulations and will increase its capacity to monitor water quality changes in the reservoirs. But assessing the overall effectiveness of the measures will be difficult. Monitoring whether water quality is changing, understanding which of the many non–point source variables contribute to the change, and determining a baseline, or standards, against which the effectiveness of current measures can be compared are complex. The *New York Times* stated the difficulty succinctly by saying, "Scientists have only embryonic understanding of the forces that keep water pure or allow pollution to accumulate" (Revkin 1997). Assessing the effectiveness of agreement to achieve economic development goals is even more difficult since few measures currently exist as a basis for monitoring. Officials involved in the agreement have only begun to think about how to monitor social and economic variables (Alan White and Ira Stern, personal communication).

The layers of federal, state, and local government and the various agencies involved in the agreement—health, environmental protection, agriculture, and economic development—make it so extraordinarily broad and complex that the agreement is difficult to implement. While the agreement seeks to coordinate the efforts of these various government agencies, it is challenged to deal with the jurisdictional and organizational issues among these different agencies. Since top-level officials have been the ones involved in developing the agreement while lower-level officials will be the ones implementing the programs, a disconnection between policy and program implementation is apparent in terms of understanding and expectations, thus increasing the challenges and difficulties.

Outcomes and Successes

At this point in implementing the agreement, outcomes and successes are reflected in changes in relationships, processes, and programs rather than measurable improvements in water quality. Gaining commitments from federal, state, and city governments; developing a comprehensive agreement with rural watershed communities; and implementing the agreement through new institutions and programs over five years represents a significant success. Perhaps the most important indicator of success is the granting of another five-year filtration waiver from the EPA. This waiver recognizes that investments made, the institutions created, and the programs initiated under the agreement continue to hold promise. Other elements of success include the following:

- A reduction of the historic distrust between the city and rural watershed communities (The leadership and facilitation processes are noteworthy.)
- A change in the regulatory culture of the DEP and the EPA to allow the agreement to emerge
- The creation of new institutions to design and maintain the partnership between the city and rural watershed communities, especially the Watershed Protection and Partnership Council, the CWC, and the Watershed Agricultural Council
- The iterative approach through which the agreement was built, such as bringing in the forestry community and putting together the Watershed Forest Ad Hoc Task Force report despite an early reluctance of the forestry community to be involved
- The leveraging of financial commitments under the agreement with increased support from other organizations, such as more than $3 million that the USDA Forest Service provided to the Watershed Agricultural Center

Success can also be seen in the responsiveness of farm, forest, and other property owners to the agreement. Greater awareness concerning changes in practices, behavior, and infrastructure that are needed to protect water quality has been created in the watersheds. This awareness may be motivated by self-interest and financial incentives, which form the basis for the agreement's approach and help maintain rural land uses through voluntary, incentive-based measures. The ten farmers who volunteered to pilot test whole-farm planning responded favorably to it and became advocates among their peers despite significant initial cynicism among farmers about cooperating with the city (Richard Coombe, personal communication). By the end of 2000, more than 90 percent of the eligible farmers had enrolled in the whole-farm planning program (*Watershed Farm & Forest* 2001).

From a process perspective, the openness with which people involved in developing the agreement have responded to critics and skeptics can also be seen as a success. They speak with enthusiasm about the agreement but openly recognize the challenges and uncertainties that lie ahead. They describe the agreement as a new approach for dealing with water quality issues, one that seeks sustainable watershed communities and integrates social and economic issues. For example, Ira Stern, the DEP's primary official working in the rural watersheds, acknowledges the uncertainties: "Common sense tells me that all the things we're doing add up to something, but will you see a difference in a glass of water in the City? I don't know" (Revkin 1997).

Water quality is the bottom line. Officials acknowledge that but are willing to implement this innovative approach and learn from it.

Future of the Project

"Now we're entering the scariest time of all," said Nancy Wolf shortly after the agreement was completed. Her statement implied a level of excitement about the agreement among people close to it and was a mixture of hope and fear. The agreement exceeded the expectations of many in the rural watershed communities. Vast financial resources were being directed to the rural watersheds through the agreement; the ways in which the new partnership institutions in the watersheds handled these resources and the watershed residents responded would ultimately determine the success of the agreement.

Although the agreement has made progress, diverse interests agree that its true success will be seen only over the long term. Along the way, the EPA and the city will reassess whether the actions taken have been sufficient, whether new investments are warranted, or whether regulations need to be strengthened. Proponents of the agreement suggest that significant flexibility is built into the agreement for making changes as new information emerges and participants discover what works and what does not.

Skeptics contend that the agreement may still fall apart because of shifting political currents, economic pressures, or environmental results indicating that the measures are insufficient. However, no groups have directly opposed the agreement. Eric Goldstein of the National Resources Defense Council, one of the environmental groups that expressed strong doubts and maintained distance from the agreement, nevertheless recognized a short-term benefit to the approach: "It's one of the most important and complicated issues facing the region. We are fooling ourselves if we think this current round will solve it. This is a stopgap initiative that buys us a little time, and that's useful" (*New York Times,* June 24, 1996). The ability of institutions and individuals implementing the agreement to deal with emerging technical and political issues and openly share information will greatly affect how skeptics respond over time. The Watershed Agricultural Council, which administers key farm and forestry programs in the watersheds, recognizes the importance of maintaining good relationships and open communication with diverse entities involved or interested in the agreement. Richard Coombe highlights these relationships in a recent "Chair's Report" by the council:

> An ambitious outreach schedule, coupled with our program's excellence, has strengthened WAC's [Watershed Agricultural Council's] visibility as a national model. I am proud to report that WAC continues to enjoy excellent rapport with the New York City Department of Environmental Protection, U.S. Department of Agriculture, U.S. Environmental Protection Agency, New York state agencies, the environmental community, and most importantly, the farmers and foresters. (*Watershed Farm & Forest* 2001)

A critical element for long-term success is education. Many participants in the agreement, city officials, and rural watershed residents recognize the need for more information, active communication, and educational programs to build common understanding among people in the city and the rural watersheds about the agreement's voluntary, incentive-based approach. If the agreement is to work, it has to be sustainable over the long term, which will require that future generations and political leadership understand it (Nancy Wolf, personal communication). The new filtration waiver granted by the EPA reflects the importance of education by requiring a continued commitment by New York City to fund the CWC's Education Program, providing grants to schools and nonprofit organizations (*The Watershed Advocate* 2002). An important educational goal is to develop a sense of community among people from the rural watersheds to the city: "Hopefully," says Alan White of the Watershed Agricultural Council, "people here in the watersheds are beginning to recognize New York City as part of our community, and City officials and residents are beginning to recognize farmers, forest landowners, and loggers as part of their community." Educational efforts need to focus on how water links people in the city and rural watershed communities and how their mutual environmental, social, and economic well-being is connected through actions in the Catskill and Delaware watersheds. The Watershed Agreement is a premier example of a major urban area and rural communities working together to bridge their differences and experiment with an incentive-based, natural systems approach, seeking to protect environmental resources and maintain rural working landscapes. It is an agreement that will chart the course of resource management and environmental protection in a highly influential region of the United States and provide many lessons for people in other parts of the country and the world.

References

Coombe, Richard. 1994. "Watershed Protection: A Better Way." Prepared for the Groundwater Protection Council Symposium, Watershed Agricultural Council, Grahamsville, N.Y.

"Delaware County Profile: Income and Poverty. 1995." Southern Tier East Regional Planning Development Board, Binghamton, N.Y.

Department of Environmental Protection, New York State. N.d. "Description of Forestry Management Program and Agricultural and Forestry Economic Development Activities with the Watershed Agricultural Council.

Krudner, Maureen. 1997. "New York City: Case Study in Watershed Management." In *People, Places, and Partnerships: A Progress Report on Community-Based Environmental Protection.* Washington, D.C.: U.S. Environmental Protection Agency.

New York City Watershed Agreement. 1996. Public Review Draft. New York City Department of Environmental Protection.

Powell, Michael, and Andrea Bernstein. 1996. "Is Watershed Deal Springing Leaks?" *New York Observer,* June 24, 1.

Ray, Joel, and Nola Heidlebaugh. 1996. "Cows in the Creek: The Dispute between New York City and the Watershed Farmers." Unpublished paper. Program on Environmental Conflict Management, Cornell Center for the Environment, Cornell University, Ithaca, N.Y.

Revkin, Andrew C. 1997. "A Billion-Dollar Plan to Clean the City's Water at Its Source." *New York Times,* August 31, 25.

Summers, Carolyn. 1995. "Incorporating Natural Systems into Urban Infrastructure." In *Proceedings of the 7th National Urban Forest Conference.* Washington, D.C.: American Forests.

The Watershed Advocate. 2002, Summer. Newsletter of the Catskill Watershed Corporation, Margaretville, N.Y.

U.S. Department of Agriculture Forest Service. 2002. Summary data on federal funding of New York City Watersheds (August 6). Northeastern Area State and Private Forestry, Newtown Square, Pa.

Watershed Farm & Forest. 2001, Winter. Newsletter of the Watershed Agricultural Council, Walton, N.Y.

Watershed Forest Ad Hoc Task Force. 1996. "Policy Recommendations for the Watersheds of New York City's Water Supply." New York State Water Resources Institute, Cornell University, Ithaca, N.Y.

CHAPTER 2

Against the Odds

(RE)BUILDING COMMUNITY THROUGH
FORESTRY ON THE HOOPA RESERVATION

Mark Baker

For millennia, the Hupa people have inhabited the "twelve-mile square" that today is the Hoopa Reservation. This land, an hour inland from the Pacific Ocean in northwestern California, is a mix of forested mountains and river bottoms that bears the scars of destructive Anglo timber harvest and other resource-extraction activities. The first wave of Anglo miners arrived in the mid-nineteenth century, followed by soldiers, more miners, and later bureaucrats who tried to subjugate, forcibly assimilate, or kill the Hupa people. In the early years, the Hupa were spared the brunt of destructive Anglo incursions as a result of being off the main mining supply trails, and utilizing their fighting prowess and the protection of the dense forests. By the late 1800s, the Hupa, having secured the right—however tenuous—to remain in the valley, shifted the battle for survival to a battle with the U.S. government for the survival of their culture and identity. The tribe faced efforts by the federal government to forcibly remove Hupa children from their homes and the reservation and to ban displays of Hupa culture, among other acts. The Hupa continued to struggle for self-determination and autonomy throughout the twentieth century, finally achieving clarity regarding their reservation and rights to the benefit of their resource steward-ship with the passage of the 1988 Hoopa-Yurok Settlement Act, which followed a legal battle begun in 1963.

It is against this backdrop that the Hupa people are advancing management of the forest as a way of rebuilding community. The Hoopa tribe views enhancement of the forest ecosystem and enhancing human community health as interdependent goals. The forest landscape is treated as both an ecological landscape and a cultural landscape. This review of the Hoopa experience highlights projects associated with the Northwest Economic Adjustment Initiative, the socioeconomic side of the Clinton administration's Northwest Forest Plan, that are part of the Hoopa tribe's effort to jointly address community health and the destructive forest logging practices of the past 100 years. On the ecosystem side, the erosion from roads and forest management of the past have received particular

while at the local level a richly textured and culturally informed forest management regime has been adopted by the tribe, economic growth, particularly in the private sector, continues to stagnate, and nonlocal forces threaten to undermine the tribe's autonomy and resource base. Perhaps the most dramatic examples of the latter are the upstream water diversions in both the Trinity and the Klamath River basins for irrigation and power generation purposes and the continuing legal battles over them. For years, downstream Native American groups and coastal communities dependent on commercial and sport fishing have suffered as a result of these diversions. The recent unprecedented salmon kill during the summer of 2002 (more than 33,000 Chinook as well as steelhead and Endangered Species Act–listed coho) on the Klamath River is only the most recent sign of the ill health of the overall watershed and the unequal distribution of benefits and costs of its management. While the Hoopa tribe is supporting positive community–forest relations on reservation, off-reservation political processes, institutional structures, and resource management agencies continue to undermine efforts to advance community forestry and sustainable development on the reservation.

Background

The Hoopa Valley Indian Reservation is comprised of the Hoopa Square, a block twelve miles by twelve miles that contains 91,647 acres of land, of which approximately 75,000 acres are commercial timberland. The Hoopa Square is located in the northeast corner of Humboldt County in northwest California. The square is bisected in a north–south fashion by both the Trinity River and State Highway 96. The nearest moderately large towns are Eureka and Arcata, approximately an hour's drive from Hoopa west on State Highway 299. Redding, a much larger commercial center at the north end of California's Central Valley, is about two and a quarter hours from Hoopa east on State Highway 299. Other than the valley formed by the Trinity River floodplain, the reservation is comprised of relatively steep but highly productive interior coast range forestlands. Almost all the residences on the reservation are located on the valley floor.

There are approximately 2,000 enrolled members in the Hoopa Valley tribe. About 1,500 tribal members live on the Hoopa Valley Reservation, whose total population is 2,633 (U.S. Bureau of the Census 2000). Of the total reservation population, 2,230, or 84.7 percent, are American Indian. Nontribal reservation residents are Yurok and Karuk Tribal members, members of other tribes, nontribal member Native Americans, and non-Indians (U.S. Bureau of the Census 2000).

People–Forest Relations and Their Role in Enabling Hupa to Resist Violent Incursions

The residents of Hoopa Valley, known as Hupa after the Yurok word for their territory, have inhabited the Hoopa Valley for thousands of years. A dense web of complex and multilayered relations linking the Hupa people with the forest have evolved over time. Other than the redwood dugout canoes that were obtained through trade with the downstream Yurok people and the salmon harvested from the Trinity River, it is hard to think of any item of material culture that is not directly linked with the forest ecosystem. Previously, the forest provides timbers and planks for housing. It still provides fuelwood for heating; countless items of material culture fashioned from wood and nontimber forest products; plants that are managed and used for making the renowned Hupa baskets; staple food items, such as acorns, game animals, and a wide array of cultivated and managed edible plants and mushrooms; and a full suite of medicinal and sacred herbs, roots, and plants. Not surprisingly, many core aspects of Hupa cultural identity are also tied to the forest. These include the large repertoire of stories and myths associated with the forest, its inhabitants, and the sacred landscape they together comprise, as well as the key dances so central to creating and reinforcing Hupa lifeways, such as the White Deerskin Dance, the Jump Dance, and the Brush Dance, which are in many ways inextricably linked with the forest. The forest is also where Hupa people went and still go today to gain knowledge. Fasting at sacred locations, vision quests, and training sessions for aspiring medicinal practitioners and healers are all intimately connected to the forest and the broader landscape of which it is a part. These connections between forest and people have sustained the Hupa over millennia—materially, culturally, and in the realm of the sacred.

The multifaceted people–forest relationship was one factor that enabled the Hupa to survive the depredations against themselves and their land that began in the mid-nineteenth century following the first Anglo incursions and that continued through the beginning of the twentieth. Unlike other native groups in the region, the Hoopa Valley's residents successfully defended their land and their rights to live in their valley, resisted the attempts of outsiders to control and benefit from the valley's resources, and maintained the integrity of their cultural traditions and identity. Prior to the invasion of Anglo miners, agriculturists, entrepreneurs, and others triggered by the discovery of gold in California in 1849, the primary contacts between Anglos and Hupa consisted of peaceful interactions with early explorers and trappers, such as Jedediah Smith, who passed through the area in 1828. The discovery of gold and the opening of the Trinity mines and the Klamath and Salmon River mines in 1849–1850 dramatically transformed relations between American Indians of the region and Anglo outsiders. Fortunately for the

Hupa, the supply lines for the Klamath and Salmon River mines lay to the north of the Hoopa Valley through Yurok and Redwood Creek (Chilula) territory. Early miners and settlers may have avoided the Hoopa Valley because of rumors concerning Hupa military strength and prowess. Partly because of this, the Hupa people were spared the brutal massacres and horrific genocide that decimated the Wiyots of the Humboldt Bay area and devastated the populations of neighboring groups, such as the Yurok, Chilula, Mattole, and Sinkyone American Indians. Wherever American Indians either resisted Anglo incursions into their territory or were simply in the way, the Anglo response was systematically brutal. For example, a northern California newspaper, in the following chilling way, reported an incident in which Yurok villages at Weitchpec (at the confluence of the Trinity and Klamath Rivers) were attacked in retaliation for disrupting miners' supply trains and because those who lived there wanted to continue to erect fishing weirs: "The Indians are hostile at the forks of the Klamath and Trinity and it has been found necessary to administer to them the same rebuke we did to those on the coast. Some 50 or 60 Indians were killed and three villages burned. Effect good" (Alta, California, August 20, 1850, cited in Fredrickson 1982, 48).

In response to the growing violence that came to be referred to as the Indian Wars, the U.S. Congress sent Commissioner Redick McKee to the area in 1851 to establish treaties with American Indian groups of the area that would "protect" and "domesticate" them through the creation of reservations. McKee negotiated eighteen treaties in the region, including one with representatives of the Hupa, Yurok, and Karuk groups. However, none of the treaties was ratified by Congress, which rejected all of them in 1852, partly in response to public opinion that too much valuable land would be locked up by the reservation system (Fredrickson 1982). The Anglo settlers of the region opposed the establishment of reservations because it reserved land from potential settlement. Their desire was for the indigenous inhabitants to be either removed or exterminated to free up valuable resources for the Anglo influx to exploit (Huntsinger 1994, 13).

The Anglo influx continued apace. By 1860, there were twenty-five Anglo farmsteads and forty-five Anglo households in the Hoopa Valley. These early settlers were fearful of possible attacks. They knew that many Hupa men were well armed, having acquired arms and munitions from miners and traders (Fredrickson 1982, 59). Hupa families and clans staunchly resisted attempts to relocate them outside their ancestral homelands. During this period, the forest served as a haven to which Hupa fighters and families could flee. The forest and the Hupa people's knowledge of it facilitated their efforts to successfully resist attempts by the U.S. Army to relocate them to the Klamath Reservation (established by executive order in 1855).[2] Eventually realizing the futility of evicting the Hupa from their home and seeking to secure protection and their land claims, in 1858 settlers successfully petitioned the federal government to establish Fort Gaston in the Hoopa Valley. There followed several years of armed conflict, including the burning of Hupa villages and other scorched-earth tactics by vigilantes and the U.S. Army. Opposition to forced removal culminated in 1863 and 1864 with the successful resistance of Hupa fighters, based in the forest, against U.S. soldiers and their local guides. This resistance came to an end with the negotiation of the treaty of 1864 that established the Hoopa Valley Reservation (the reservation was not confirmed by executive order until 1876). In February 1865, most white settlers in the valley were given ten days' notice to leave the valley and were provided compensation for the assets they left behind. In 1867, "the last farm was turned over to the government" (Fredrickson 1982, 64).

Ongoing Struggles to Maintain Cultural Integrity and Control of Tribal Natural Resources

While the Hupa people had fought and won their struggle against Anglo settlers and the federal government to remain in their valley, the costs of the struggle had been enormous. By 1864, the number of Hupa villages had been reduced from eleven to four. This was due to a combination of factors, including consolidation for defensive purposes and population decline resulting from the combined effects of the slave trade in young boys and girls, war, disease, starvation, and migration due to fear of forced removal from the valley. By 1870, the estimated precontact Hupa population of 2,000 had been reduced to 601, which was further reduced to 460 by 1887 (Fredrickson 1982, 96).

Having won the initial struggle to remain in the Hoopa Valley, in the following decades the Hupa endured systematic efforts by the federal government to stamp out Hupa culture and identity. The primary vehicles for these efforts were the schools established by the BIA to which Hupa children were forcibly taken and taught to disdain their own ways and adopt those of the dominant culture. Some of these schools were as far away as Los Angeles and Oklahoma (Norton 1979, 113). Additionally, most BIA agents tried to ban the ceremonial dances central to Hupa culture and identity. Those who insisted on maintaining the Hupa way of life were punished by withholding their rations and supplies. Many were forced to rely on their knowledge of the forest to sustain themselves. In 1876, the Hupa people successfully resisted the coercive attempts of the BIA agent to relocate them (with planned military support) to the Round Valley Reservation, roughly one hundred miles to the south in what is now Mendocino County. While some Hupa sought safety by moving up into the forests, others planned violent resistance in response to this attempt to yet again remove them from their valley. Realizing the violence that would ensue if relocation were forcibly implemented, the agent, J. L. Broaddus, eventually dropped the relocation plan.

In addition to the attacks on their cultural identity, this period also witnessed a continued undermining of the natural resource base on which the Hupa people had previously depended. Miners, ranchers, and settlers encroached within the reservation boundary. These encroachers were ineffectively repelled by the reservation's administration, whose dual Interior and War Department jurisdiction only exacerbated problems, such as graft, corruption, and mismanagement. Furthermore, commercial salmon fishing and canneries had become established on the Klamath River by the 1880s. Soon after, the salmon runs on the Trinity River declined precipitously. They have yet to recover. The historically unprecedented salmon kill on the Klamath River in 2002 underlines the extent to which native people in northwestern California have still not been able to reclaim their water rights.

While native water rights claims remain contested, the Hupa people were able to solidify and reassert territorial rights in the form of private land titles and communal control over the reservation's forestlands near the end of the nineteenth century. Somewhat ironically, the vehicle for solidifying these tenurial claims was the Dawes, or General Allotment, Act of 1887. Based on the assumption that individual landownership would facilitate the assimilation of American Indians into the dominant culture, the Dawes Act authorized the allotment of forty- to sixty-acre tracts of land to assigned heads of households and individual American Indians. In most cases, implementation of the Dawes Act not only did not achieve the hoped-for objective of assimilating American Indians into mainstream American but also undermined the territorial integrity of many tribal groups and weakened their cultural integrity.

However, at Hoopa the opposite results were obtained. Rather than being a mechanism that resulted in land loss and undermined cultural integrity, the Dawes Act was used as an instrument for securing private tenurial rights and reserving most of the tribe's land base to be managed in perpetuity for the collective benefit of the tribal members. While the first surveys were made in 1889 and allotments soon followed, the allotment process was not finalized until 1919, and allotment schedules were not finalized until 1922–1923 (Norton 1973). Tribal timber lands, comprising most of the lands within the reservation, were reserved from allotment. This was exceedingly important because it meant that as the Hoopa tribe gradually developed their own "modern" institutional structures of governance and internal capacity for technically sophisticated resource management, they had a relatively large land base of collectively owned intact forestlands that they could manage—once they regained control over them.

Political Autonomy, Emerging Governance Structures, and Increasing Control over Natural Resources

The institutional structures through which the Hupa strengthened their autonomy, sovereignty, and self-governance evolved gradually throughout the twentieth century. The first formal Hoopa Valley Tribal Council was created through elections in 1911 at the instigation of the BIA superintendent (Roschmann 1991, 114). The early council activities focused on maintenance and construction of reservation infrastructure. They also provided early opportunities for familiarizing members with government processes. However, as Roschmann (1991) notes, the council possessed relatively limited power and autonomy; "self-government took place only to the degree that . . . Hupas did not undermine the status quo . . . the council's real purpose was to relieve the Superintendent of a 'great number of small matters,' not to institute a self-governing political body competing with the agent's authority" (118). Eventually, in 1927 the council was dissolved by the BIA because, as outgoing Superintendent Keeley stated in 1930, "tribal councils are the biggest source of agitation of anything in the Indian Service. They are usually made up of the hand picked agitators, and for the most part, the ones who can not, or will not, work or do anything for themselves" (cited in Roschmann 1991, 118).

Throughout this period, an informal "council of the people," some of whom were members of the earlier formal council, continued to meet and press for political self-determination and economic self-sufficiency. Many of these council members were elected to the 1933 BIA-approved seven-member Hoopa Valley Business Council. Support for tribal councils had been growing throughout the 1920s as reformers such as John Collier, commissioner of Indian Affairs for the new Roosevelt administration, publicized the disastrous impacts of the Dawes Act and called for greater American Indian autonomy and self-governance through the creation of tribal councils that demonstrated principles of indirect rule. However, as with other colonial examples of indirect rule, tribal council authority stopped far short of true self-governance. As a sign of protest against the limited authority granted the tribal council, most of the 1933 Business Council members chose not to run in the 1935 election.

In a related move, the tribe, in a referendum held in 1934, voted 174 to 8 to reject the 1934 Indian Reorganization Act (IRA), which repealed the Dawes Act (and the allotment system) and contained several provisions to support education, economic development, and tribal self-governance. The resounding rejection of the IRA was out of step with most Indian tribes who stood to benefit from its provisions. Roschmann (1991) explains this apparent anomaly by arguing that the

Hupa people had strategically employed provisions of the Dawes Act to secure their landownership claims and that by rejecting the IRA they sought to retain their tenurial security. Other reasons included the rejection of the self-governance provisions of the IRA that fell short of government-to-government relations and concerns that accepting the IRA would possibly weaken Hupa claims based on the unratified 1851 and related treaties. Seen in this light, the anomalous rejection of the IRA by the Hupa was consistent with Hupa efforts to strengthen their control over forest and other natural resources within the reservation as well as to advance their self-determination and self-governing capacities. Meanwhile, the Hoopa Valley Business Council continued to assert its authority in arenas where it could, such as the use of tribal money in a revolving loan fund and "in local matters, such as inheritance claims, land disputes, the protection of fish and game, and the observance of tribal customs . . . but in larger issues they found that the government would approve only those resolutions which echoed national policies" (Norton 1979, 177).

The following years were marked by continuing efforts by the Hupa to advance their self-determination and their ability to control and benefit from the reservation's natural resource base. In 1952, the constitution and bylaws of the Hoopa Valley Tribe were approved by the commissioner of Indian affairs (Hostler and Hostler 1967). In 1955, the commissioner authorized per capita payments to Hoopa Valley tribal members from revenues associated with the increased timber harvesting occurring on the Hoopa Square under BIA management. Passage of Public Law 280 in 1953 transferred jurisdiction over many Indian lands as well as civil and criminal matter to the states and ushered in the "termination era" of federal Indian policy history. While termination policies had relatively little effect on the Hoopa Valley Indian Reservation, this was a period of tremendous land loss by the downstream Klamath River–based Yurok people; many Yurok allottees took their allotments out of trust status and fee patented them to loggers or logging companies (Huntsinger 1994, 27). The termination era came to an end in the 1960s and was replaced with a federal emphasis on Indian self-determination, including tribal authority for natural resources management. Principles of self-determination and self-governance were further advanced by the Indian Self-Determination and Education Act of 1975, which, among other things, included provisions for tribal contracting for services that the BIA and other government services previously provided.

Throughout this period and until passage of the 1988 Hoopa-Yurok Settlement Act, there existed significant unresolved issues concerning whether the Hoopa Valley Reservation created in 1864 and its subsequent enlargement in 1891 to include the downstream Klamath Reservation and the connecting strip between the two was a single, integrated reservation and whether Yurok tribal members were entitled to a portion of the timber revenues generated by timber sales on the original Hoopa Valley Reservation (the Hoopa Square). Legal action in 1963 brought by downstream Yurok tribal members who claimed a share of the revenues from the square was not resolved until the 1988 Hoopa-Yurok Settlement Act. Until 1978, the BIA had used the Hoopa Valley Business Council to manage the tribal timber resources and profits, but in that year it took over the management of the assets from the timber management program and held them in trust for both groups until the passage of the 1988 Settlement Act. The act divided the trust account between the two tribes, partitioned the land into two distinct reservations, and mandated that the Yurok form their own tribal government (Huntsinger 1994, 32).

Forest Management and Its Social and Ecological Legacy

After World War II, the Hoopa Valley tribe became increasingly dependent on industrial-scale timber harvesting for generating economic revenue. Until the early 1980s, timber harvesting and processing remained the mainstay of the reservation economy. Until 1991, forestry and timber harvesting was managed by the BIA. The short-run dividend was a plethora of jobs and revenue that benefited community well-being if narrowly construed in economic terms. However, the industrial-scale focus of forest management at Hoopa for much of this period was associated with a number of factors that ran contrary to the historically diverse and culturally informed community–forest relations that had existed previously. For example, industrial-scale timber harvesting disrupted the abundance and collection of many nontimber forest products. Indeed, until more participatory forest management processes were adopted following the assumption of the Hoopa Valley tribe's control over forestry operations, there was minimal incorporation of culturally informed values and forest management practices with the forest management plan. In addition, the intensive harvesting pressure, combined with the dominant forestry practices of the time, bequeathed the tribe a host of ecological problems, including poorly stocked hardwood and brush-dominated conifer stands and a dense network of roads, landings, and crossings that contribute large amounts of sediment to streams that support salmonid species and are used for domestic water supply. In short, while providing short-run economic benefits, the dominant model of BIA-managed forestry at Hoopa weakened the dense web of relations that bind the community and forests and generated negative environmental effects, both of which constitute much of the forest legacy with which the tribe must now contend.

For the three decades following World War II, timber harvest levels exceeded sustained yield. Despite an early timber inventory by a BIA forester in 1947 that suggested that the timber base could support an annual allowable cut of 15 million board feet (mm b.f.) per year, actual harvest levels for the next thirty years were much higher. During the 1950s, the allowable cut hovered around 35 mm b.f.; this was increased to 40 mm b.f. during the 1960s. After destructive floods in 1955, 1962, and 1964, salvage harvesting operations, supported by both the BIA and the Tribal Council, were authorized, and the allowable cut increased to 60 mm b.f. In the mid-1970s, information from forest inventory plots installed in 1971 led to a revised allowable cut of 26 mm b.f.; however, the Sacramento BIA office rejected this estimate and retained the 40 mm b.f. as the allowable cut. Throughout the 1950s, 1960s, and 1970s, logging and millwork provided the great majority of nontribal government–related jobs for reservation residents. Although management and other supervisory positions were almost always held by nonlocal non-Indians, logging and millwork were the economic engines during this period. As a result of reductions in the allowable cut, by 1981 all five mills on the reservation had closed, and employment opportunities in logging were reduced by 85 percent (Office of Research and Development 1996, 23). Finally, in 1986, in response to further documentation of actual growth and yield of timber and reductions in timber harvest areas due to withdrawals or restrictions of commercial forest management, the Sacramento BIA office adopted a reduced annual allowable cut of 13.4 mm b.f. in its Interim Operating Plan, 1983–1992. This plan, however, was rejected by the Tribal Council in 1984, primarily because of unacceptable references within the plan to Yurok claims and other more technical issues.

The history of the rise and decline and stabilization of reservation timber harvest levels has several implications for current efforts to promote economic development. First, timber harvest levels are more likely to drop than increase in the future. This means that the timber industry, in the foreseeable future, will not be the primary economic engine that it was in recent decades. Thus, economic diversification, while fraught with challenges, likely is the most promising approach for stimulating investment and economic growth. Second, the existing forest condition bears the marks of long-term disinvestment and liquidation of the forest asset. On the basis of analyses of regeneration survey data in the late 1980s, the Forestry Division of the tribe's Natural Resources Department concluded that approximately 10,000 acres of timberland were taken over by brush and hardwoods with little or no conifer stocking and that the conifers on more than 7,000 acres were being outcompeted by brush. Third, the reservation's timberland area is characterized by extremely dense road networks (in excess of 4.5 miles per square mile overall, and in some watersheds the density approaches 6 miles per square mile). These road networks constitute the primary source of sediment delivery to

streams and a direct threat to aquatic ecosystems. Road restoration and forest rehabilitation are therefore high priorities for the tribe.

Restoring the Forest and Reinvigorating the Community–Forest Relationship

For more than a decade, the Hoopa Valley tribe has had full authority for managing the reservation's forestlands. Following the 1988 Hoopa-Yurok Settlement
Act, the tribe increased its control over forest management, initially by contracting with the BIA for various aspects of forest planning and management. By
1991, all aspects of the tribe's forest management program were tribally managed, including timber sale layout, administration, scaling, wildland fire, silviculture, and forest development (Hoopa Valley Tribal Forestry Division 1994,
169). Seen from a historical perspective, this is the culmination of more than
150 years of struggle for political autonomy, self-determination, and the right to
remain in the valley they inhabited for thousands of years. Having successfully
defended their claims to the forest resources within the reservation and maintained communal ownership of those resources, the Hoopa Valley Indian Reservation, through the Forestry Division, now faces the challenging task of maintaining an economically viable forest management regime while contending with
the destructive ecological legacies of past management practices and striving to
reintegrate the full suite of community–forest relationships into the formal forest management process. A further challenge is the need to, within a context of
long-term reductions in timber harvest levels, develop innovative ways to generate maximum forest-related employment and small-business opportunities related to forest products. The resumption of full control over their forest resources
allows the Hupa to reintegrate and fashion new forest–people relations. As will
be discussed shortly, the grant and funding opportunities offered by the NEAI
facilitated this process in numerous ways.

One of the first priorities of the tribe was to develop their own forest management plan, as distinct from the BIA forest management plan, which had hith-
erto governed forest management on the reservation. An important feature of the
plan development process (which lasted from 1992 to 1994) consisted of the efforts to solicit input from tribal members. Numerous avenues were pursued for
soliciting tribal input. In April 1992, a written questionnaire was sent to all tribal
members asking about their concerns and for their input on forest management
issues; the results were sent back to the membership in October of that year.

This extensive outreach and tribal member input associated with the forest
plan development process built on earlier intensive collaborative efforts between

the Forestry Division of the Natural Resources Department and the Hoopa Valley Tribal Council. By 1993, a video was made of different forest management options, and a copy was sent (nine hundred in total) to each tribal member's household. The purpose of the video was to provide visual images of what different forest management alternatives would look like and to solicit additional input regarding tribal member preferences. Innovative relationships were also developed at this time between the University of California Cooperative Extension as well as with the University of California, Berkeley, faculty. These collaborative links facilitated the tribe's efforts and abilities to compile their own geographic information systems database for forest management planning and to conduct an allowable harvest analysis. The combination of in-house forest management technical capacity, Tribal Council input, and solicitation of tribal member perspectives enabled the Tribal Forestry Division to develop a forest management plan that reflected the full spectrum of interests and values with respect to the tribe's forest resources. These interests and values were translated into a set of general goals and minimum management requirements that would be applicable regardless of which plan alternative was eventually chosen.

The extensive outreach process resulted in the identification of nearly 1,000 "issue, concern, or opportunity statements" that were grouped into several subject areas, such as cultural, socioeconomic, and biodiversity areas (Hoopa Valley Tribal Forestry Division 1994:3). Cultural issues, concerns, and opportunities included the need to burn for the maintenance of traditional plants and to protect traditionally important nontimber forest product sites, such as tanoak and mushroom areas. Socioeconomic issues, concerns, and opportunities included the need to maintain an economically viable timber harvesting regime that provided quality jobs, fire protection and arson control, and road management and construction, among others. Biodiversity issues, concerns, and opportunities focused on the effects of timber management on water quality and fisheries and timber management's cumulative impacts on water quality as transmitted through direct impacts on soils and watershed conditions. Other biodiversity-related issues related to past, present, and future silvicultural practices and the effects of timber management on wildlife.

The forest plan alternative that was eventually chosen for the 1994–2003 period sets the annual allowable cut at 10.4 mm b.f., significantly lower than any prior post–World War II allowable cut level. The plan prioritizes stand rehabilitation and conifer restocking of areas that were captured by brush and tanoak following previous timber harvesting activities using manual release and planting methods (herbicide application was banned by a tribal resolution in the late 1970s). It identifies a wide variety of watershed restoration activities needed to protect domestic water sources and to protect and enhance salmonid habitat. In response to issues raised by tribal members concerning cultural and socioeconomic issues, the plan identifies a large number of archaeological and ceremonial sites as well as eight specific cultural areas that include mushroom gathering areas, Port Orford Cedar areas, and camps and campgrounds, in which little or no timber harvesting is allowed. These cultural areas total more than 6,000 acres. Additionally, silvicultural prescriptions for timber harvesting in areas that produce mushrooms and other nontimber forest products but that are outside designated cultural areas are developed in a manner that is sensitive to the need to maintain and/or enhance their abundance. The plan also identifies forest areas important as viewsheds, wildlife areas (such as riparian corridors, travel corridors, falcon activity centers, and traditional species activity areas), and riparian areas in which timber harvesting is also restricted or not allowed at all. In short, the current forest plan effectively maps onto the tribe's forest ecosystem a wide variety of culturally informed and traditional forest management practices and uses. The extent to which a cultural overlay modifies, shapes, and conditions the tribe's timber harvest operations is unprecedented. It represents the landscape effects of the integration of sovereignty, technical forest management capacity, and a participatory process that encourages the expression of culturally rooted values and interests that pertain to the forest resource.[3]

The NEAI at Hoopa: Its Role in Strengthening Community–Forest Relations

Many of the NEAI projects at Hoopa touch on or engage directly with the dense web of relations that bind together the community and the forest ecosystem. In general, these projects were advanced on the assumption that enhancing community well-being and improving forest ecosystem health are interdependent goals. The focus of the following discussion is on those projects that most directly address the community–forest relationship. These include several grants by the Economic Development Administration to the tribe's Office of Research and Development for capacity-building and training purposes, a grant from the U.S. Department of Agriculture's (USDA's) Rural Development Department for a revolving loan program, U.S. Forest Service support for the Hoopa Valley Tribe's Tsemeta Forest Nursery to expand its native seed and medicinal herb collection and processing capabilities, and a Forest Service grant to support an oral history research effort of the Hupa Language, Culture, and Education Program, among others. The largest NEAI grants, provided to the tribe by the BIA, were for a variety of forest restoration efforts. The purpose of this discussion is to illuminate both the nature of the relationship and some of the ways in which the tribe is currently trying to reinvigorate it.[4]

OFFICE OF RESEARCH AND DEVELOPMENT
FOREST-RELATED GRANTS

The Office of Research and Development (until 1995 known as the Planning, Research, and Development Division) is responsible for planning and coordination of economic development activities. Its purpose is to stimulate private and public investments that provide employment and economic growth opportunities. All but two of the NEAI grants received by the Office of Research and Development came from the Economic Development Administration of the Department of Commerce; the non–Economic Development Administration grants came from the USDA's Rural Business Enterprise Grant program. Several of the grants that the Office of Research and Development received were for economic development planning, specifically to reduce the tribe's economic dependence on timber harvesting and to promote private sector growth. Some of the grants that the Office of Research and Development received did directly relate to the forest ecosystem. For example, a 1995 Economic Development Administration planning grant enabled the tribe to develop a feasibility study of a log-sort yard for value-added wood processing and a small mill. While the log-sort yard and mill has not been developed, there are currently efforts under way to develop value-added processing facilities for the tribe's SmartWood-certified hardwood resource (primarily oak and madrone).

Recent Economic Development Administration grants to the Office of Research and Development include provisions for developing a small-business incubator facility that will be managed in association with the Business Service Center. The business incubator will, among other things, provide floor space, kilns, metalwork facilities, and woodworking equipment to complement the business center's technical and financial analysis services as well as sales and marketing support for emerging and expanding small-scale business entrepreneurs. The incubator would also facilitate the development of food processing businesses, such as a cannery, through the provision of a commercial kitchen and other services. Many Hupa entrepreneurs are artisans (basket weavers, metalworkers, woodworkers) whose work, materials, and creativity is closely linked with the forest ecosystem, both as a source of raw materials and as culturally mediated inspiration and artistic design.

ORAL HISTORY, HUPA IDENTITY, AND FOREST RELATIONS

In 1998, the U.S. Forest Service, through its Rural Community Assistance program, made a grant to the Office of Research and Development and the Hupa Language, Culture, and Education Program, which focused on recording and preserving Hupa oral history, customs, and traditions. The grant was supplemented by contributions from the Hoopa Valley tribe and the National Endowment for the Arts. The purpose of the effort was to preserve existing Hupa oral histories, to interview elders, and to prepare a publication about Hupa oral history that could be used in educational contexts.

A primary thrust of this effort was a focus on women elders and the transmission of knowledge concerning Hupa values, traditions, and culture from women elders to younger women and girls. Organizers of the project wanted to provide a vehicle for communicating to Hupa girls the "everyday Native American worldview" of Hupa women who were seventy to eighty years old, and to help Hupa girls find ways of being Hupa in the contemporary world. Hupa women college graduates interviewed several women elders as part of this project. In addition to recollections concerning their own lives, such as their experiences as children in the BIA boarding schools, many of the women elders spoke about the importance to them of the sacred dances and their role in some of these dances. Many also described their memories of making trips to the forest with older woman to collect materials for basket weaving and the strong relations that bound elder and younger Hupa women. Portions of the interviews with three women elders were developed into a booklet titled *Collecting, Preserving, and Sharing Our Heritage* (Hoopa Language, Culture, and Education Program 2000).

The results of this effort, including but not limited to the published booklet, have been used as the basis for a Hoopa summer school program for children in grade school, particularly those between the ages of nine and fifteen. About thirty girls participate in the summer program. Part of the effort to equip young Hupa women and girls to learn how to be Hupa in the contemporary world involves revitalizing and reacquainting their relationship with the forest. To accomplish this, the summer program includes trips into the forest to learn and practice some of the things the women elders discussed in their interviews. The links between identity, education, and the forest are reflected in this project.

A REVOLVING LOAN PROGRAM
AND FOREST-BASED EMPLOYMENT

In 1998, USDA Rural Development granted the Tribal Loan Department $105,000 to be used as a revolving loan fund. Joyce Johnson, a loan officer in the department, applied for, received, and managed the grant. In managing the grant, she made a concerted effort to make as many small loans to as large a number of people as possible. Of the approximately thirty loans made from this grant, the majority of them were for $2,000 or less. All the loans were made to individuals who were either starting or expanding a business. Many of the small loans supported small businesses that were directly or indirectly related to the forest. For example, several forest contractors used small loans to purchase equipment and supplies or for the bond money required to bid on jobs. And self-employed artisans, such as woodworkers, metalworkers, basket weavers, and jewelry craftspeople were also able to purchase needed equipment and supplies. Some of the larger loans were used for purposes such as the purchase of a dump truck for a self-employed contractor, remodeling a downtown restaurant that had been damaged by fire, and helping establish a new downtown coffeehouse. These latter two establishments are both owned and managed by Hupa women entrepreneurs. Additionally, many of the artisans who were able to purchase supplies and equipment using this loan fund were also women. Consistent with other microcredit programs around the world, repayment rates were very high, approaching 100 percent. That many of the loans were made to forest-related businesses underscores the close links between community, economy, and the forest at Hoopa.

TSEMETA FOREST NURSERY: EXPANDING FROM CONIFER SEEDLINGS TO THE DIVERSITY OF NONTIMBER FOREST PRODUCTS

Tsemeta Forest Nursery was initially constructed in the late 1980s as a state-of-the-art glass-covered greenhouse for growing containerized forest planting stock. For the first ten years of its operation, the nursery staff concentrated on producing containerized forest seedlings that were purchased under contract by the Hoopa Valley Tribal Forestry Division, the U.S. Forest Service, the Bureau of Land Management, and the California Department of Forestry for reforestation and forest restoration projects. However, by the late 1990s, with the dramatic reduction in forest harvest levels, especially clear-cutting practices, the demand for forest seedlings for replanting purposes sharply declined. Nursery manager Elton Baldy, recognizing the need to diversify the range of products and plants produced by the nursery, began exploring the potential for producing ornamental plants, shrubs and trees, native plants and grasses, and medicinal herbs. As part of this diversification effort, in 1997 Elton Baldy applied for a Forest Service grant to support native seed and medicinal plant drying and processing facilities. In 1998, the U.S. Forest Service Rural Community Assistance program provided such a grant. By this time, relationships had been developed with wildcrafters in the region, including the High Mountain Herb Cooperative, Trinity Alps Botanicals, and other individual wildcrafters. It was envisioned that Tsemeta Forest Nursery would be able to enter into partnerships with these wildcrafters through the purchase of their raw product and then drying, processing, and marketing it. Additionally, the nursery anticipated on-site production and processing of medicinal herbs and native grasses. To this end, a plot of land was certified for organic production by the California Certified Organic Growers Association.

The enhanced nursery infrastructure that the grant enabled has allowed the nursery to purchase, process, and sell a variety of different native grasses and medicinal herbs. The propagation of native grasses and other native plants used in ecosystem restoration projects has been relatively successful and is consistent with the forest restoration needs of the Hoopa tribe and of adjacent public and industrial forestland owners. However, several challenges have beset the nursery's efforts to grow, process, and market medicinal herbs. For example, the High Mountain Herb Cooperative, at one time a promising partner for medicinal herb collecting and processing, is no longer in operation. One of the reasons for the cooperative's demise is the fickle and cyclical market for medicinal herbs. Unpredictable market shifts, in part due to the globalization of the medicinal herb market, have made it difficult for wildcrafters and the nursery alike to identify products whose prices are stable and that are economically viable to grow or wildcraft, process, and sell. While the Forest Service grant has helped Tsemeta Forest Nursery diversify its operation, the nursery has been challenged to diversify its operation to ensure its survival. Successful economic development that draws on people's local forest knowledge is constrained by both nonlocal factors and the ability of a small, local enterprise to respond to these dynamic and challenging conditions and local relationships. A healthy people–forest relationship may be a necessary but not sufficient condition for sustainable community-based development.

HOOPA VALLEY TRIBAL FORESTRY DIVISION, FOREST RESTORATION, AND CREATING JOBS IN THE WOODS

The dominant post–World War II forest management practices have bequeathed the Hoopa tribe a legacy of thousands of acres of brush- or oak-dominated land that once supported old-growth conifers, a heavily roaded landscape, and a current and potential sediment delivery problem that threatens the tribe's vital fishery as well as domestic water supply sources. It is widely accepted that erosion rates on reservation lands are quite high. For example, the magnitude of erosion from reservation roads is three times higher than for roads in the adjacent Redwood Creek watershed, which is mostly under industrial timberland management (Oldenburg 2001). Oldenburg, a tribal forestry hydrologist, suggests that this difference is not surprising given the "size, type, location, and maintenance levels on these roads" (2001, 9). There is clearly a need to pursue vigorous forest and watershed restoration work and with that work to provide employment to former timber workers. The Hoopa Valley Tribal Forestry Division has been working aggressively on these fronts, and support from the NEAI has helped them do so. The watershed restoration projects funded by the NEAI clearly illustrate the link between ecosystem restoration and employment generation.

Between 1994 and 1998, the Forestry Division of the Natural Resources Department received five Jobs-in-the-Woods grants, all through the BIA. The grants funded a combination of watershed assessment and restoration, monitoring, and contractor/worker training in Mill Creek, Bull Creek, Tish Tang, and Pine Creek. These four watersheds were prioritized for restoration work on the basis of watershed assessments across the reservation. The assessments also guided the restoration activities within each watershed. The goals and objectives of these efforts were to reduce sediment delivery to high priority streams by treating sites of chronic or potentially catastrophic sediment production; to create jobs for heavy-equipment operators and contractors previously employed by the timber industry; and to set up long-term monitoring stations to assess effectiveness of restoration efforts and general aquatic ecosystem health (Blomstrom 1996, 1).

By the end of 1996, these watershed restoration efforts had produced impressive results. A 1997 watershed restoration status report notes that a total of 90,580 cubic yards of material had been removed from the Mill Creek, Pine Creek, and Tish Tang Creek drainages and that 129,305 cubic yards of material were estimated to have been saved from entering streams (Blomstrom 1997, 1). This latter figure represents a sizable proportion of the total treatable sediment volume of 192,670 cubic yards estimated by Pacific Watershed Associates (a private consulting firm) for these three drainages. Prior watershed assessment work by Pacific Watershed Associates, as modified, updated, and mapped with geographic information systems (GIS) by the Tribal Forestry Division, provided the basis for prioritizing drainages and individual sites for restoration work. This allowed restoration funds allocated to the tribe to be used most effectively.

Because provision of employment was a key goal of these projects, contractor training for restoration work was made a priority for this work. Training workshops for road restoration, decommissioning, and obliteration were provided to local contractors. Not only were these free of charge, but contractors received a stipend for participating in them. Restoration efforts for calendar years 1995 and 1996 provided a total of nine full-time jobs for the four-month restoration season. All these individuals had previously been employed by the timber industry. One of the contractors who participated in the restoration workshops and who was contracted to decommission several roads has subsequently been able to successfully bid on Bureau of Land Management watershed restoration contracts in other parts of Humboldt County.

While the first grants to the Tribal Forestry Division focused on watershed restoration efforts, the later grants addressed ongoing assessment and monitoring needs. One example of this is Supply Creek, which currently has impaired anadromous fish habitat and impaired domestic water supplies. Research by the Tribal Forestry Division shows that, on average, Supply Creek background sediment yields were 4,585 tons per year between 1954 and 1993, while sediment yields from roads and log loading sites were 25,930 tons per year. This high level of sedimentation has compromised the water supply of about 1,500 valley residents. The watershed assessment grant from the BIA enabled Tribal Forestry to identify fifteen major issues concerning the current condition of the watershed. The watershed assessment developed watershed restoration project objectives and then specified restoration activities, complete with field reviews and tentative restoration prescriptions. This work provided the basis for the next Jobs-in-the-Woods NEAI grant, which requested funding for implementing restoration activities on Supply Creek.

In 1998, the tribe received a grant from the BIA to conduct watershed restoration activities in Supply Creek. The restoration work was designed to stabilize upland slopes and reduce the potential for future sediment delivery to Supply Creek. This approach is based on the assumption that it is more cost effective to prevent the input of new material into already degraded streams and allow the normal stream energy to flush previous sediment inputs rather than attempting to excavate sediment from the stream. The proposed restoration work (most of which is now complete) is anticipated to prevent 193,000 cubic yards of material from entering the stream, thus reducing the time needed for the stream to recover from past sediment inputs, which currently total approximately 800,000 cubic yards of material. The work includes activities such as removal of stream crossings, reconstruction of existing rolling dips in forest roads and construction of new ones, reconstruction and stabilization of failing road fills and gullies, culvert installation, road decommissioning, and brush removal and moderate road construction work. All the on-the-ground watershed rehabilitation work was contracted out to local Indian contractors, most of whom had attended the "Watershed Restoration for Heavy Equipment Operators" training workshops offered as part of the previous NEAI grants to the Forestry Division.

The last NEAI grant from the BIA was awarded to the tribe in 1999 to fund baseline implementation and effectiveness monitoring of the last five years of watershed restoration work and timber harvesting activities on the reservation. Monitoring will take place in those watersheds in which NEAI-funded restoration work has taken place since the early 1990s plus a fifth watershed, Captain John Creek, which is relatively pristine and can function as a reference watershed. Captain John Creek is also an important domestic water supply. The project aims to test the implementation and effectiveness of forest and road management practices in terms of effects on water quality and fish productivity or habitat, to gather baseline data regarding total maximum daily limits for the tribe's water quality control plan, and to support GIS mapping of forest management activity cumulative effects. By assessing the effectiveness of current best management practices governing forest management in terms of their ability to maintain or enhance water quality, the monitoring will enable determination of whether adjustments are needed in these practices in order to protect water quality and fish habitat.

Conclusion: When Healthy Community–Forest Relations Are Not Enough

Community–forest relations at Hoopa once again emphasize the interdependence of community and forest health. The synergy between political sovereignty, cultural identity, and the control, management, and use of tribal forest resources is clearly evident. At Hoopa, culture is encoded through the diverse ways in which Hupa people use, value, and manage the natural resources on their reservation. The forest landscape of the reservation is as much a cultural landscape as it is an ecological landscape. Its structure and function in many ways encodes and reflects culturally informed resource management practices. Species important for basket weaving are actively managed for, as are a wide variety of medicinal herbs and other plants. Subsistence-oriented uses of the reservation's natural resources, such as fishing for salmon and the gathering of other foodstuffs, are both crucial safety nets for unemployed or underemployed people and their dependents as well as activities that are important vehicles for transmitting lifeways and practices central to Hupa identity. Not surprisingly, the tribe's Forest Management Plan acknowledges, provides for, and facilitates the cultural practices associated with these elements of Hupa culture; those species that are particularly valued within this culturally attuned natural resource management framework are actively managed.

However, a vital relationship between community and forest does not guarantee economic well-being. Even before the decline in timber harvesting in the late 1980s, low income levels and high unemployment characterized the reservation economy. In 1971, the median family income was $3,389, one-third of the national median family income of $11,106. The 1971 per capita income was $1,430, about one-third of the state per capita income of $4,610, while unemployment hovered around 30 percent (Hoopa Valley Business Council 1973, 2.202). Following the regional and reservation declines in timber harvests that began in the 1980s and the closure of all five mills located on the reservation, unemployment and associated hardships skyrocketed. Estimates of unemployment rate vary, but they are all high. A 1988 BIA Labor Force Report estimates unemployment at 81.43 percent (Office of Research and Development 1996, 23). Estimates of the heads of households whose income is below the established poverty income level range as high as 81.57 percent (Office of Research and Development 1996, 23). The 1990 census indicates a 40.7 percent poverty rate for households and a 29.6 percent unemployment rate for the reservation. The 1999 Tribal Census Project of the Tribal Data Resources Division reports an unemployment rate of 32.4 percent with an additional 5.3 percent employed only seasonally and 9.7 percent employed only part time for tribal members.

By almost any measure, poverty and unemployment rates are several times higher than county, state, or national averages. Private sector investment and job creation continues to stagnate, and addressing drug and alcohol abuse issues continues to be identified by the Tribal Council as a top priority. In short, traveling from the coastal portion of Humboldt County to the Hoopa Valley Indian Reservation is still, in many respects, analogous to moving from a First to a Third or Fourth World context, history, and economy.

At least two sets of implications concerning community well-being can be drawn from these statistics. The first concerns the fact that developing a vital and self-sustaining community–forest relationship, as has been accomplished at Hoopa, is not enough to ensure community well-being because of the off-reservation factors that hinder or support economic development, the exercise of political autonomy, and the control and management of tribal natural resources. As the example of the difficulties that Tsemeta Forest Nursery faced with processing and marketing of medicinal herbs illustrates, the local effects of globalization can seriously constrain reservation-based economic development initiatives. Other off-reservation factors also determine the sideboards of what can and cannot be accomplished on the reservation. Perhaps the most dramatic example of this is the 2002 salmon kill on the Klamath River. As of the time of this writing, approximately 33,000 dead Chinook salmon, many weighing more than forty pounds and laden with eggs, are rotting in the lower reaches of the Klamath River; many more carcasses will never be counted. More than 300 coho salmon and 600 steelhead, both listed as threatened under the Endangered Species Act, have also died. These fish, returning from the ocean to spawn in the gravel bars from which they hatched in prior years, have succumbed to diseases that have run rampant because of a lack of clean, cold water flows in the river and the consequent crowding and increased vulnerability of the salmon runs. While the science is predictably unclear, many suspect that upstream water diversions from the Klamath and Trinity Rivers for irrigation and hydroelectric power generation are at least partly responsible for the lethal low flows and warm temperatures in the Klamath River. While the Bureau of Reclamation has agreed to a request by the National Marine Fisheries Service to a temporary release of water from upstream reservoirs on the Klamath River, many suggest that this is too little too late and that while the release may enable fish to make it farther upstream, they will simply be trapped in smaller pools and holes when the pulse of water subsides. Downstream communities also question an Interior Department decision last year to restore water deliveries for upstream irrigators who depend on Bureau of Reclamation water for farming and ranching. This decision reduced this year's water flow in the Klamath to 76 percent of last year's, which was already considered a drought-year flow level. Furthermore, legal battles between the federal government and those who appropriate water from the Trinity River, such as Westlands Water District (in the arid San Joaquin Valley) and power generators, prevent the federal government from releasing water from the Trinity River to save the fish.

While the current crisis is acute, it is only the most recent manifestation of a process that began in the 1880s, when salmon overharvesting to supply the canneries on the lower Klamath decimated the upstream salmon runs in Hupa territory. And while it is not possible to convey in words what these historically unprecedented fish kills mean to native groups such as the Yurok and Hupa, for whom salmon constitute material, symbolic, and spiritual sustenance, it is clear that the struggles of the Hupa and neighboring tribes for self-determination and the right to maintain their traditional lifeways and culture are far from over. For while the Hupa may have embarked on a cutting-edge and sophisticated watershed restoration regime on their reservation, the cleanest gravels and purest cold pools and riffles will be useless for spawning fish if upstream diversions prevent the returning salmon from reaching them. Thus, achieving the goals for which the Hupa have long struggled requires an ability to reach beyond the reservation boundaries and effectively engage with some of the most powerful vested interest groups in the western United States: hydroelectric power generators and corporate agriculture. When community well-being, through the presence or absence of salmon, is linked with political and economic forces of this magnitude, it is clear that healthy community–forest relations are necessary but not sufficient for its realization.

The second set of implications regarding community well-being at Hoopa point to processes that are internal to the reservation and relate primarily to its economy. They concern the need for economic diversification, developing a strong private sector within the reservation economy, and attracting outside investment. Even in the early 1970s, when the timber industry was "healthy," the Hoopa Valley Business Council recognized the need for economic diversification to expand job opportunities, raise personal income levels, and reduce dependence on the timber industry. These goals remain a high priority for the tribe, and they constitute the guiding principles for tribal entities such as the Office of Research and Development, the Loan Department, and others.

They also inform the tribe's innovative efforts to understand and respond to the implications of tribal sovereignty for tribal economic development. As articulated by Daniel Jordan, self-governance coordinator and director of the tribe's Department of Commerce, the crucial and missing link in the calculus of tribal economic development is acknowledgment of the importance of the relationship between sustainable economic development and tribal sovereignty. Jordan and others argue that the central impediment to sustainable economic growth on reservations is the lack of understanding of the implications of tribal sovereignty for economic development. The fact that tribes are sovereign entities fundamentally differentiates them from other, nontribal communities. Because tribes are sovereign entities, state laws and institutions such as business codes, court systems, and other legal frameworks governing business transactions do not apply on reservation lands. The federal government has constitutionally reserved the right to conduct relations with tribes, but it does not regulate business relations. The state government does regulate business transactions, but it has no jurisdiction on reservations. The result is a void of uncertainty on reservations regarding business activity unless the tribe itself has enacted its own business and other codes. Because of this essential difference between reservation and nonreservation communities, Jordan argues that economic development programs and initiatives will never succeed in bringing about sustainable economic growth unless they first acknowledge these differences, understand the implications for policies that promote economic development, and then tailor programs and interventions accordingly.

Acknowledging the institutional and legal void at Hoopa, the tribe has recently taken the lead in developing its own set of comprehensive business codes. This is part of its effort to develop the court rules and business codes and associated infrastructure necessary for supporting tribal and nontribal business and economic development. These codes provide the "broad infrastructure and framework under tribal law that is needed by any business to be successful" (Jordan 1999, 4). The tribe has developed at least ten different business codes. For example, Title 50, the Tribal Comprehensive Business Policy Code, approved in 1998, sets out tribal and private sector business policies, tax policies, and preferences for supporting local businesses through local purchasing agreements and establishes a 1 percent business tax on gross revenues to help maintain the Tribal Department of Commerce. Other business codes include the Tribal Corporations and Entities Code, Tribal Non-Profit Corporations Code, and Tribal Small Business Incentive Program, among others. The tribe has also developed model articles of incorporation, by-laws, and commercial leases as well as a publication titled *Creating Business Opportunities on Indian Reservations*. With respect to court rules, the tribe has developed and adopted a comprehensive set of rules concerning the structure and operation of a tribal court system; procedures for the appointment and removal of judges; the structure and function of a tribal appellate court, clerk, and records; personnel policies; and jurisdictional issues.

Hoopa Valley Business Council. 1973. *Hoopa Valley Indian Reservation Comprehensive Plan.* Hoopa, Calif.: Hoopa Valley Business Council.

Hoopa Valley Tribal Council. 1998. *Tribal Comprehensive Business Policy Code.* Title 50 of the Hoopa Tribal Code. Hoopa, Calif.: Hoopa Valley Tribal Council.

Hoopa Valley Tribal Forestry Division. 1994. *Hoopa Valley Indian Reservation Forest Management Plan for the Period 1994–2003.* Hoopa, Calif.: Hoopa Valley Tribal Forestry Division.

Hostler, Patricia, and Byron Hostler. 1967. *History of the Hoopa Tribe.* Willow Creek, Calif.: Hoopa Valley Business Council.

Huntsinger, Lynn. 1994. *A Yurok Forest History.* Berkeley: University of California, Department of Environmental Science, Policy, and Management.

Hupa Language, Culture, and Education Program. 2000. *Collecting, Preserving, and Sharing Our Heritage.* Hoopa, Calif.: Hupa Language, Culture, and Education Program.

Jordan, Daniel. 1999. "Hoopa Valley Tribe Moves beyond Self-Governance to Create Business Environment." *Sovereign Nations: Newsletter of Tribal Self-Governance,* November/December.

Nelson, Byron, Jr. 1978. *Our Home Forever: The Hupa Indians of Northern California.* Hoopa, Calif.: Hupa Tribe.

Norton, Jack. 1964. "A Historical Review of the Hoopa Reservation and the First Allotting Program." Manuscript, Humboldt State University.

———. 1973. "A Land and Her People: A Summary Account of the Hupa." In Hoopa Valley Business Council, *Hoopa Valley Indian Reservation Comprehensive Plan.* Hoopa Valley, Calif.: Hupa Valley Business Council.

———. 1979. *Genocide in Northwestern California: When Our Worlds Cried.* San Francisco: Historian Press.

Norton, Jack, III. 2001. *Proposed Strategic Plan for Tsemeta Forest Nursery.* Hoopa, Calif.: Office of Research and Development.

Office of Research and Development. 1996. *Hoopa Valley Indian Reservation Transportation Plan.* Hoopa, Calif.: Office of Research and Development.

———. 1998. *Hoopa Valley Indian Reservation 1999 Overall Economic Development Strategy.* Hoopa, Calif.: Office of Research and Development.

Oldenburg, Edward. 2001. *Erosion Rates and Sediment Delivery Ratio of Forest Roads on the Hoopa Valley Indian Reservation, Hoopa, California.* Hoopa, Calif.: Hoopa Valley Tribal Forestry Division.

Roschmann, Joachim. 1991. "No Red Atlantis on the Trinity: The Rejection of the Indian Reorganization Act on the Hoopa Valley Indian Reservation in Northwestern California." Ph.D. diss., University of California, Davis.

U.S. Bureau of the Census. 2000. *Profile of General Demographic Characteristics, Hoopa Valley Reservation, California.* Washington, D.C.: U.S. Bureau of the Census.

U.S. Congress. 1988. Public Law 100-580, Hoopa-Yurok Settlement Act. Washington, D.C.: U.S. Government Printing Office.

CHAPTER 3

Revolutionizing County Forest Management in Minnesota
AITKIN COUNTY AND SMARTWOOD CERTIFICATION

Peter Lavigne

In 1997, Aitkin County, Minnesota, forestlands became the first county lands in the United States to be certified for sustainable forest management. Their certification has inspired other local-level agencies to pursue certification as a way to meet the increasing demand for "responsibly" produced forest products.

The story of Aitkin County certification begins with a local entrepreneur, county-level land managers, and local and nonlocal nonprofit organizations who were able to meld their ideas about good business, community development, and environmental responsibility with community and north-woods restoration and sustainable management of the local forest. A young owner of a small, wood products manufacturing operation announced that his company would eventually purchase only certified wood and began what he refers to as a "crusade" to open the market for certified forest products in Minnesota. At about the same time, the long-term commissioner and vice commissioner of the Aitkin County Land Department, who had been overseeing innovative forest management on county lands for a broad variety of ecosystem values (including wildlife, water, recreation, and native forest restoration), were promoting a vision of forest management as "heroic reintervention" with a two-hundred-year time horizon. Certification was a way to get there. Enter resources and assistance from a couple of local nonprofit organizations and one international trade research institute, and the Forest Stewardship Council's SmartWood certification process was under way. Certified forest sources soon became the rule rather than the exception in Aitkin County. Most major environmental organizations historically opposed certification of public lands because they believe that it insufficiently addresses historic abuse and habitat values while allowing for degrading industrial practices. Over the five-year period covered in this chapter, environmental opposition to the certification of public lands declined significantly. Some regional and national environmental organizations are now exploring and supporting sustainable use and restoration forestry as a means to restore forest ecosystems. The Aitkin County Land

Department can be considered a model agency for other public agencies attempting to promote both community development and ecosystem restoration while marrying business opportunities to forest restoration and sustainability.

In the fall of 1997, the Aitkin County, Minnesota, Land Department became only the second public forest manager, and the first at the county level, to be SmartWood certified as an environmentally responsible timber provider. Managing over 220,000 acres of forestland for a variety of purposes, including timber production, wildlife habitat, and recreation, the Aitkin County certification by the SmartWood program of the Rainforest Alliance was followed closely by SmartWood certification of 400,000 acres of Minnesota lands in Aitkin County managed by the Division of Forestry of the Department of Natural Resources. In July 2002, Aitkin County recertification by SmartWood was accepted and approved by the county commissioners. In the five years since the original Aitkin County certification, interest in "green certification" of publicly owned forestlands in the region has exploded.

In 1998, nine additional Minnesota counties approached the Minnesota legislature for $700,000 from a "sin" tax fund to pursue SmartWood certification. Despite strong support from a variety of interests, Sierra Club activists lobbied heavily against the appropriation, and it was defeated. The former Midwest regional director of the Sierra Club, Carl Zichella, currently working for the Sierra Club as California director, strongly opposed the efforts in 1998 but now supports public lands certification in the Great Lakes. Because of the loss of the state appropriation in 1998 and subsequent state budget deficits, only the Cass County Land Department (adjacent to Aitkin County) has been certified. In the late 1990s, many U.S. national forest districts began pursuit of Forest Stewardship Council certification . After lobbying by the Sierra Club and other organizations, the U.S. Forest Service imposed an initial one-year moratorium on federal land certification, and the American Forest and Paper Association successfully lobbied against other public land certification attempts in Wisconsin and Michigan. In 2002, national forest certification discussions remain off the table, though discussion of restoration forestry efforts and forest-thinning sales has gained significant momentum in Congress in the aftermath of a disastrous series of enormous forest fires throughout the West in 2002.

The story of the Aitkin County Land Department certification involves a number of key players and factors from the wood products industry, nonprofit organizations, the Forest Stewardship Council, the SmartWood program, institutions of higher education, the Institute for Agriculture and Trade Policy, and private foundations. The key factors include rules of the European (and especially the British) markets, consumer willingness to pay a premium for certified wood, and a decade-plus history of the Aitkin County Land Department's work in trying to manage for true multiple uses in a forest suffering the legacy of 150 years of clear-cutting, high grading, devastating fires, and general abuse.

Industry Kicks Off the "Revolution"— and the Demand

Eric Bloomquist does not look like a crusader. No suits of armor, no tilting at windmills. The self-effacing and enormously successful owner of Colonial Craft, a wood products manufacturer headquartered in Minneapolis–St. Paul, disclaims any revolutionary intent. Yet Eric and Colonial Craft, like Ben Cohen and Jerry Greenfield of Ben and Jerry's Ice Cream, have started a revolution in the wood products business—probably influencing the way this entire industry will operate in the future. At the same time, Eric is one of a handful of key individuals— including Roger Howard and Mark Jacobs of the Aitkin County Land Department; Mark Ritchie of the Institute of Agriculture and Trade Policy in Minneapolis; Bob Brander, former director of the Sigurd Olson Environmental Institute in Ashland, Wisconsin; Jon Jickling and Richard Donovan of SmartWood; Catherine Mater of Mater Engineering; and John Krantz of the Minnesota Department of Natural Resources—who kicked off a process that has revolutionized state and county land management in Minnesota.

Understanding the seventy-five-plus years of clear-cutting and devastation of the once-great pine forests of the upper Midwest in Michigan, Wisconsin, and Minnesota from the 1840s to the 1920s is essential to comprehending the end-of-the-century forest products business in Aitkin County and the upper Midwest. That history is documented in small community museums across the region. For just one example, the lumbering exhibit covering two floors of the Castle Museum in downtown Saginaw, Michigan, covers in apologetic detail[1] the numerous logging camps, sawmills, and river drives that turned the once-rich forests, swamps, and river systems of the region into the farming and manufacturing center of glorified ditches and contaminant-laden canals, factory sites, neatly plowed fields, and remnant woodlots characterizing the area today. As local fisherman and autoworker Jim Fauver said on a 1998 tour of Saginaw County, "There's hardly a place to fish in the entire state where there isn't a fish consumption advisory due to some contaminant or other." Saginaw County today, like many of its cousins in Michigan, Wisconsin, and Minnesota, consists of endless farmed fields, narrow wood rows, small villages, and an urban industrial center interrupted by heavily channelized and contaminated ditches that once were rivers.[2]

Historian Frederick Turner, in his insightful book *Rediscovering America: John Muir in His Time and Ours,* discusses a folk truth from the time of initial

European settlement of the East that related that "a squirrel could start in a tree on the seaboard and travel west all the way to the Mississippi without having to touch the earth." By 1800, according to Turner, the more than 400,000 square miles of gigantic climax forest reaching to the Mississippi had "been broken to the western portions of Pennsylvania,"[3] and by the 1880s, thirty years after Muir's teenage upbringing in central Wisconsin, "the great eastern forests had been logged out, and so had most of those in the Midwest."[4] Turner characterizes the clearing of the great woods harshly: "The way [the settlers] went about using up the forests of the eastern half of the continent had about it a kind of thoughtless rage, as if they really were at war with the wilderness, as Thoreau said."[5] By the late 1920s, the headwaters of the Mississippi River in Minnesota and Wisconsin had been thoroughly logged; the soils played out by poor farming practices caused spring floods to scour soil from the Mississippi watershed's north woods to the Gulf of Mexico with increasing regularity. Environmental and economic devastation followed as the land and its peoples entered the Great Depression—documented in such movies as the disturbing and starkly beautiful, award-winning 1937 movie *The River,* directed by Pare Lorentz, and books by Steinbeck, McWilliams, and others.[6]

Out of this context of devastation, in 1993, Colonial Craft, which manufactures window grille inserts, moldings, and casings; high-quality picture frames; and specialty wood parts like the racks on gas barbecue grills, announced to its wood suppliers that it intended eventually to buy only wood certified to have been grown and harvested in an environmentally sound and sustainable manner. It was a bold move, given that none of their suppliers were certified by either of the two assessors in the United States accredited by the Forest Stewardship Council, Scientific Certification Systems (SCS), or the SmartWood program.

In the late 1960s, Bloomquist, like so many of his north-country contemporaries, went to work during high school in a small manufacturing business. Rasmussen Millwork Inc. was a small operation specializing in making window grille inserts. In 1972, Bloomquist dropped out of college to buy the then-six-employee company doing business as Colonial Craft.[7] In 1980, with the first contract with Anderson Windows, the business really began its major growth. Over the years, Bloomquist built Colonial Craft into a $30 million three-state (Minnesota, Wisconsin, and Alabama) business with more than 250 employees and with customers in the United States and Europe.[8]

Bloomquist notes that none of the company's business success was preordained. "In our youth, young and impressionable, we were environmentalists more than businesspeople . . . we would never consider being a member of the Chamber [of Commerce] or anything like that . . . we said 'you're not lobbying for what we want—we want something else.'"[9] Bloomquist said that within the company they thought there was a contradiction. "We're in the wood products business, we're killing trees. . . . We were always concerned about where our product came from, but to be really honest we didn't have a clue. We didn't have the knowledge. But we were always concerned, supported all the environmental groups, anybody that walked up to the door."

Bloomquist did belong to a small trade association, the Minnesota Wood Promotion Council. In 1992, forestry professor Jim Bowyer of the University of Minnesota spoke at a council meeting and talked about the new concept of "green certification" that he had just heard about. Bloomquist was sold on the idea of having a way to verify where Colonial Craft's raw material was coming from. The council formed a "Green Certification Task Force" consisting of Bloomquist, who promptly hired a student intern from the University of Minnesota to find out about the fledgling certification organizations.

The task force published a four-page brochure in 1992 for the council titled *What Is Certification?*, and what Bloomquist refers to as "the crusade" began. Colonial Craft and the council participated in the founding events of the Forest Stewardship Council and had early conversations with both Scientific Certification Systems (SCS) and SmartWood Bloomquist found that with one exception—the SCS certification of the Menominee Tribal Enterprises forest in Wisconsin—neither SCS nor SmartWood had certified any land managers in the United States. Midwest Hardwood Corporation, one of Colonial Craft's suppliers, had nonexclusive chain-of-custody certification in 1994 but did not manage land. Bloomquist then went with Richard Donovan of Smart-Wood; Jeanne Germain, marketing manager of Colonial Craft; and John Krantz of the Minnesota Department of Natural Resources (DNR) and made a presentation to the Keweenaw Land Association, Ltd., a forest management ownership group in the western Upper Peninsula of Michigan. Keweenaw Land produces logs, some of which enter the SmartWood-certified chain of custody and was one of Colonial Craft's major suppliers. Bloomquist asked them to pursue source certification.

Keweenaw received SmartWood source certification in 1994,[10] and Colonial Craft received nonexclusive chain-of-custody certification from SmartWood in 1995.

In 1998, Bloomquist said of the results for Colonial Craft, "We like the notoriety we have gotten. It has been very good for our business. . . . I don't have the dollars in my pocket yet, but we got a couple of opportunities we're working on that are there only because of certification. I think in the long run it's going to prove that it was the right thing to do." Bloomquist also noted that Colonial Craft would not be on any major new customer's radar screen except for the certification. SmartWood certification has led to some interesting new business opportunities, particularly in Europe because of the European Union's requirement that all imported wood be green certified.

opportunity to accomplish restoration forestry with a long-term perspective in the county. As Jacobs comments, "In other Minnesota counties the land commissioner position is fairly competitive, but here it is pretty stable, and we have been able to sustain good forestry and land management practices as a result."

Jacobs says that one key factor in the county's reputation for progressive management has been their willingness to partner with organizations like the Mississippi Headwaters Board, various educational institutions, and economic development agencies to try out and learn new approaches for inherited land management challenges. Support of the county's economic base was a major reason for the Aitkin County Land Department's pursuit of SmartWood certification. Jacobs said, "There were three reasons we always talked about in this certification: One of them is public confidence. We felt that there are often misguided public concerns about management in this area of northeastern Minnesota. We thought that if we could go through this process, stick our necks out, and meet the standards, it would give the public a lot more confidence in what we do."[12] Jacobs's second reason was prestige. "Aitkin County has been a downtrodden county over the years. Seems like whenever we make the news it is something bad, murder, or flood or something like that, so we thought this would be a real feather in the cap."

Finally, from an economic standpoint, Jacobs and Howard thought that the prospect of higher prices for certified wood had the potential "to boost some of the local wood products industries . . . to give them a little step up in potential value added for the products that they will be able to market as green certified wood." Early results in 1998 auctions in Aitkin County show wood prices up slightly, but, Jacobs says, "most of it will not enter the 'certified stream.' We are too early in the game. We have received a lot of inquiries about certified wood from our lands and have several local sawmills seriously looking into certification."[13] The Palisade Supply Inc. "Green Hardwood Dimension" mill received approval for chain-of-custody certification in July 1998.[14]

Sustainable forestry at the turn of the twenty-first century of any kind, and particularly forestry with a view toward true multiple use management and with a landscape view of the region, has many biological challenges in Aitkin County according to wildlife ecologist Robert Brander. "In Northern Minnesota, the land was grossly misused through flawed public policies. The resultant poorly formed forest was inherited by the State Conservation Department and the Aitkin County Land Department when they began their forest management program in the 1930s."[15]

At the turn of the twenty-first century, the forests of Aitkin County are changing from a predominance of aspen to northern hardwoods. Brander, who was leader of the Aitkin County and Keweenaw SmartWood assessment teams, argues that responsible forest management in Aitkin County will have to keep all silvicultural options open in order to achieve fully productive forests over the next one hundred to two hundred years. Because human intervention throughout the northern Great Lakes forest in the last century was so destructive, the only hope of regaining a fully structured and productive forest is through an equally intense human reintervention.

But this time, Brander says, "we must proceed with the best silvicultural science and the emerging scientific disciplines of conservation biology and landscape ecology, and we must proceed with forest management planning that doesn't quail at horizons that may be one hundred or two hundred years into the future."

The SmartWood Certification Process

SmartWood certification of forest "sources" is based on field review by approved local groups (including the Sigurd Olson Environmental Institute in Ashland, Wisconsin, and the Rogue Institute for Ecology and Economy in Oregon) using SmartWood's generic guidelines or, when available, country or bioregional guidelines that have been written in consultation with local experts and organizations, often in collaboration with the Forest Stewardship Council. Aitkin County's certification was conducted under the "Lake States Guidelines for Assessing Natural Forest Management" published by the Smart-Wood regional certification partner, the Sigurd Olson Environmental Institute (SOEI). In 1994, Bob Brander, a former director of the SOEI, and Bob Simeone, a consulting forester in Wisconsin, put together a draft for the Great Lakes states based on the Smart-Wood generic guidelines and then convened a group of fifteen scientists and practitioners, including loggers and foresters, for a two-day meeting to refine the draft and finalize the guidelines.

In general, candidate operations must meet the following broad principles:

1. Long-term security for the forest (that is, it will not be cleared in the foreseeable future)
2. Maintenance or improvement of environmental functions, including watershed stability and biological conservation
3. Sustained-yield forestry production
4. Positive impact on local communities
5. The existence of a plan for long-term forest management planning, management, and monitoring, including a written forest management plan

In the case of plantations, SmartWood does not endorse the conversion of standing forests to tree plantations but will certify those that have been developed on previously

continued

deforested lands and/or that are a first step toward forest restoration. SmartWood sees this as a means to restore tree cover, protect soils and watersheds, and reduce pressure on natural forests.

SmartWood sources are certified according to how closely they adhere to SmartWood principles and guidelines. Sources operating in strict adherence to those principles and having long-term data to support their practices are classified as "sustainable." Sources that can demonstrate a strong operational commitment to the principles and guidelines are classified as "well managed."

Chain-of-Custody Certification

Certification of companies marketing SmartWood products (such as wholesalers, processors such as Colonial Craft, retailers, and brokers) is granted after a chain-of-custody audit confirms that certified wood is being used in certified product lines. The SmartWood name, logo, and certification mark are the property of the Rainforest Alliance; their use for marketing and advertising purposes must be certified, licensed, or authorized by the Rainforest Alliance.

Modified from Rainforest Alliance, *Description of the SmartWood Program* (June 1996).

Brander is passionate about a long-term view of acceptable forest management in the Great Lakes region. He says,

Minnesota forests have been managed for fiber. And for good reason. That is what the land use history drove the land to. But that is beginning to change. In "ripped over" mismanaged, unmanaged forest approaches, which existed right up to the 1960s in the northern Great Lakes, the only hope of restoring anything resembling a fully productive forest is a well-directed reintervention. And it may include every silvicultural system that we have—some that some of us may find repulsive, such as clear-cuts for massive white pine restoration. If there is public will for white pine restoration in Minnesota, it will require heroic reinterventions. But this time with a purpose. The previous reinterventions were ill directed or strictly economic.

The real question in Brander's mind is whether the forest succession currently under way in Aitkin County is going to be actively managed or whether it happens in natural succession. The aspen or pulp forest is going to disappear. To return it to a sustainable, selective cut forest, without high grading, is a one-hundred-year process. Brander noted another transition challenge:

Aitkin County is right at the cusp of losing the Aspen forest and transitioning to a northern hardwoods forest and maybe then back to white pine. One hundred years out we can see this returning to a productive white pine forest. That has tremendous implications for the wood products industry in terms of keeping the pulp mills and the operator base alive until there are enough saw logs to justify investment in new machinery and equipment. That entails a lot of transition management.

Land Use History[16]

Aitkin County encompasses 1.2 million acres of land. Three major ecological subsections intersect within the county: the St. Louis Moraines, which in presettlement time supported white pine, red pine, and aspen–birch forests and some of the best northern hardwood forest in Minnesota; the Tamarack Lowlands, a glacial lake plain and ground moraine that supported conifer swamp, bog, and aspen–birch forest (a large part of the lowlands was dominated by sedge meadow); and the Mille Lacs Uplands, ground and end moraines that in presettlement times supported white pine and red pine forests and aspen, white birch, and white pine forests in the uplands, with equally as much conifer swamp (tamarack, black spruce, and white cedar) in the lowlands.

The composition, structure, and to a lesser degree distribution of present-day forests in Aitkin County are largely the result of excessive logging that began late in the nineteenth century, the massive fires that followed, and the extensive drainage of wetlands for agriculture. By the late 1920s, these events culminated in a northern landscape largely unable to support agriculture or logging, landowners unable or unwilling to pay their land taxes, and massive tax forfeitures of private ownerships. A series of complex and unique state statutes were promulgated, and much of the tax-forfeited land was transferred into state and county ownership and/or management.

In 1935, the state legislature authorized each county board to appoint a land commissioner "to gather data and information on tax-forfeited lands; make classifications and appraisals of land, timber and other products . . . and such other duties concerning tax-forfeited lands as the County Board may direct." Forest management as a responsibility of the land commissioner was implied but not specified in the statute. Aitkin County appointed its first land commissioner in 1939 and thus set the foundation for the Aitkin County Land Department and formal authority for the county to engage in forest management. The Aitkin County Land Department offered its first timber sale in November 1939.

In 1990, 754,200 acres of the total were classified as forested. Of the forested land, 700,500 acres were classified timberland capable of producing

What Is the SmartWood Network?

In 1994, the SmartWood Network was established by the Rainforest Alliance and several independent nonprofit organizations to promote forest product certification worldwide. SmartWood works in collaboration on a region-specific basis with various independent, nonprofit organizations that focus on bringing innovative certification opportunities to forest managers in tropical, temperate, and far-northern regions.

SmartWood Network Partners and Collaborators

California, USA: Institute for Sustainable Forestry (ISF)
Vermont, USA: National Wildlife Federation (NWF)
Washington, USA: Northwest Natural Resource Group (NNRG)
Brazil: Instituto de Manejo e Certificação Florestal e Agrícola (IMAFLORA)
Denmark: NEPCon
Indonesia: Lembaga Alam Tropika Indonesia (LATIN)
Mexico: Consejo Civil Mexicano para la Silvicultura Sostenible (CCMSS)
SmartWood, Goodwin-Baker Building, 65 Millet St., Suite 201, Richmond, VT 05477, USA; tel: 802-434-5491; fax: 802-434-3116

more than twenty cubic feet per acre per year of wood crops. Ownership of the 700,500 acres of timberland in 1990 was as follows (in thousands of acres):

Federal: 7.9
State: 249.9
County and municipal: 96.3
Forest industry: 11.3
Individual: 228.8
Corporate: 6.3
Total: 700.5

While reforestation since the 1930s is impressive, the "new forest" is quite unlike it was one hundred years ago. Before scientifically based forest management could be put in place by state and county agencies, two or three more decades of nonselective "logger's choice" logging continued to threaten the recovery of forests in Aitkin and surrounding counties.

Aspens, a minor component in the 1800s, occupied 31.6 percent of Aitkin County's timberland in 1990, while the once-vast white, red, jack pine type occupied only 1.3 percent. Many aspen stands, however, are overmature and unless harvested soon will convert to shade-tolerant types. On the other hand, increasing commercial demand for wood fiber since the late 1970s has led to a substantial area of young (under twenty years old) aspen stands. The northern hardwood type (sugar maple, basswood, ash, red maple, and elm), whose distribution in presettlement Aitkin County is not well understood, is increasing its range on many sites through succession from other types; these northern hardwoods now occupy approximately 32 percent of the county's timberland. The "new forest" of Aitkin County contains a small (less than 4 percent) but economically lucrative red oak type, much on a successional path that will likely lead to the northern hardwood.

Lowland conifers (black spruce, tamarack, and white cedar) occupy 22 percent of the county's timberland. While the lowland conifers acreage is less than it was one hundred years ago, it approximates its natural distribution, stocking, and age more than any other forest type in the county. Finally, it appears that the only management strategy to ensure survival of northern Minnesota's signature white pine type is an intensive public and private restoration program. While blister rust and other problems particular to white pine will be distinctive challenges, silvicultural scientists and pathologists optimistically predict that a properly designed restoration program will be successful.

Tax Law and Policy[17]

Both the Minnesota DNR and the Aitkin County Land Department are governed in their management of forestlands by a long series of state laws that addressed unparalleled tax delinquency in the northern counties during the 1920s and 1930s. Two acts that were passed in 1935 are most important in this regard: 1) Chapter 278 gave the state absolute title to tax-forfeited land after the specified tax redemption period expired, and 2) Chapter 282 (formerly Chapter 386) provided details for the administration of parcels that forfeit to the state, including the requirements that the county board classify all tax-forfeited parcels as agricultural or nonagricultural and that the classification be approved by the Conservation Commission (now the Commissioner of Natural Resources). Later acts enlarged on the significance of nonagricultural lands and increasingly emphasized timber values. The act of 1945 authorized county boards to set aside tax-forfeited land more suitable for forest purposes than for any other purpose and provided for the establishment of county memorial forests.

In addition to tax-forfeited lands, the state took legislative actions on the titles of other lands by assuming responsibility for the drainage bonds in Aitkin, Roseau, and Mahnomen Counties. The lands thus acquired are commonly known as "reforestation areas" or "reforestation and flood control areas." In 1949, the legislature combined receipts from the lands acquired by these means in a "Consolidated Conservation Areas Fund." Lands within the 1949 act are commonly called "con-con lands."

The upshot of this lengthy "forfeiture legislation" is absolute state ownership of much of Aitkin County's timberland but with title to the forfeited lands "impressed with a trust in favor of the county and other local taxing districts." Thus, the framework for public forest management in Aitkin County includes a tacit partnership of the DNR and the Aitkin County Land Department. The partnership works well according to Aitkin County's Assistant Land Commissioner Mark Jacobs, who says that the partners "share several joint management areas and work together on issues such as fire succession and wildlife management."[18]

The perceived relationship between northern Minnesota's economy and the forest ecosystem has provided the impetus for new forest law and policy. Technological advances by the 1970s elevated aspen from a "weed" species to the primary component in the manufacture of wafer board and oriented strand board. Subsequent massive harvests of aspen and other species to feed the demand for wood fiber and chips in northern Minnesota led concerned citizens to ask the state to assess the potential environmental impacts of continued harvests of this magnitude. The state responded in 1989 with the commissioning of a generic environmental impact statement. Approved by the state in 1994, the statement now provides important background information for the long-term management of Minnesota's northern forests. In 1995, it prompted the Minnesota Sustainable Forest Resources Act, which authorized the creation of the Forest Resources Council and the Forest Resources Partnership, to coordinate partnerships in which landowners, managers, and loggers work together on implementing sound forestry practices.

In 1994, the DNR issued guidance on "old-growth forests." The guidance proposed definitions of old growth, set goals for old-growth management on state lands, and reserved stands identified as old growth until they could be evaluated in the field. In 1995, the guidance was expanded to establish DNR teams for each landscape subsection, with the charge of "selecting and designating old-growth and future old-growth stands."

In response to widespread concern about the white pine resource in Minnesota, a White Pine Regeneration Strategies Work Group was appointed by the DNR in early 1996, with a charge to report their findings to the Forest Resources Council. In January 1997, the Forest Resources Council endorsed the recommendations of the work group. A biennial appropriation of $1.5 million

Colonial Craft and "Bloomquist's Crusade"

Colonial Craft is an unusually progressive operation in its emphasis on employee education, its extensive list of employee benefits, and its general sense of corporate responsibility. As owner and chief executive officer Eric Bloomquist says, "Basically, if there is [an employee] benefit we offer it." Colonial Craft offers extensive education benefits, health coverage, and three kinds of profit sharing (a traditional annual pension profit sharing, a 401[k] hourly profit sharing matching 50 percent of what an employee puts in, and "gain sharing" each month) along with a high degree of training in teamwork and relationship building. Company financial information is shared with employees every month, and in 1996, Colonial Craft paid out 60 percent of its profits back to employees. For Bloomquist, one of the joys of the expansion and success of Colonial Craft since he bought the company in 1974 is that "we're way bigger but we are not a lot different."

One benefit that Bloomquist is especially proud of is a learning center built in Colonial Craft's Luck, Wisconsin, facility named with the intentional pun "The Mind Molding Center." The center, built partly with a grant from the state technical schools in Wisconsin, is a dedicated space including a number of computer learning stations. It is open to any employee and their families, during hours and off hours, to go in and do anything else available through the remote learning network. Bloomquist says the key to facility success is having instructors on-site a few days a week. Two of 100 employees in the facility got their general equivalency degree (GED) the first year. People, Bloomquist says, had never considered it before. Bloomquist adds, "We offer training down to a pretty deep level in the company in all our facilities. We've done some things with the university where people work with us to put together a whole day unit and we send maybe half the company to it, put them in college for a day or two. . . . We're doing everything we can think of and become aware of. There's always something different and there's always somebody doing something neat. You can't get too smug in this because there are way too many neat things you haven't thought of or become aware of and it changes fast."

So, it is no surprise that Bloomquist calls his quest to find certified lumber for his manufacturing plants a "crusade." After meeting with SmartWood's Richard Donovan for the first time in 1994, Bloomquist said, "Look we really want to do this, but there is no certified wood out there so what do we do? So we went out on a couple year crusade, the vast majority of my personal time, I had an assistant who worked with me an awful lot, and we spoke to anybody who would listen. . . . So we pushed, cajoled some of our traditional vendors, asked them to get involved in it."

The audience often was not rushing to sign up. "We went to all the trade organizations, Hardwood Lumber Association, etc., and because we got visibility quickly, and because we were willing to just say what we thought, talk about it, tell the numbers, tell the stories (there weren't a lot of people around willing to do that—and in the Hardwood Lumber Association well, we're a pretty significant customer), so they tended, whether they wanted to or not, to be gracious and let us in and not necessarily agree with us. And we got in to the Hardwood Research Council, the NHOA annual meeting, to tell the story, make the pitch. [We would

continued

say] this is good for us, we think it's good for the industry, we need some of you to get on this bus because we can't do it ourselves, we can't do it without you and we pushed really hard. It wasn't somebody coming in telling them to clean up their act; it was us standing there with $10 million in purchase orders. . . . In a crass sort of way, I said in the beginning, all you need to participate in certification is a purchase order and checkbook."

As to the actual costs of certification, Bloomquist says, "The 'crusade' had been very, very expensive, [and] the actual certification process had been reasonable."

was appropriated by the legislature in 1997, and in the 1998 capital budget, the legislature appropriated an additional $600,000 for various purposes related to white pine restoration.[19] Aitkin County received $11,000 for fiscal year 1998 (which covered the planting of approximately 20,000 white pine seedlings along with pruning, thinning, and other site preparation and disease and deer and insect predation prevention practices) and received $14,000 in fiscal year 1999. The white pine restoration funds are shared statewide by the DNR, the counties, the University of Minnesota, and private forest stewards.

Economic and Social Context

The management of forests by the DNR and the Aitkin County Land Department contributes to a major segment of the Aitkin County economy. The forestry sector in Aitkin County generated full- and part-time employment for an estimated 202 persons in 1994 (excluding sole proprietorships or family partnerships).[20] This represents 3.6 percent of total employment in the county and 47 percent of the manufacturing sector employment. According to estimates made by the Minnesota DNR, each $1.00 in stumpage sold results in $40.17 in value added to the state's economy ($28.62 to $1.00 in impact for sawtimber, $42.99 to $1.00 in stumpage for pulpwood). Based on these figures, the estimated impact of the forest products industry on Aitkin County in 1994 was $11,673,810 in direct impact of actual spending (202 jobs), plus $10,389,690 as a multiplier effect of this spending on other trades and services (269 jobs), resulting in a total impact of over $22 million (471 jobs in the county).

Because of expansion of the wood products industry in northern Minnesota and Wisconsin over the past twenty years, Aitkin County currently has extensive markets for its timber. Aitkin County lies within the "woodshed" of numerous large wood-using plants that, consequently, are the major consumers of wood harvested from Aitkin County public lands. While each plant has different requirements, these fiber-based industries use large volumes of aspen, though they also consume mixed hardwood and conifer species. Competitive demand for these fibers keeps timber prices (principally aspen) high, with prices driven by global commodity prices. Markets for hard and softwood sawtimber have likewise expanded over this period with a clear trend toward increased use of smaller-diameter and lower-quality logs. This trend is especially significant given the relatively young age of most of Aitkin County's hardwood resource. These market opportunities help increase management options for hardwood intensification and stand improvement initiatives currently under way.

The 1995 analysis of Minnesota's fifth forest resources inventory appears to support the view that hardwood sawtimber will increase in economic importance in Aitkin County. Eleven percent of Aitkin's net growing stock (expressed in thousands of cubic feet) is "soft hardwoods," which includes species such as aspen and basswood. Maintenance of soft hardwoods stock has been the primary objective of forest managers in northern Minnesota since new wood products technologies appeared in the 1970s. However, as the 1995 inventory shows, 19 percent of Aitkin's growing stock is now "hard hardwoods"—sugar maple, oak, ash, and other high-density woods. At 214 million cubic feet, Aitkin's inventory of hard hardwoods is the largest of any county in the state. Moreover, Aitkin County contains 16 percent of the stock (expressed in thousands of board feet) of hardwood sawtimber in the seventeen counties in northern and northeastern Minnesota. This finding that Aitkin County is a major repository of hard hardwood sawtimber is supported by the analysis of presettlement forests in the St. Louis Moraines ecoregion, which extends southwest well into Aitkin County.

Fast-moving social and demographic events also have the potential to "direct," to some degree, forest management in Aitkin County. The U.S. Bureau of the Census tracked Minnesota population shifts from 1990 to 1996. Aitkin County's estimated population increased from 12,425 to 13,715, a 10.4 percent increase and fifteenth highest of the eighty-eight counties in the state and second highest of the northern counties. The Aitkin Area Chamber of Commerce and others believe that the recent surge in population growth is due to development of new businesses and to the influx of retirees and "metropolitan transplants." The University of Minnesota Department of Applied Economics, however, projects that Aitkin County's population will decrease approximately 23 percent between 1995 and 2020, in large part because of declining birthrates and a rapid drop in kindergarten-age children. Aitkin County reached a high of 17,865 people in 1940, when nearly three-fourths of the population was classified as "rural farm." In contrast, less than 7 percent of the population was classified that way in the 1990s.

Aitkin County is also within territory ceded by several bands of Ojibwa through mid-nineteenth-century treaties with the U.S. government. Traditional rights retained, as specified in the various treaties, include the right to hunt, fish,

and gather within ceded territory. Recent federal court decisions uphold the retained rights. Because the right to "gather" implies harvests of wild herbaceous
foods, medicinal plants, and structural materials, there are implications for management of public forest lands in Aitkin County. According to John Landis of
SmartWood,[21] there seem to be no major conflicts of interest with tribal rights
in Aitkin County.

The Aitkin County Land Department's Forest Management Administrative Structure and Scope of Operations[22]

The structure of the Aitkin County Land Department's forest management administration has been in place since 1989. While Land Commissioner Roger
Howard has county board–delegated responsibility for forest management, day-
to-day operations are under the direct supervision of the assistant land commissioner, Mark Jacobs. Three district foresters normally do fieldwork. District 1 is
115,510 acres, District 2 is 71,732 acres, and District 3 is 34,517 acres, which
averages approximately 74,100 acres for each of the three foresters. The commissioner's office and the district foresters receive technical support from a geographic information system (GIS) specialist and a forestry inventory specialist.

   Some 221,000 acres are within administrative oversight of the Aitkin
County Land Department. Of that total acreage, approximately 134,000 are
dedicated "memorial forest," that is, a statutory multiple-use forest. Most of the
memorial forest dedications occurred in the 1960s. County parks (a relatively
minor acreage) were also dedicated according to statute. Large blocks of county
land are neither dedicated forest nor park. Thus, there are three broad categories
of land administered by the Aitkin County Land Department: memorial forest,
county park, and "other." Removal of lands from memorial forest or park status
requires public hearing and affirmative decision by the county board, but such
removals rarely occur. The department often permits timber sales on lands in the
category of "other." Another option often used by the department is to use
"other" lands as exchanges for privately held lands within or adjacent to memorial forest.

   Through county board resolutions, the Aitkin County Land Department
participates with the Division of Fish and Wildlife and the Division of Forestry
of the DNR in joint management of nine of the twenty-five state wildlife management areas in Aitkin County. Those nine wildlife management areas total approximately 18,911 acres, or 39 percent of the total 47,962 acres of wildlife
management area in the county.

Aitkin County is one of several in northern Minnesota that in 1990 formed county forest advisory committees. The Forest Advisory Committee advises the County Board of Commissioners and the DNR on management of the county's forestlands and, in particular, the harvest schedules proposed by the county and the DNR. The DNR provides the secretarial support for the committee. Jacobs says that the "department staff brought the certification idea to the Forest Advisory Committee," and they "had a pretty active role in deciding to go ahead with the certification process." The fourteen-member committee consists of eight citizen seats (one each appointed by the five county commissioners and three at large) along with four industry professionals and two county commissioners.

In 1994, the Forest Advisory Committee commissioned a public perception survey that included direct mail and surveys at meetings with stakeholder groups, such as the lake associations, snowmobile clubs, a loggers group, and others. The survey reinforced early discussions about certification. According to Jacobs, water quality issues were the number one concern overall in the surveys, while jobs and wildlife habitat came in a close second and third, respectively. Recreation in general and visual quality were behind the top three, while old growth rated a poor response, and soil productivity was last.

In addition to its obligations for generating timber revenues on tax-forfeited lands, the Aitkin County Land Department has a broader mission, including providing recreation, water quality, wildlife habitat management, and environmental education on its public lands. The broad focus on ecosystem management for uses other than timber is unusual among Minnesota counties. Aitkin County's leadership in promoting wildlife management, recreation, water quality, and healthy natural systems has evolved over the past two decades under the influence of Commissioner Howard. He says that the evolution from a singular economic analysis of the revenues from timber harvest to the broader cost/benefit appreciation of the values of recreation, wildlife, safe drinking water, and related ecosystem restoration issues has been relatively painless in Aitkin County. "We've had to answer many questions from the county commissioners over the years, and we've done a lot of educational outreach, and the political support has been good." He notes that the economic benefits of the county's broadly based approach to management of its lands grow over time as the land becomes more productive for wildlife and timber harvest at sustainable levels.

The department's thirteen-person staff oversees four major county-developed and county-owned campgrounds and Minnesota's oldest residential environmental education facility, the Long Lake Conservation Center. (The Conservation Center's total 1996 attendance included 5,553 students and 1,338 adult participants in its programs.) It also contracts with clubs for maintenance of over six hundred miles of snowmobile trails and itself maintains one hundred miles of all-terrain vehicle (ATV) summer trails and two cross-country ski trails. The department also maintains twenty-one county-owned river and lake accesses and maintains, under contracts with the state, an additional twenty-seven state-owned river and lake accesses.

Jacobs is particularly proud of the county's GIS that has developed since 1995. The computerized modeling system includes a variety of data layers used to create maps, to project timber growth and sales and recreation impacts, and for a number of other uses. Data layers include watershed and subwatershed boundaries, soil types and distribution, forest inventory, roads, tax districts, public campgrounds, public ditches, major landmarks, settlement restricted areas, zoning, public accesses, and many others. The GIS serves a number of county departments, including the Sheriff's Department and the Department of Planning and Zoning. Jacobs says that the maps and reports created from the GIS data layers were essential in assisting the SmartWood assessment team in the certification process.

In September 2001, Howard and Jacobs celebrated the adoption of the Aitkin County Land Department Strategic Plan. The several-hundred-page plan provides "an outlook stretching for one hundred years" to manage the county's 222,000 acres of tax-forfeited land. The mission statement adopted in the plan calls for responsible stewardship, sustaining "the forest for future generations" while generating income for the county and local government and properly using the "land base and renewable forest resources to sustain the region's economic and social well-being." The plan "recognizes that the current forest is primarily the result of human disturbances over the past century" and articulates the county's approach to managing its forest as "working with the current forest to create a future forest that has a more 'natural' character."

Local Processors and Certification

Bob Bartz,[23] a retired state forester and self-described tinkerer, got out of forestry in the early 1960s to start up a mill making pallets and precut pallet parts. The pallet company grew to a high of twenty-five employees before it shut down in the 1980–1982 recession. In 1985, Bartz restarted his mill with one employee in a crating lumber business. Employment gained until 1990, when he cut back again to three or four employees and went on an extended road trip to research other lumber markets.

In 1991, Bartz attended a "hardwood dimension" workshop in Green Bay, Wisconsin, that gave him an awareness of the hardwood dimension industry. He later heard of a process used in Japan and Germany in which raw logs were cut into precise dimensional pieces, kiln dried, and sold ready for use in a variety of products. Wainscoting made by these processes, for instance, resulted in 94 percent of what previously would be waste products being used in final manufacturing. After years of experimentation with low-grade logs and lumber and with building and customizing precision cutting equipment, small dry kilns, and wood-waste fuel systems, Bartz is now operating his own Palisade Supply Inc. "Green Hardwood Dimension" business outside the town of Palisade, Minnesota.

Bartz, who in twenty-five years of business in Aitkin County had almost no contact with the Aitkin County Land Department until he was asked to serve on the Forest Advisory Committee in 1990, said at first he thought it was "going to be a big waste of my time. I've got to go in and sit in some meeting just because some environmental group says we have to." But he soon became a fan of the Forest Advisory Committee. "It didn't take very long before I realized that this was a meeting that wasn't interested in just screwing the logger. By getting private citizens involved, getting them to learn about forestry, getting the state Department of Natural Resources people, the county people, the fisheries and wildlife people, and the refuge manager, all these different entities, sitting down at the same table and talking to each other," they got some good work done. "That first couple of years there was some hard words and yelling. But after they got through that stage and decided that they were going to work together, things got accomplished."

Bartz, also a member of the Minnesota Woods Promotion Council, is impressed with what the Aitkin County Land Department staff have accomplished. He emphasized Jacobs's and Howard's strategic thinking and persuasive abilities. He also provided an overview of the timber harvest in Aitkin county over the years:

> When I first started buying logs, most of it was cut by part-time loggers, construction workers, in the wintertime. And then it progressed into full-time loggers, and the full-time loggers got bigger and bigger and the John Deere equipment got bigger and bigger. We started with 420 model dozers, and now you're up to humongous grapple skidders and all that equipment. This is fine for large tracts of industrial timber, but it doesn't mix, it doesn't work in our type of timber around here. Our timber is in small tracts, largely aspen and mixed hardwoods and you take that pulpwood logger and that pulpwood mentality and put him in one of our stands down here, before long you've got damage. So we need to change the way we do things.

Bartz says only a small percentage of loggers in Aitkin County are still causing major damage to the resource. When apprised of a citation that Jacobs had issued to a logger who had skidded trees out of the woods, across a gravel county road, and into a neighboring pasture, causing deep ruts in the forest soils, the gravel road, and the turf in the pasture, Bartz exclaims, "That's something else . . . this type of a butcher. The percentage of the logger population, this type of operation, is getting less and less. But there's still a few out there."

Bartz and others say, however, that the incentive to invest in new logging equipment is still marginal given the partial transition in the forest types from pulp to hardwoods. Bob Brander maintains that the fragmented nature of the landownership in the county and the small, highly personalized logging outfits can work to the county's advantage in restoration efforts, particularly in white pine restoration:

> Because the forest lacks a lot of structure the only people you can get in are one or two person operators who do highly personalized logging. They have the ability to do micromanagement. What we're suggesting, for example, is to begin to experiment, let's say with white pine, and you are into a thinning operation and part of the prescription is that you will do the operation in the fall or spring and deliberately prepare the seed bed through the harvest operation of the white pine. That would be an attempt to emulate wind throw for example. . . .
>
> So much of this has to do with the equipment available and the skill of the logger. In upper Michigan, cable skidding was once considered state of the art. Or if not state of the art, that was just how people did it. But then we go and see an operator with some of the new wood processing equipment, and other than the slashings and stumps in the stand, you can't tell he's been there. That's a half-million-dollar investment. The loggers have to gear up and have the right equipment to simulate wind throw and other natural regeneration systems.

Bartz's Palisade Supply Inc. mill went on "voluntary suspension" of its Smart-Wood chain-of-custody certification in 2002. Bartz explains that he is still a strong supporter of certification because "the health of the forest is what it is all about" but that he was inching toward retirement and that his small operation—which does a lot of custom drying and milling—was not producing enough certified product to justify the $700 to $1,000 annual recertification fee. "Business is so good with my other products," he says. "I can't justify the additional paperwork and other requirements when I am shrinking my business and moving toward retirement." Bartz sees good incremental changes with harvesting methods in the region and has only "minor complaints" with the certification process.

Rich Peterson is another former forester (and current business management teacher) who started a small value-added processing mill in the county, Master Millwork and Lumber. Peterson was appointed to the Forest Advisory Committee in 1996 and was an early strong supporter of the certification efforts: "a very forward-looking step." In 1997, he saw the SmartWood certification as an opportunity to help the timber industry add value, though with no guarantees on price. "The timber industry in Minnesota historically never added value by processing here. Most wood shipped out to Wisconsin and points elsewhere because of the tax climate and workers compensation costs." Peterson says that the "jury is still out on the promise of higher sales prices on certified wood. Lots of higher-quality sites are available." He maintained that the certified material would be best used within the county to generate quality products and industry locally. "Manufacturing could and should provide a major portion of the local economy."

Peterson's initial faith has proved profitable for several Aitkin County region businesses—and especially so for the newly certified (2001) Tviet Logging and Lumber in Palisade, Minnesota. Bartz, despite his own cutback in certification efforts, persuaded the Tviet brothers to certify their much larger mill a few miles from his own in the town of Palisade, and their effort has given them a great new business selling certified pallets to Summit Brewing Company in St. Paul.

Pallets are a great product for certified forests in the process of restoring healthy tree stands after decades of mismanagement. The relatively low-grade lumber that comes from initial restoration forestry thinning can be readily used for pallets and other low-grade wood products. Phil Guillery, forester and director of forest certification for the Institute for Agriculture and Trade Policy in Minneapolis, says that "the ever-present pallet may seem like an insignificant market, but close to half of all hardwood harvested in the United States is made into pallets."

The Institute for Agriculture and Trade Policy: The Global View

The Aitkin County story is incomplete without an understanding of the role that the nonprofit Institute for Agriculture and Trade Policy (IATP) played in the regional certification effort. The IATP's president, Mark Ritchie, explains[24] that "the institute was founded in 1986 to link rural communities and environmental organizations, particularly family farms with environmental issues as directly and closely as possible. The IATP's primary focus over the last decade has been on the connections between local policy and global policy. Over the years, the institute has worked in relation to various natural resource issues affecting rural people, including water, watershed issues, and forestry, including the impact of forest management and forest products on local family farmers and in other countries."

The IATP's involvement in wood certification grew out of one of their major projects, a systematic analysis of product sustainability labeling around the world. Ritchie explains,

> In 1995, we began to expand from our work on eco-labeling which was in the
> agricultural area, particularly organic, organic culture, to an expanded look at

eco-labels and how they might be used in the farm community both for sustainably produced agriculture products . . . and value-added goods, especially if there was an environmental component to that value-added or an economic sustainability component. That led us into looking more carefully at eco-labeling and certification in forest products and how that might be useful and helpful to farmers. . . . I believe there are a lot of lessons in forest certification that can be useful for farmers active in sustainable agriculture labeling.

One of the important issues the IATP looked at early in its study of forest certification was supply and demand for certified wood. Ritchie says, "There was an argument, back and forth, the chicken and the egg, not enough product couldn't get a big enough market—and without a big enough market, couldn't get enough product. So one of the answers proposed is that certification of wood from state- and county-owned forests would increase the supply enough to the point that the market would grow."

The IATP then began to act as a conduit for funds in the Great Lakes states from several private foundations[25] that were pushing the effort to get timber producers to meet environmentally sustainable forestry practices. Acting as a funds conduit led the IATP to a partnership with SmartWood and Bob Brander and the Sigurd Olson Environmental Institute and ultimately to involvement with the Aitkin County Land Department. Bloomquist believes that the demand for certified wood arises from a variety of sources, including government requirements, as in the case of the European Union, and consumer demand. He says that supply originally was his biggest problem. Ritchie now says,

> We know 10 times as much as we did when this effort started seven to eight years ago. There is a long way between a certified forest and harvested wood being turned into a certified product in the marketplace. IATP is now putting its money into market makers, people who can put buyers together with producers. We didn't know this in the beginning.

The other major lesson is that all certifications that are worth their "green" label begin with timber stand improvement. That means very low-quality wood in the beginning. So certification of large forests needs first to be coupled with that market in mind.

Conclusions

Supply of certified timber in 2002 is increasing quickly with the addition of Cass County and the formation of several private landowner cooperatives looking into certification. Ritchie says that the big setback in the Minnesota process was when the Sierra Club killed the funding to nine counties. He explains that "one of the implications was that we couldn't expand certification to the really big forest that it would take to run a big certified paper mill." He adds, "Slowly we are getting to that stage and several paper mills in Wisconsin and Michigan that have recently been purchased by a corporation that is operating certified mills in Canada are on everybody's mind as steps to certified paper. . . . It's all about turning a certified forest into products in the market, and all elements of that process have been a learning curve."

Ritchie also says that consumers and producers are finding ways to communicate a new social compact around agricultural and forest products:

> Farmers are, of course, large owners of land and big influencers of water, so we deal with that constituency, and we see the SmartWood label as a really effective tool for that constituency. At the same time, we are in relationship to the wood products industry and the buyers. This is a tremendous tool for the industry doing its own niching, [product] differentiation and rate sustaining in general. . . . And then . . . there are the individual values of people ranging from the folks who don't want the forests cut unless there's somebody they can really trust, all the way to people who are in this industry who love wood, and are attached to the idea that there is a process that could express that love—like people who love the land, who love trout, who love cows, who want to live and work in a way consistent with their heart. If they're home making furniture and love wood, a label that then gives you assurance that at each stage of the process of growing and getting that wood there was someone else who loved wood and who was operating according to sustainable principles—then it makes the process so much more satisfying.

Ritchie, Bartz, and Brander, among others, see the Aitkin County Land Department's success with its progressive forestry practices and emphasis on a wide range of uses and services for county residents and the larger public as the "story" in Aitkin County. Says Ritchie, "The story is the advanced thinking in Aitkin County. They have developed many public amenities; they know the importance of wildlife management and all the broad list of values that the Land Department supports. Most of the counties don't even begin to think about many of these issues."

Aitkin County's influence continues to spread. In the six years since initial certification, the Aitkin County Land Department received numerous awards, including the Minnesota Association of Counties Achievement Award, a 1998 Achievement Award from the National Association of County Officials, and a Governor's Partnership Award from the State of Minnesota. Mark Jacobs received the JC "Buzz" Ryan Award as Forest Manager of the Year from the Minnesota Forest Employees Association.

More important than the awards are the hundreds of inquiries Jacobs reports coming into his office from interested organizations, state and county agencies, universities, and certified industries throughout the world. In the first six months of 2002, visitors came for tours of Aitkin County's forests from as close as Canada and as far away as India. Assistant Land Commissioner Jacobs noted the dozens of letters of support from businesses and environmental groups that poured into the county commissioners' mailboxes in support of the recertification of Aitkin County lands in May, June, and July 2002. A small sampling included effusive praise from the World Wildlife Fund, Aveda Corporation, the National Wildlife Federation, the Minnesota Center for Environmental Advocacy, and The Nature Conservancy.

Meanwhile, Bloomquist continues his speaking engagements and advocacy for certification in front of any audience that will listen. Finding enough certified lumber for Colonial Craft's expanding business is an ongoing problem. Most important, the success with certification of the public lands in the county will likely provide continuing support from county residents and political leaders of the efforts by county and DNR foresters to restore a naturally balanced and productive forest for timber, recreation, water quality, and wildlife out of Aitkin's misshapen, severely high-graded, poor-quality forests.

Acknowledgments

This chapter would not have been possible without generous donations of time and patience from Bob Brander, Mark Jacobs, Mark Ritchie, Eric Bloomquist, Bob Bartz, Rich Peterson, Mollie MacGregor, and SmartWood staff Jon Jickling, John Landis, and Richard Donovan as I tracked them down on vacation; in their offices in Wisconsin, Minnesota, and Vermont; and between trips abroad.

Useful background material on a variety of related topics was provided by Don Arnosti, Minnesota state director for the National Audubon Society; Kim Bro, director of the Sigurd Olson Environmental Institute; Jonathan Kusel of Forest Community Research; Professor Craig Shinn of Portland State University; Professor Steve Born of the University of Wisconsin–Madison; Secretary Trudy Coxe of the Massachusetts Executive Office of Environmental Affairs; Professor Alden Lind of the University of Minnesota–Duluth; Jay Moynihan of Ashland, Wisconsin; Sara Johnson of the River Alliance of Wisconsin; and Gayle Peterson, former director of the Project Environment Foundation, now the Minnesota Center for Environmental Advocacy.

Special thanks are due to University of British Columbia forestry graduate Jeffrey Hayward, who graciously shared travel and interview time in Wisconsin and Minnesota and came through with crucial replacements of destroyed interview transcripts. Paul Koberstein, editor of *Cascadia Times,* provided much encouragement along the way and his ever-so-skilled suggestions for editing the first draft.

Reviewers Mark Ritchie, Craig Shinn, Jeanne Germaine, Eric Bloomquist, Bob Bartz, Jeff Hayward, Mark Jacobs, Bob Brander, Jill Belsky, Elisa Adler, and Jonathan Kusel provided many corrections and suggestions to improve initial drafts.

Extraordinary thanks are due to two people without whom this case study would not exist. First, to my wife, Nancy Parent, who cheerfully endured my absences for fieldwork and the fits and starts of research and writing, for her unwavering stand for my work. Finally, thanks to Jonathan Kusel, friend, colleague, and Community Forestry Case Studies project director, for his support, risk taking, and cheerful patience.

Notes

1. One entrance to the exhibit states in large text, "The era of 'green gold' is over. It would be easy to condemn those who were involved in lumbering for the destruction of the pine forest, but this 20/20 hindsight does not do these people justice. Although greed and ignorance were involved in the lumbering industry, there was also a solid belief that what they were doing was right."

2. Soil samples taken from the bottoms of the Pine, Chippewa, Tittabawassee, and Saginaw Rivers in 2000 and 2001 showed high levels of dioxin in fifty-five of sixty-nine locations tested. The "normal" background concentration for dioxin in soil in Michigan is about 33 parts per trillion, while the highest levels found among river sediment samples was 1,500 parts per trillion. *Saginaw News,* June 8, 2002, 1.

3. Frederick Turner, *Rediscovering America: John Muir in His Time and Ours* (New York: Viking Penguin, 1985), 305.

4. Turner, *Rediscovering America,* 305.

5. Turner, *Rediscovering America,* 305.

6. See the video *Power and The Land: Four Documentary Portraits of the Great Depression* (1994), which includes the Lorentz films *The River* and *The Plow That Broke the Plains.* The films, narrated with epic poetry and musical scores by Virgil Thompson, include rare footage of logging camps and river drives and documents the deforestation of the Mississippi valley. See also books by Carey McWilliams, including *Factories in the Fields* (Boston: Little, Brown, 1939) and *Ill Fares the Land* (Boston: Little, Brown, 1942), and, of course, John Steinbeck's *The Grapes of Wrath* (1939).

7. Rasmussen Millwork, after Bloomquist's purchase, was eventually officially incorporated as Colonial Craft. Bloomquist also notes that he did go back and finish college in the first few years he owned the business.

8. In 2002, Colonial Craft was acquired by Quanex Corporation, based in Houston. Quanex is a manufacturer of engineered materials and components for the vehicular and

building products markets. As of August 2002, Quanex was still emphasizing Colonial Craft's commitment to SmartWood-certified products on its corporate website.

9. All Bloomquist quotes from an in-person interview taped and transcribed in July 1997 and a follow-up telephone interview in July 1998.

10. All certification dates referenced from the *1996 Good Wood Directory.*

11. All references and quotes from Mark Jacobs and Roger Howard from in-person interviews taped and transcribed June 14–16, 1997, unless otherwise cited.

12. Quotes from personal interviews with Mark Jacobs taped and transcribed July 14–16, 1997, and July and August 2002 unless otherwise cited.

13. E-mail communication from Mark Jacobs, July 21, 1998.

14. Telephone interview with Eric Bloomquist, July 22, 1998.

15. All quotes from taped and transcribed personal interview with Robert Brander, July 12, 1997, unless otherwise cited.

16. This section has been adapted from the SmartWood and Sigurd Olson Environmental Institute *Certification Assessment Report of the Aitkin County (Minnesota) Land Department's Management of County Forest Lands,* July 1, 1997, 8–9.

17. This section has been adapted from the *Certification Assessment Report . . .,*9–11.

18. Quotes from personal interviews with Mark Jacobs taped and transcribed July 14–16, 1997.

19. Telephone interview with Bruce ZumBahlen of the Minnesota DNR, July 22, 1998.

20. Parts of this section have been adapted from the *Certification Assessment Report . . .,* 11–13.

21. Interview with John Landis, forest health specialist, Richmond, Vermont, June 26, 1997.

22. Parts of this section have been adapted from the *Certification Assessment Report . . .,* 13–15.

23. Information and quotes from an in-person interview with Bob Bartz at the Palisade Supply Inc. mill, July 14, 1997, and a telephone interview, August 9, 2002.

24. Quotes from in-person and telephone interviews with Mark Ritchie in 1997, 1998, 2000, and August 2002.

25. The Rockefeller Brothers Fund provided funding to help pay for Aitkin County's certification assessment, while the Heinz Endowments provided funds for an assessment on public lands in Pennsylvania. A public foundation, the Great Lakes Protection Fund, provided funding for a 1997 market survey in the region.

Bibliography

Aitkin County Tax-Forfeited Lands Forest Management Plan, September 9, 2001.

Abramovitz, Janet N. *Taking A Stand: Cultivating a New Relationship with the World's Forests.* Worldwatch Paper 140. Washington, D.C.: Worldwatch Institute, April 1998.

A Guide to Specifying Certified Forest Products. Beaverton, Ore.: Certified Forest Products Council. Brochure.

Aitkin County Land Department (209 Second St. N.W., Aitkin, MN 56431)
Aitkin County Forestry Advisory Committee Report—1996.
Aitkin County Land Department Annual Report—1996 in Review.
5th Annual Itasca Community College Hardwood Management Field Tour. Booklet, 1997.
American Forests (P.O. Box 2000, Washington, DC 20013; www.amfor.org.
Brinckman, Jonathan. "Many Shun 'Feel-Good' Approach in Timber." *The Oregonian,* April 26, 1998, D1.
Communities and Forests. Newsletter of the Communities Committee of the Seventh American Forest Congress, vol. 1, no. 1 (Fall 1997).
Durbin, Kathie. *Tree Huggers: Victory-Defeat and Renewal in the Northwest Ancient Forest Campaign.* Seattle: The Mountaineers, 1996.
Earth SENSE. Newsletter vol. 1, no. 4 (1996) (Earth SENSE, A Fund of the St. Paul, Minnesota Foundation, Minneapolis).
Forest Stewardship Council (Avenida Hidalgo 502, 68000 Oaxaca, Mexico; http://antequera.antequera.com/FSC).
Forest Stewardship Council. *U.S. Initiative UPDATE* 1, nos. 2 and 3 (FSC, RD 1, Box 182, Waterbury, VT 05676).
———. "Status of FSC-Endorsed Certification in the United States." August 2, 2001, www.fscus.org.
FSC Notes. Newsletter, no. 5 (April/May 1997).
Forest Voice: Protecting Forests and Defending Wildlife. Newsletter, vol. 11, no. 1 (Winter 1998) (Native Forest Council, P.O. Box 2190, Eugene, OR 97402).
Here Are a Few Stories about CollinsWood. Booklet (Collins Pine Company, 1618 S.W. First Ave., Suite 300, Portland, OR 97201; www.CollinsWood.com).
Institute for Agriculture and Trade Policy (2105 First Ave. S., Minneapolis, MN 55404). *Annual Report 1996* (draft).
Certified Forestry News. Newsletter, vol. 2, no. 2 (April 1, 1998).
"State Certification Project Success." *IATP News* 1, no. 2 (October 20, 1997).
Watershed Currents. Newsletter, vol. 1, no. 8 (November 21, 1997).
LABELS. Newsletter, vol. 1, no. 1 (July 8, 1997).
Kliebenstein, Bob. "Sustainable Forestry Gains Steam." *The Country Today,* August 12, 1998.
Lake States Regional Guidelines for Assessing Natural Forest Management. Smart Wood Certification Program, Sigurd Olson Environmental Institute, Northland College, Ashland, Wisconsin (February 14, 1994, draft).
"Minnesota Chosen for Landmark Study of Public Forest Lands." DNR News Press Release, n.d.
Minnesota Pioneers Responsible Forestry. 2002 booklet sponsored by the Minnesota Department of Natural Resources, Aitkin County Land Department, Cass County Land Department, the Institute for Agriculture and Trade Policy, and the McKnight Foundation.
Mississippi Headwaters Board (Cass County Courthouse, Walker, MN 56484).
Mississippi Headwaters Forest Steward booklets: *Harvesting Your Woodlot* and *Protecting Your Shoreline.*

Organized to Protect the Mississippi through Interlocal Cooperation. Brochure.

TIDINGS. Newsletter, vol. 13, nos. 4/5 (April/June 1997).

Visual Quality Best Management Practices for Forest Management in Minnesota. Booklet, May 1994.

Wanted: Scenic Beauty. Brochure.

1996 Good Wood Directory (Good Wood Alliance, 289 College St., Burlington, VT 05401; www.goodwood.org).

The Northern Forest: A Legacy for the Future. Brochure, 1995 (Northern Forest Alliance, 58 State St., Montpelier, VT 05602).

Oregon SmartWood: Practical Conservation through Certified Forestry. Brochure (Rogue Institute for Ecology and Economy, 762 A St. Ashland, OR 97520).

Power and the Land: Four Documentary Portraits of the Great Depression. Video, 1994 (Kino Video, 333 W. 39th St., Suite 503, New York, NY 10018; 800-562-3330).

"Protecting Forests through Certification: The Good Wood Crusade." Issue Brief, World Wildlife Fund, Washington, D.C., August 1998.

Rice, Richard E., Raymond E. Gullison, and John W. Reid. "Can Sustainable Management Save Tropical Forests?" *Scientific American,* April 1997.

The Rivers Advocate. Newsletter, various issue, 1996–1998 (Rivers Council of Minnesota, 1313 5th St. S.E., Minneapolis, MN 55414).

"Samples Indicate Rivers Tainted." *Saginaw News,* June 8, 2002, 1.

Seventh American Forest Congress Final Report. Washington, D.C., February 20–26, 1996.

Shanks, Bernard. *This Land is Your Land: The Struggle to Save America's Public Lands.* San Francisco: Sierra Club Books, 1984.

Sigurd Olson Environmental Institute of Northland College and the Rainforest Alliance's SmartWood Program. *Certification Assessment Report of the Aitkin County (Minnesota) Land Department's Management of County Forest Lands.* July 1, 1997.

SmartWood Program (3 Millet St., Goodwin Baker Building, Richmond, VT 05477; e-mail: smartwood@ra.org).

Confidential Draft SmartWood Forest Assessor Manual. September 27, 1996.

Description of the SmartWood Program. Monograph, Rainforest Alliance, June 1996.

SmartWood Certified Forestry Press Pak. January 1997.

SmartWood: Effective Conservation through Innovative Forest Management. Brochure of the SmartWood Program (c/o Rainforest Alliance, 65 Bleecker St., New York, NY 10012).

The SmartWood Network: A Worldwide System of Region-Specific, Non-Profit Organizations Conducting Independent Forest Assessments, Evaluations, Monitoring and Certification. June 1996.

SmartWood Perspectives on Certification of Public Forest Lands. www.rainforest-alliance .org/swr13.html (accessed May 4, 1998).

SmartWood List. February,1997.

SmartWood Network List of Members and Collaborators. April 1997.

What Is the SmartWood Program? Booklet, 1997.

State of Minnesota Office Memorandum: DNR-Forestry. "Reaching a Decision on Aitkin County Certification." From John Krantz, June 20, 1997.

Sustaining Profits and Forests: The Business of Sustainable Forestry. Booklet (Sustainable Forestry Working Group, John D. and Catherine T. MacArthur Foundation, 1997).

Turner, Frederick. *Rediscovering America: John Muir in His Time and Ours.* New York: Viking Penguin, 1985.

UNDERSTORY: Developments from the Sustainable World of Wood. Vol. 6, no. 3 (Summer 1996) (Good Wood Alliance, P.O. Box 1525, Burlington, VT 05402-1525).

Vance, Nan C., and Jane Thomas, eds. *Special Forest Products: Biodiversity Meets the Marketplace.* General Technical Report GTR-WO-63. USDA Forest Service, Washington, D.C., October 1977.

Vileisis, Ann. *Discovering the Unknown Landscape: A History of America's Wetlands.* Washington, D.C.: Island Press, 1997.

www.colonialcraft.com

www.fcresearch.org

www.iatp.org

www.quanex.com

www.rainforestalliance.org

www.smartwood.org

Part II

FROM PROCESS TO PRACTICE

CHAPTER 4

Catron County, New Mexico
MIRRORING THE WEST, HEALING THE LAND, REBUILDING COMMUNITY

Sam Burns

Land management in the American West remains contentious, a result of the inevitable clash between traditional natural resource–based lifeways and the rapidly accelerating body of knowledge regarding ecosystem health and proper stewardship. As the largest county in New Mexico, Catron County also has over 65 percent of its land in federal holdings. Ranchers, loggers, and other area residents perceive use of these lands as a necessary right rather than as a privilege granted by a distant public agency. As is the story told throughout the West, Catron County was hit particularly hard by the reduction in allowable timber harvest, other restrictions related to the Endangered Species Act, and the many court battles associated with resource management. These changes—and perceived changes to a less local, more top-down, federally mandated management—proved disorienting and frustrating to locals.

A place-based community, Catron County was rent by local conflict that tore at the very base of the cooperative, rural society. Out of roiling disagreement and public lambasting between interest groups, the Catron County Citizen's Group emerged to air issues, rebuild trust, diversify the economy, and attempt to secure a voice in decisions regarding the use of "their" federal lands. With hard-won successes and deeply frustrating failures, the Citizen's Group offers lessons to collaborative efforts throughout the country. Seeking to rebuild its economic and social fabric and to sustain and adapt its identity and integrity in an age of rapid sociocultural change, Catron County's renewal depends on reshaping the interrelationships between the community's values, economic base, and natural environment. In Catron County, as in many small, rural places in the West, the as-yet-untold chapters of the story will revolve around the interplay between economy, ecology, community, and equity.

A Story of Change

The story of the West is almost always about land—land and its many forms and features: open range, water, timber, wildlife, wilderness, cattle, mountains, and mesas as far as the eye can see. In Catron County, New Mexico, the story of the West is being retold as passionately as ever. Its central theme is social, economic, and cultural change at the beginning of the twenty-first century.

Catron County is the largest county in New Mexico. Seven thousand eight hundred square miles of valleys, hillsides, and mesas dominate the landscape. A population of 3,000 live here, with deep cultural roots in agriculture and Spanish-American history. They have held on to a way of life grounded in rural traditions—looking out for friends and family, utilizing the products and resources of the land, desiring political autonomy, and striving for local community control.

Turning southwest by auto from Albuquerque, through Socorro, it is a three- to four-hour drive to Reserve, the county's seat. For a long while, travel is along straight, flat roads and then up through high plateau grasslands, mostly dry, rocky, and empty. Coming from the northwest through Grants, the land is similarly open and austere, punctuated by black lava flows within Malpais National Monument. As one draws within the last 30 miles, New Mexico Highway 12 winds across ridges and down drainages before descending beyond the Continental Divide to the west into the San Francisco River valley. Here the landscape changes first to piñon/juniper country, then to ponderosa pine.

Here on the southern edge of the Colorado Plateau, beyond a high-desert plain, rim country tumbles downward, collecting scarce precipitation and forming a watershed fertile enough to sustain a forested ecosystem with creeks, meadows, mountain vistas, large trees, and riparian areas. In the span of a few dozen miles, after becoming accustomed to the barren terrain of the previous two hundred miles, the extent of the ponderosa pine forest is utterly surprising.

As the road continues to twist and turn toward Reserve, farther and farther from the interstate highways and main thoroughfares, Catron County's physical remoteness becomes most obvious. It is not an easy place to get to. And that is how most people seem to like it—somewhat out of the way, a place where you have to want to be, a place where your social roots may go back several generations, a place where hopefully no one will bother you, especially about formal rules.

At the northerly edge of Reserve, Highway 12 turns abruptly westward toward Arizona. Here "Main Street" begins with its small grocery store, bar, and gas station. As it continues southward, there is a medium-size motel and a few smaller ones, a couple of locally owned cafes, and several car repair shops. Alongside most houses are woodpiles. In the yards rest children's toys, religious objects, and an old pickup truck. On the front porch of one house, an elderly Hispanic couple eat their summer evening dinner, bidding passersby hello, willing to talk to a stranger. "Main Street" continues south out into a broad valley, punctuated on the edge of town by the Catholic Church, Santo Nino.

On a rising mesa on the west side of Reserve are the school, the community center, a few more houses, and a medical center operated by the Presbyterian Medical Services under contract with the county government. Along the east side of the valley runs the San Francisco River. Out along the highway, as it runs west toward Alpine, Arizona, is the county fairground. Across the highway, the Reserve Ranger District of the Gila National Forest is surrounded by groves of gambel oak. Here lies a key to the story of Catron County and the changing culture of the Rocky Mountain West.

The Gila National Forest—Changes in Public Land Management

As is the case with many small villages and towns in the region, much of Catron County consists of federally owned public lands. Like Kalispell, Montana; Sheridan, Wyoming; Dolores, Colorado; Moab, Utah; and dozens of other places in the Rocky Mountain states, Reserve, New Mexico is tied socially, economically, and culturally to large tracts of public land. Sixty-five percent of the land in Catron County is owned and managed by the federal government.

Community attachments to these lands run deep and are pervasive. Such attachments have gone unnoticed and been taken for granted because they have been so informal and unbroken for decades. Only as these ties to place have been challenged, weakened, or broken have they become visible to the ordinary citizen in Catron County. Only as they have become a matter of rancorous political debate here and in other places throughout the western United States have the patterns and vulnerabilities of traditional, land-based, cultural ties become fully recognized. They are traditional in the sense that they reflect the long-standing patterns of making a living directly from the land and its resources.

The 3.3-million-acre Gila National Forest is divided into five ranger districts, one of which is headquartered in Reserve. Within this forest is the 558,065-acre Gila Wilderness, located forty-four miles south of Reserve, twenty-five miles north of Silver City. It was the first Forest Service wilderness area, administratively selected in 1924 and officially designated by Congress in 1964 after passage of the Wilderness Act. The Aldo Leopold Wilderness with 202,016 acres and the Blue Range Wilderness with 29,034 acres also lie within the Gila National Forest.

According to Mike Gardner, the Reserve District ranger until 2001, in 1988 the Gila National Forest produced 30 million board feet of timber per year. The volume of logging, in part, set the stage for environmental appeals of timber sales. The first Gila National Forest plan, which had been completed in 1986, identified species, including the Mexican spotted owl, which needed protection. Species protection required by the Endangered Species Act led to a dramatic reduction in the Gila National Forest's timber program.

With continuous reduction in the sale and availability of timber, the sawmill operated by Stone Container Corporation (now US Industries) closed in 1993. More than one hundred jobs in the community were lost. While some reports suggest that the sawmill closed, at least in part, because of Stone Container's financial problems (Davis 1996), the fact remains that instead of 30 million board feet cut per year, the Forest Service commercial timber program was virtually dismantled. The loss of the timber program led to a corresponding reduction in Forest Service silviculturists, ecologists, and sale administrators, especially on the Reserve District. After ten years of decline in activity and capacity, the Gila National Forest was not able, with its own staff, to carry out a wide range of management objectives, from small timber sales and restoration projects to broader ecosystem stewardship.

Simultaneously, during the early 1990s, Gila National Forest staff in the Reserve area conducted an analysis of the forest resource conditions through the Negrito Ecosystem Management Plan. According to Donal Weaver, a recently retired silviculturist on the Reserve District, about thirty members of the community and staff had met to address the issues and concerns regarding ecosystem conditions in an area surrounding Negrito Creek. This forest and community planning process was one of the earliest Forest Service attempts to advance ecosystemwide management analysis, initiated under the 1992 U.S. Forest Service's New Perspectives program.

The purposes of the Negrito Ecosystem Management Plan were to address "abnormally dense, even aged ponderosa stands," "pinyon and juniper encroachment on meadows and grasslands," "erosion damage," and "landscape fragmentations" (Yaffee et al. 1996). Representatives of the Gila National Forest believed they were "out in front" of the national movement to look at "ecosystem level" issues, but their efforts were sidetracked and delayed by contentious debate and criticism that occurred between divergent commodity and environmental interests.

Ecological Perspectives—Pressures to Change

In contrast to traditional users of the Gila National Forest, such as ranchers and loggers, people with ecological or environmental perspectives began to speak out about the degraded conditions of the land and vegetation. They were critical of overgrazing, logging in unroaded areas, removing large trees, and negative impacts on certain endangered species. Both in speeches and in studies, references were made to stream bank erosion, the invasion of piñon and juniper species into rangelands, and the loss of old-growth and that the land could not support the number of cattle permitted by federal grazing allotments:

> These types of degradation were those also named in the Negrito Ecosystem Management Plan, but with a higher level of urgency: . . . in the late 1980s, Peter Galvin and Kieran Suckling, environmentalists who had moved to the Reserve area from out of state to count owls, as Forest Service field biologists, started pushing for federal protection of the owl. "I'd go to a timber sale before it was cut and walk around, then I'd go back and see what happened to the beautiful forest, and it was completely trashed," Suckling recalled. "All the big trees were cut and the ground was ripped up by tractors. It looked like a war zone." (Davis 1996, 10)

Whether intended or not, ecological or environmental perspectives ran headlong into the traditional views of longtime residents who saw public lands as part of their birthright. In the eyes of long-term residents, environmental activists were relying on the power of the federal government, namely, the National Environmental Policy Act of 1970 and the Endangered Species Act of 1973, to undermine their economic livelihood. Use of such power was viewed by locals as invasive and threatening to their community's well-being.

Contentious rhetoric swept the West as the environmental movement and rural community economies clashed in ideological confrontation. By the late 1980s, words were being heard that continue to resound today, over a decade later—the Diamond Bar range allotment, Earth First!, Wise Use, custom and culture, private property rights, Mexican spotted owls, county sovereignty, and the county supremacy movement: "[In 1995,] Arizona State University zoologist W. L. Minckley wrote that the Gila River Basin—which includes the San Francisco River slashing north-south through Catron—is the only riparian area in the world where every native fish species has been extirpated or has been listed or recommended for listing as endangered or threatened" (Davis 1996, 9). Davis also writes,

> But many local residents, and especially county leaders, deny that they're in a natural-resource crisis. They say they're in a regulatory crisis. They blame the Fish and Wildlife Service for listing the owl, Gila trout, southwestern willow flycatcher, the spiked dace, and loach minnow as threatened or endangered. They say "New-Nazi" federal officials harass people by driving around county roads in law enforcement vehicles. They blame environmentalists who sue to protect birds and fish and to stop ranchers from building livestock watering tanks in the wilderness. (1996, 9)

Local ranchers felt they were the objects of finger-pointing by "enviros" and government employees. Rather than being to blame for the loss of fish species and water resources, the more common local belief was that, in the words of Hugh B. McKeen, former Catron County commissioner and rancher, it was "Forest Service management that protected trees and put out fires for so many years [that] has left us with springs that no longer exist and rivers and streams that no longer function."

At a critical time when common ground might have been found, when the "Old West" and the "New West" might have benefited from a dialogue with each other, a learning moment was lost. Caught up in a sea of ideological debate, with opposing sides claiming the high ground of community ideals or ecological values, the middle ground of positive community adaptation was squeezed out. Without a middle ground, ideologies that should have been transformed into a healthy debate about social, economic, and public policy adaptations deteriorated and instead fueled a cultural war. The war was fought with blunt tools of rhetorical criticism:

> "Those people in Catron County are looking for the wrong place to blame," said Susan Schock, a Silver City environmental activist whose Gila Watch group has battled Catron County since 1992. "They're trashing the land. They won't diversify their economy. They think everything can be fixed with more money and more manipulation." (Davis 1996, 9)

While the forest ecosystems were suffering cumulative degradation caused by resource utilization, years of drought, and federal resource management policy, to claim that the people of Catron County were "trashing the land" merely led to further inflammatory statements, not a willingness to engage and consider the actual conditions of the land.

Hugh B. McKeen noted, "All we got in those days was bad press." What he meant was that the press focused mainly on the polarized and reactionary side of the story. During the early and most conflicted years, as the moderate voices were pushed aside by rhetoric on the poles of the divisive argument, the debate became more and more extreme, and the respective advocates backed each other farther and farther into separate corners. Neighborly problem solving was lost, the land did not heal, and the community began to break apart.

Escalating conflicts and political rhetoric were accompanied by increased tension between adversaries, physical symptoms of stress, and even the fear of violence. Elena Gellert, longtime environmentalist and resident of Luna, New Mexico, recalled "a dangerous kind of undercurrent that could have erupted any time." Gellert remembers,

I went to public meetings where I spoke in favor of the Endangered Species Act, and listing certain species and that was at a meeting where there were threats of using bullets and shooting. I remember leaving that meeting being concerned for my vehicle, concerned for my own safety. I was very concerned for the safety of the people who are now the Southwest Center for Biodiversity. (Smith 1998, 3)

Trust was lost; fear took over. Coercion took the place of mutual discovery and community conversation.

The County Land Use Plan— Loss of Community

By 1989, Catron County government sought, through the adoption of ordinances and a land use plan, to limit the federal government's power to manage public lands within the county. The county's central argument was that its laws could nullify the management direction and actions of the Forest Service regarding wilderness protection, grazing permits, timber harvesting, and endangered species habitat protection.

The county land use plan claimed authority to arrest Forest Service employees for "trespassing" on federal forestlands while performing their regular resource management duties. County government proposed to take control of Forest Service lands within its jurisdiction in order to manage them for commodity utilization based on the principle of "custom and culture," a phrase that has been widely appropriated from National Environmental Policy Act language. The original intent of the phrase was to address how federal decisions impacted traditional ways of life or historic, social, and economic community practices. County leaders who sought increased local control over federal lands to protect their "customs and culture" became known as "county supremacists."

From the perspective of county elected officials, to label them as "county supremacists" was erroneous and a consequence of government officials and outsiders dominating the media. Rather than supremacy over federal lands, what they sought was a role in public land planning activities in Catron County and participation in public decision-making processes that otherwise appeared to them to be "a stacked deck" where local voices were outnumbered by what they viewed as extreme environmental positions.

From the perspective of county leaders, federal land managers' decisions to reduce grazing, timber, and mining in response to legal environmental mandates and political pressures were threats to the county's long-standing rural lifestyles and ultimately its economic survival. They viewed the increasing restrictions of historic uses of public lands as undermining the community's economic and social patterns. Over many decades, these patterns had become so much a part of the community that they were viewed as rights, not a "permitted use." Some citizens trace these "rights" back to the 1848 Treaty of Guadalupe Hidalgo (see Tate Gallery 1953). The restriction of a timber sale on Forest Service land, reduction of a grazing allotment, or road closure was viewed as a violation of individual property rights, not as an appropriate, rational action to manage public resources derived from legitimate authority or based in scientific resource management.

Issues and decisions that had previously been informally addressed between a commodity user and local Forest Service district staff, such as between a rancher and a Forest Service range conservationist, now required public review under the National Environmental Policy Act. Resource decisions were increasingly based on new scientific information and analysis intended to achieve better ecosystem management. Most community members were neither aware of nor understood this new information, nor were they invited to discuss it except in the most formal of terms. Decisions that had once been made locally by resource managers had to be taken to higher levels where they took many times longer to make, often with limited certainty and finality, and ultimately did not appear to consider local community needs and knowledge. The requirements of the National Environmental Policy Act and the Endangered Species Act forced local resource managers to be accountable to higher authorities and regulations, and this was perceived by many community members as an unwarranted imposition by a distant, insensitive, Washington-based government. These were the same laws, for instance, that enabled the environmental group Southwest Center for Biodiversity to file a series of lawsuits to enforce species and habitat protection and that resulted in an injunction prohibiting logging on Arizona and New Mexico national forests for eighteen months during 1995 and 1996.

Social and political forces and economic interests, internal and external to Catron County, wittingly and unwittingly conspired to set the stage for deep polarization and discordant discourse. The story told in the media inflamed the debate, and the world outside Catron County heard about a community drama of threats, counterthreats, fear, and anxiety. While Catron County's story has become infamous and the county somewhat notorious for its oppositions to the Forest Service, most of what has been told thus far has been defined by the most extreme poles on a broad continuum of interests. While opposing advocates argued their positions as they saw them—and indeed there was some truth in each set of claims—the middle ground, the community as a place for families, children, working, making a living, healing, neighboring, and future well-being—was largely absent. Where a middle ground might have been constructed there now resided alienating pain and loss. Blaming, charging and countercharging, rhetoric, and denial became the focus rather than beginning, early on, to talk about what the land, trees, and streams needed so the community could sustain itself.

Catron County Citizens' Group—
From Pain to Process

From the midst of individual pain and loss of community, the Catron County Citizens' Group emerged. It grew out of concerns about how local residents were suffering from stress, increased tensions, and fear of violence between opposing factions, all of which affected the health and well-being of the community, including relations among schoolchildren. What had begun as a dispute over preferred approaches to resource management became a social crisis manifested by higher rates of alcohol and spousal abuse, depression, and a loss of control over one's life. What had begun as a conflict over trees, water, and dirt became a war that tore at the relationships, roots, and dreams of people's lives.

After the husbands and wives of Forest Service staff approached him about their concerns, Mike Gardner, the Reserve District ranger throughout the 1990s, sought the assistance of a counselor to assist family members, including children who felt intimidated by classmates. While local ranchers and loggers had felt social and economic exclusion for some time, finally the official trustees of the forestland became victims of the social and political conflicts themselves, and the need to rebuild relationships within the social community became manifest.

Dr. Mark Unverzagt, who operated the Presbyterian Medical Service Clinic in Reserve, with the advice and assistance of Dr. Ben Daitz at the University of New Mexico Medical School, obtained the help of Melinda Smith of the New Mexico Center for Dispute Resolution and John Folk Williams of the Western Network to pull together community members. In 1995, this group became known as the Catron County Citizens' Group (hereafter Citizens' Group). Dr. "Mark" was motivated by what he saw as worsening health impacts stemming from the social, political, and environmental conflict.

The Citizens' Group membership initially included county elected officials and staff, Forest Service employees, ranchers, environmental representatives, loggers, and citizens in the county who were concerned about the economy, job training, overcoming the past and current tensions, or the future health of the area. In an account of the Citizens' Group's work, Melinda Smith (1998), wrote,

> Despite differences, the group quickly established common ground and shared interests about the need for economic development and diversification, the maintenance of rural lifestyles and values, the importance of sound land stewardship, and the importance of participation in the decision that affected the county.

There is a sense of relief among some of the participants that there was finally a forum to deal with these issues. Reserve district ranger Mike Gardner expressed it this way: "It was five years of pretty harrowing times with nobody really coming to your aid. Nobody saying, you know, 'attaboy Mike, hang in there, things are going to change pretty soon.' Now with this group, I feel like I'm not just dealing with somebody with opposing views from mine or somebody saying things intentionally to make me mad." (Smith 1998, 5)

The Citizens' Group developed a mission statement: "to come together to openly and honestly discuss and deal with the diverse situations we face, finding common ground from our different points of view to ensure an economic, social, and an environmentally sound future for us all" (Smith 1998, 5).

The early days and months of the Citizens' Group were spent in establishing dialogue, finding common ground, and developing two "on-the-ground" projects: piñon and juniper removal on a range allotment and attempting to develop a business park on five acres of designated Forest Service land. At the February 1996 meeting, about fifty people, working in small groups, brainstormed concerns and desired outcomes. According to Smith (1998, 7), these included the following:

- Job availability
- Youth opportunities/parental and community support of youth
- Environmental issues and land management
- Lack of cooperation between communities and divergent groups
- Diversification of the economy
- Reduction of social polarization between long-term and new residents
- Reduction of hostility and development of tolerance for different views
- Maintenance of culture and acceptance of change
- Control change that happens and diminish negative influences
- Maintain work ethic
- Public education about land management from a local perspective
- Relief of tension/stress
- Good conflict resolution
- More effective decision-making processes about land management
- People in the county deciding the future of the county

Working committees were established to address five priority areas (Smith 1998, 7):

1. Education, including educating each other about their different points of view and values as well as the public about issues and conflicts the county is experiencing

2. Dispute resolution—finding processes for resolving differences and preventing threats of violence or destructive behavior
3. Land stewardship—finding common ground for maintaining healthy range and environmental conditions everyone can agree on
4. Economic development—developing new sources of revenue for the county and its residents
5. Youth development—creating a means for full participation of the county's youth in the current process and future of the county

Support from the Hewlett Foundation enabled Dr. Daitz to film the community discussion and development process as a means of reflecting more clearly to the community its conflicts and means of resolving them. A grant from the Surdna Foundation allowed Melinda Smith to continue the conflict resolution and community building processes and also enabled the Citizens' Group to hire a local coordinator in April 1996.

Building a Track Record— A Long, Winding Road

As is true of many community-based coalitions attempting to resolve the long-developing conflicts between commodity producers and users, environmental interests, and local government and federal land agencies, the process of rebuilding community and healing the land has been a challenging one in Catron County. After establishing its vision and direction during its formative months, the Citizens' Group needed to simultaneously facilitate a process that would demonstrate progress, keep the parties at the table, build community support, and increase trust within the group. These are high expectations where community economic dependencies on federal lands have become so deeply ingrained, where public land ecosystem management practices have brought dramatic changes, and where long-held and well-established community beliefs have been confronted so pointedly by regional and national interests, laws, and powers. In Catron County, expectations for change and improvement became especially challenging because the "line in the sand" had been so emphatically drawn between radically different views of local and federal government powers, responsibilities, and actions, breeding fear among citizens and a lack of conversation, all of which ultimately led to a loss of well-being.

When asked to convey an example of the success of the Citizens' Group, one member said, "We're still here." Another said, "No one's gotten hurt." Progress? Yes—but are these "successes" enough to sustain a collaborative process? What then are the appropriate ways to define the process of building a track record, of describing the accomplishments that the local community and the public land agencies have achieved and that opposing groups and funding sources will accept as measures of success? How can these actions and outcomes be measured?

Typically, there is some combination of key concrete events within which certain definable actions occurred, followed by outcomes, both expected and unexpected. These often lead to change in attitudes, beliefs, or behaviors that usually can occur only in a cauldron of community conflict. In many situations of deep value-oriented polarization, the social and political heat is turned up very high. Such contexts are often messy, personally painful, and exhausting, yet somehow, finally and ironically, they emerge as hopeful. What were these times and actions, "ways and means," for Catron County and the Citizens' Group?

February to March 1996—Early Mistrust

In the nearby town of Eagar, Arizona, at a meeting attended by one Citizens' Group member, Catron County commissioners and grazing permittees met "to pursue litigation against the Forest Service for restricting grazing permits" (Smith 1998, 8). A Forest Service employee was escorted out of the building where the meeting was taking place. This event renewed hostility among the parties, but through many hours of mediated discussion, an endorsement of appropriate group social behaviors was achieved by the Citizens' Group: "hearing all sides with respect and speaking the truth," "having direct communications before categorizing people," and "respecting everyone's value to each other and to the community" (Smith 1998, 8).

That this endorsement needed to occur to allow the Citizens' Group to move forward is an indication of the degree to which community relationships and social trust had been undermined. Supported by some suggestions from the supervisor's office of the Gila National Forest about the needs for scientific analysis, understanding of grazing standards and cooperative monitoring of range conditions, and the resolution of the conflict that had begun at the Eagar meeting, while not a pleasant beginning to a community rebuilding process, led to field trips to discuss actual land conditions. Once out on the land, it was considerably easier to listen to each other and achieve some "common understanding" (Smith 1998, 9). Engaging with real situations on the land appears to have enabled those who were at odds relative to resource management issues to begin to work on solutions to specific problems. People who were quite far apart because of their rhetorical positions found they were much closer with regard to identifying needed ecological improvements on the land. Paying attention to the land changed the context and tenor of a polarized debate such that it became a dialogue about community stewardship. To make this single adaptation was nevertheless a big step for the Citizens' Group.

Spring 1996—
New Environmental Perspectives

A number of people who might be identified as "environmentalists" had lived in the Reserve area prior to the increase in community tensions but moved away because of social discomfort and tension based on the same anxieties expressed earlier by children and families of Forest Service employees and by Elena Gellert. Todd Schulke was one these. In 1996, he was living near Silver City, New Mexico, a drive of a couple of hours to the south of Reserve. After discussions between Citizen's Group representatives and the leadership of the Southwest Center for Biological Diversity, Todd agreed to begin attending the Citizens' Group meetings during the spring of 1996. From the perspective of those responsible for developing the collaborative process in Catron County, it was essential to have a representative of the Southwest Center if mutual understanding between environmentalists and traditional forest users was to occur. During times when it was challenging for Catron County to maintain a viable relationship with the Southwest Center, Todd has remained a member of the Citizens' Group. About his involvement in the group, Todd has stated, "My intention is to develop understanding and trust in each other so at least there is enough common ground that we can move together" (Smith 1998, 10).

Schulke has continually placed considerable emphasis on sound ecological assessment, and this has brought an important perspective to the Citizens' Group. However, his advocacy of the Southwest Center's positions, such as preserving old growth, keeping all timbering out of roadless areas, and the organization's lawsuit against the Forest Service over range conditions, has made it difficult for Todd to bridge from the Southwest Center to the Citizens' Group, where he has at times been viewed as a regional representative of the Southwest Center, not simply as a local member of the Citizens' Group.

The Eagle Peak Fire

The H. B. Salvage sale was proposed in an old-growth forest on the Gila National Forest's Reserve District after the Eagle Peak fire. The Southwest Center opposed the sale because it was in an area with old-growth characteristics, while others viewed the sale as a salvage operation in an area that had been burned.

During the planning phase, the local Forest Service timber staff reduced the sale area by removing some of the unroaded portions in order to make it more ecologically acceptable. The sale was projected to produce about six million board feet and was therefore desirable from the perspective of providing jobs for local, unemployed citizens.

Although there was disagreement about the outcome of the sale, removal of some of the unroaded areas led to recognition that a lot of work had been done to make the sale more ecologically balanced. Some local community leaders were therefore disappointed when U.S. Department of Agriculture Undersecretary James Lyons rescinded implementation of the salvage rider, thus canceling authority for the sale. Lyons's action added to community frustrations that decisions, plans, and proposed actions that had been improved by intensive local comment and the Forest Service's response to it could be ignored by external federal actions. This fueled the notion that communities and Forest Service districts will not be allowed to develop collaborative initiatives.

Whether Catron County community members could have anticipated the depth of political opposition to the unappealable timber sales associated with the "salvage rider" is debatable. The rider was attached to the 1995 Omnibus Appropriations and Rescissions Act, which was designed to "expedite salvage timber sales in order to achieve, to the maximum extent feasible, a salvage sale volume above the programmed level to reduce the backlogged volume." But while they saw a reasonable connection between the Eagle Peak fire, the H. B. Salvage sale, and the "salvage rider," they could not grasp the national environmental reaction to a provision that made such sales "not appealable." Catron County, a large place with a small population and a deeply traditional western worldview, was caught between a local objective, perceived as reasonable and well founded, and numerous national interests and values with far more power.

Mediation of Range Conflicts

In addition to unresolved timber issues between the Forest Service and citizens of Catron County, there were also environmental concerns about overgrazing and the power and control of the ranching industry over federal lands. At the same time, ranchers remained concerned about regulatory powers being exercised by the courts that reduced grazing and, in particular, the Forest Service's reduction of eight hundred head of cattle from the Diamond Bar allotment, the largest on the Gila National Forest.

The Citizens' Group decided that a mediation committee might be useful in reducing range conflicts. Its members believed that the conflicts had mostly to do with "interpersonal" issues, such as differing expectations of ranchers and the Forest Service—"differences in attitudes, cultures, and backgrounds of Forest Service personnel and ranchers, trust, and perceptions of uneven power among the parties" (Smith 1998, 10–11). While some progress was made on the interpersonal issues using mediation techniques, the participants also concluded more education was needed among all the parties about the mediation process. Greater attention was also needed to getting all parties to the table, which would balance the power on the mediation committee so that parties would be more satisfied with the results (Smith 1998, 10–11).

Overall, the mediation committee's work was viewed as a qualified success with the clear need for more resources to carry on the process, for more reflection and learning among Citizens' Group members, and for more diverse public involvement to keep the mediation committee from being viewed as an "advisory" committee under the Federal Advisory Committee Act (Smith 1998, 11–12).

While it may be desirable and sometimes feasible for the Citizens' Group to attempt to reduce the "interpersonal" issues between some of the ranchers and the Forest Service, such efforts need to be timely. Once the relationship between ranchers and the Forest Service escalates into conflicts, legal processes typically overtake the collaborative ones. In the case of the Diamond Bar allotment, the reduction in cattle numbers eventually ended up being decided by the court. Kit and Sherry Laney, owners of the Diamond Bar, sued the Forest Service over their allotment reduction, contending that "Forest Service regulators doomed their business" because they had to remove all their cattle in April 1997 (Paulson 1999). Their lawsuit was subsequently thrown out by the district court, a decision later upheld on the basis that the Forest Service has the authority to manage land uses and could limit cattle access to public lands.

Forest Health Improvement

In the fall of 1996, the Forest Service proposed several forest restoration projects. One of these was the Apache sale, a 125-acre overstocked stand of ponderosa pine infested with mistletoe yet capable of producing an estimated 450,000 board feet of timber. Donal Weaver, then the Forest Service silviculturist on the Gila's Reserve District, worked through the Citizens' Group to explain the importance of retaining an old-growth overstory, reducing the mistletoe invasion, thinning the tree density to reduce fire hazards, increasing forage, and providing forest products for the area's small loggers. The only serious debate occurred over where to cap the diameter size. While environmental representatives argued for a sixteen-inch cap, Weaver and others believed this diameter was not scientifically defensible.

Todd Schulke of the Southwest Center said he would have to hold firm on the sixteen-inch cap, commenting,

> One thing that's underestimated [with regard to the Apache sale] is how far we're sticking our necks out being out here and advocating some of this stuff . . . there are some political realities." [However,] . . . from an economic perspective, the restrictions on logging were devastating the county. County manager Adam Polley responded: "You're looking at Reserve . . . [and] at a group of people losing their living." . . . Donal Weaver stated: "To have Todd out here and trying to work with us and at least admit that there's a need for logging of some sort is a pretty big step. We just need to keep working together. . . . We're a long ways from where we were a year ago, which was nowhere." (Smith 1998, 14)

The sixteen-inch cap was eventually agreed to after the Forest Service and others insisted that it would not set a precedent for future projects. Both sides on this issue felt they were taking a risk, but most involved were encouraged by the trust that was built in order for the agreement to occur. After the agreement was reached, the then Reserve District ranger, Mike Gardner, said, "The future of public lands management [is when a] diverse group can come up with a desired future condition for an area" (Smith 1998, 14). But even with this progress through agreement at the community level, the Apache Timber sale was delayed because of contracting and administrative procedures within the Forest Service and, to the chagrin of many of the Citizens' Group members, including the local Forest Service representative, remained unthinned long after its planning was completed. After a change in the Forest Service pricing structure, the Apache sale was sold in 1998 to a local logger and timber transporter. While it had been anticipated that the thinning work would be completed in twelve to eighteen months after the sale, as of 2002 the logger has not thinned some portions of it because of higher-than-anticipated harvesting costs.

Community Visioning and Organizational Transitions—1997 Conference

In the fall and winter of 1996, numerous meetings were held to develop a community vision. These meetings resulted in focusing the Citizens' Group's work on watershed improvements, economic development, mediation, and youth by restructuring the group's committees on these areas. While progress was made in developing mediation skills within the schools where social tensions had occurred, the Citizens' Group felt that they should place primary emphasis on pressing natural resource issues, such as the Apache timber sale and grazing. This preference led some members to feel that social concerns, such as the need for a job training center, were being overshadowed, and subsequently they reduced their participation (personal conversations with Citizens' Group community members, summer 1997).

Citizens' Group members and support staff had wanted for some time to hold a conference to put in a more positive light the press's harsh characterization of Catron County's experiences and to bolster local support and the Citizens' Group's momentum. The conference was held in July 1997, with numerous presentations by natural resource specialists, a journalist, a mediator, other public land–community partnerships, environmentalists, and local spokespersons instrumental in the initiation and operation of the Citizens' Group. The conference, "Communities, Land Use, and Conflict" (July 18–19, 1997), provided an opportunity for locals and visiting groups to showcase their accomplishments, learn from each other, and reenergize members of the Citizens' Group. The conference encouraged a rededication to action within the Citizens' Group and provided an opportunity to assess progress to date relative to other collaborative efforts in the West; however, it also illustrated the variance of opinion about collaboration (see New Mexico Center for Dispute Resolution 1997). Representatives of national and regional groups in attendance stated that local collaborative processes did not adequately include national interests in protecting natural ecosystems. One of the keynote speakers, nationally recognized journalist Alston Chase, expressed his concern that historic, community and land-based culture in the West was as or more vulnerable to decline than nature; this, if true, portends additional social conflict and economic disruption as the story of western rural change continues to unfold.

Focusing on Project Development

As the Citizens' Group moved into the fall and winter of 1997–1998, it began to focus on project development and implementation. Discussion focused on the problems of marketing small-diameter pine, the need for ecological analysis acceptable to diverse perspectives, and the potential loss of the area's remaining small loggers. There was a growing realization that the loss of silvicultural and forestry staff from the Gila National Forest had practically eliminated its capacity to manage even a minimal timber program, including the smaller sales that had been agreed to for restoring ecosystem sustainability. A formidable irony had evolved: no timber program, no staff; no staff, no forest restoration capacity. Without Forest Service staff, the necessary scientific and administrative skills were not available to carry out forest restoration projects needed to return the forest to a healthier condition.

The Citizens' Group was also addressing widespread local concern about reduction in cattle and declining range conditions, caused in part by a continuing regional drought. In the midst of these community conversations, the Southwest Center filed a lawsuit against southwestern U.S. national forests. The suit sought to require the Forest Service to address grazing impacts on endangered species through consultation with the Fish and Wildlife Service. This action by the Southwest Center came as a surprise to many Citizens' Group members and led one person to walk out of the December 1997 meeting. Some members now mistrusted having a Southwest Center representative at the table who was presumably seeking a collaborative approach while the organization was pursuing litigation to obtain its objectives.

The Southwest Center, in its goal of protecting specific species and achieving broader "regional outcomes," and the Citizens' Group, in its desire to achieve common ground through a local collaborative process, had reached a point of deep uncertainty. As Melinda Smith stated, the Southwest Center lawsuit was "casting a shadow over the trust and fragile gains of the group" (Smith 1998, 17).

In the midst of that uncertainty, at a February 1998 Citizens' Group meeting with some forty to fifty persons in attendance, participants heard a presentation on the Ponderosa Pine Forest Partnership and the Forest Plan Revision for San Juan National Forest in southwest Colorado, which has utilized community study groups on each of its three districts. Small loggers, elected officials, Forest Service leadership, and environmentalists at the meeting expressed a strong sense of urgency and resolve to move forward collaboratively on as many actual forest restoration projects as possible.

Abel Camarina, then the Gila National Forest supervisor, expressed a commitment to move ahead with the proposed demonstration timber sales. There was discussion of seeking funding from the Forest Service's Rural Community Assistance Program to build capacity for further community involvement. Local loggers emphasized that they could not remain in the community unless some new economic opportunities developed soon. There was exploration of new-product development to make juniper paneling. Todd Schulke, the environmental representative from the Southwest Center, affirmed his support of restoration project development if it was based on sound ecological analysis that would improve forest sustainability. Overall, there were strong expressions of support by many Citizens' Group members and community leaders to bring about community and forest improvement through the community–forest partnership process. Many recognized that without these renewed commitments, the deep problems of economic, community, and ecological sustainability could not be addressed, much less resolved.

From Community Healing to Project Implementation

By 1999, the Citizens' Group had built a collaborative framework for action. The many years of discontent had been paid back with an equal number of years of soul searching and social reinvestment. Although not totally healed from the community and regional polarization that had occurred because of very different perspectives about how to utilize the surrounding forest and rangelands on the Gila National Forest, the community was ready to get back to work. There was a growing impatience with the "process" of collaboration and a realization that the economic situation for the remaining woodworkers was becoming even more desperate. The "woods" were still in bad shape, and work needed to get done.

About the same time, a new regional coalition was forming, known as the Four Corners Sustainable Forests Partnership (FCSFP), through a special funding arrangement to utilize the resources of the Forest Service's Economic Assistance Program. These funds are administered through the New Mexico State Forestry Program for a four-state area, including portions of Arizona, Colorado, New Mexico, and Utah. In 1999, the Citizens' Group was awarded $45,000 by the FCSFP, to be matched by $39,600. This grant increased the capacity of the Citizens' Group to work on economic development and stabilization in the community, building skills to work with small-diameter pine, expanding markets, and recruiting a wood industry back to the county. This was followed by grants in 2000 and 2001 from the FCSFP of $75,000 and $66,000, respectively, to continue to build community and economic capacity to work in forest restoration.

In 2001, the Citizens' Group also received substantial funding ($356,400) from the new Collaborative Forest Restoration Program, created through the sponsorship of Senator Bingaman (N.M.) of a federal act by the same name, Public Law 106-393. Utilizing these resources, the Citizens' Group is in the process of designing and building a small-diameter log greenhouse located at the high school, establishing a log-holding yard, providing business technical assistance, continuing a Youth Conservation Corps, publishing a community newspaper, and implementing a habitat-fragmentation monitoring assessment.

The log-holding yard is an essential component in their ongoing economic sustainability strategy, which Bob Moore, the executive director of the Citizens' Group, refers to as a "vertically integrated, community based, small diameter, forest products industry" (Catron County Citizens' Group, n.d.). Moore estimates that a sustainable industry could be developed in Catron County based on three to four million board feet of raw material. The key to success will be to process from 70 to 90 percent of this volume in the community, thus the importance of the log-holding yard. The yard is located at the old Stone Sawmill site, which was purchased by the Catron County government for $80,000. The Citizens' Group has an agreement with the county to use the site in return for making $10,000 in improvements each year for five years.

Even though there had been legal action by an environmental group to stop the sale, in late 2001 the Citizens' Group was able to purchase some fir logs from a three-hundred-acre salvage area of the 7,000-acre Corner Mountain fire (Baca and Moore 2002). Gary Harris, a small sawmiller, noted that "the Corner Mountain injunction was the first court case that has been won in 14 years" (FCSFP 2002). As of March 2002, approximately 350,000 board feet of fir logs had been hauled into the yard and sorted. The fir logs were all that was left in the burned area; the ponderosa pine had deteriorated because of several years of delay in getting the salvage sale approved.

Bob Marlin, another small sawmiller and woodcraftsman who works with alligator juniper to make furniture, sees the holding yard as a "success." "The wood sort yard enables me to get more work done. When I get a beam order, I don't have the dollars to do everything. I don't have a loader. But I can go down to the yard and get the wood I need. I can get the wood for 25 cents a board foot. I can't harvest it for that, and I can use their loader" (FCSFP 2002). While Marlin sees the holding yard as a boon, he is concerned that "we are going to reach a plateau on the log sort yard. . . . The forests are in severe trouble. They are overgrown, and the Forest Service is going to have to pay to get rid of the small trees" (FCSFP 2002). Marlin goes on to explain that new markets need to be developed for all the small-diameter materials that need to be thinned. He believes that the key to economic sustainability is what can be done with the so-called waste materials. "Let's look into building a power plant," he exclaims.

Looking down the Road

In the four years between 1998 and 2002, the Citizens' Group has made significant strides toward its goals. Not only has it opened the log-holding yard, but it is in its second year of operating a Youth Conservation Corps, is active in strengthening the local health advisory council, is assisting forest-thinning crews to prepare contracts for wildland fire mitigation, and is involved in community building and collaboration through publishing the Catron County Citizen. With ample external financial resources now coming in and a stable community base of support, the Citizens' Group is well poised to build a sustainable economy based on forest restoration. The group's mantra explains this notion well: "finding common ground to ensure an economically, socially, and environmentally sound future."

Nevertheless, even after seven years of very difficult work, several large hurdles remain. Besides the pervasive sense that forest restoration work will still be challenged by appeals and court injunctions, including the complicated question of what "management indicator species" will be used in future analysis of the National Environmental Policy Act, there are the economic barriers of a forest industry that is based on removing small-diameter, low-value raw material from the woods. Harvesting costs often exceed the value of the trees that need to be removed. Finding ways to utilize the "slash" and the sawdust may improve the economics enough to make the restoration approach to forestry feasible and maybe occasionally show a small profit.

Gary Harris, who has barely survived operating a two-man mill for several years, has recently decided to sell out, recoup his debt, and go to work for the Citizens' Group at the log yard. However, he sees that in doing so he reduces by one more business the capacity of the community to internally utilize the logs brought into the yard. Harris is concerned that it would take $300,000 to $400,000 in capital to upgrade the mill so that it could process the volume that needs to come off the Gila National Forest. "No one can make this sort of investment, and not have a log" (FCSFP 2002). In his statement. Harris is raising the dominant issue in contemporary forest restoration efforts—a stable supply of raw materials. Without long-term stewardship contracting, retooling the wood products industry to process small-diameter material efficiently will remain tenuous at best.

In this regard, the Citizens' Group has been active in a major hope for the future. Recall the Negrito Ecosystem, an analysis area of 128,000 acres designated in 1991. "Much of the analysis was driven by baseline photographs of the ecosystem taken in 1935. Comparisons show a sharp decline in the open grasslands, dramatic encroachment of pinon juniper, and an unhealthy crown-cover density. From the photos and data collected, it was determined that over 7,700 acres of grassland has been lost since 1935. Pinon-juniper has increased by almost the same amount—6,200 acres" (Coates 2002, 6). Since June 2000, through the efforts of Laura Vallejos, a new silviculturist on the Reserve District of the Gila National Forest, the Sheep Basin Unit of the Negrito Ecosystem has been analyzed for restoration treatment.

The Sheep Basin Analysis Unit contains 6,143 acres, of which 3,362 acres of ponderosa pine are proposed for treatment (Sheep Basin Restoration Project 2001). It is estimated that this treatment area would produce approximately five million board feet, 40 percent of which would be nine-inch diameter and above (Laura Vallejos, Citizens' Group public meeting, January 2002). This would be a first step in a steady supply of logs for the holding yard. The Citizens' Group has been active in field trips and other public involvement efforts to develop an eight-point strategy to insure fire risk reduction, proper tree clumping, tree species diversity, hiding and thermal cover for wildlife, old-growth integrity, wildlife "snag" trees, a nonaggressive approach to fiber production, and watershed scale resource management (Moore 2001, 1). The Sheep Basin Unit is one of several analysis areas in the Negrito Ecosystem that hold the key to a "steady supply" of trees for the new restoration industry emerging in Catron County.

Obviously, the economics of forest restoration is a major challenge to future success, as is the tenor and direction of resource management by the Forest Service of the public lands in Catron County, which will deeply affect the future sustainability of the surrounding communities. Concomitantly, the future conditions of these same forests are ultimately dependent on the capacity of the local community to undertake the much-needed fuel treatment and fire risk reduction efforts, thus the vital, persistent, and enduring need for community–public land collaboration in developing ecologically sound forest restoration.

As wildfires raged across the West in midsummer 2002, new wood processing equipment was expected to arrive soon at the log yard operated by the Citizens' Group. Gary Harris, who had worried about the salvaged fir logs deteriorating before they could be sold and that a $300,000 investment for milling equipment would possibly not be available without a "steady supply of raw material," excitedly explained, "We're getting a 5-inch double band saw that will cut a forty foot log. We will use it as a head rig, and we're also getting a debarker, and a chipper, and a molder-planer. We should be working by September or October" (personal communication, July 2002). After a decade of struggle, that has the distinct ring of success.

Standing Back—Taking Stock

In the Catron County story, one can see how locals felt when external legal actions reduced economic opportunity and when public land decisions caused families to relocate. The loss of control over the future by a once-active community was clearly visible in the stress and frustration of old-time residents and was noticed by the community's only family doctor. One could also understand the environmental or ecological perspective that the ecosystem had declined and that "overutilization of forest resources" should be halted. Each perspective was born from legitimately held values, but neither could ultimately succeed without attention to collaborative and adaptive solutions. If the forest ecosystem was in a state of decline, so too was the social and economic well-being of Catron County.

In the late 1980s and early 1990s, no person, organization, or government entity was prepared for the degree or rapidity of the change and tensions that boiled over in Catron County. In retrospect, one might fervently wish that the local government had had the means to bring all parties to the table, but its leaders believed that they had to fight for the economic and political survival of the community. It would also have been highly beneficial for all concerned if the Forest Service, the Environmental Protection Agency, and the Fish and Wildlife Service, among other federal agencies, had possessed the capacities to assist communities in adapting to changing public land management policies before the social fabric and economic well-being of public land–dependent communities became so extremely threatened. If local environmentalists had been encouraged to stay in the community during the early 1990s, community and ecological issues might have been jointly addressed before the cultural climate became volatile and the context for collaborative discourse was nearly destroyed.

It is quite doubtful, in the context of the history of the West, that such cooperative scenarios as these could have occurred. The key local voices—the leaders, both formal and informal—possessed limited social and legal tools with which to attack a pervasive, deeply ingrained national problem. Indeed, on reflection, could one expect a single community in the very heart of the "Old West" to solve a long-standing historic national issue: the appropriate role and use of public lands? How could anyone expect this when so many others, with better preparation and far more resources, have not succeeded?

What happened in Catron County is the dominant story of the West—a scenario of dramatic change, of painful social and economic upheaval, as divisive and unhealthy as any conflict in the rural western United States in the late twentieth century, no less convulsive to local communities than the siting of nuclear waste depositories and power plants or battles over state and regional water rights.

What can be learned from the story of Catron County? Clearly, in terms of generating hope, solutions, healing, and potential success, it has been the community, working through the Citizens' Group, that has provided the process and potential for cultural recovery and ecological health—not the federal, state, or local government or large business. It has not been national environmental organizations, the judicial system, or an array of formal education and technical assistance programs. Rather, it has been the community—led by a minister, a doctor, a schoolteacher, a rancher, an environmentalist, an emergency medical technician, a newcomer, a university professor, and numerous other ordinary citizens— who said and continue to say that building a healing process had to begin here and now and with us. With their initiative, it did just that—taking individual and small-group steps and holding potlucks and long meetings at night until the long-awaited and badly needed external financial assistance was made available. The people decided to no longer stand by silently and allow their community to continue to be torn apart. In 1995, the citizens of Catron County collected themselves and prepared a vision that still guides their work and that they are just beginning to have success in implementing. The past decade of unrelenting, steady work is the strongest indication of the commitment and collaboration needed to undertake community-based forest restoration.

The Success of Collaborative Public Land Processes

How does one know that collaborative processes can lead to appropriate community solutions and healthy and sustainable ecosystems? What are the indicators of success? For some people in Catron County and elsewhere, the volume of timber produced is the measure of success. For them, there will be no progress until some amount of logging resumes. When invading piñon/juniper forests are being "pushed" over to rehabilitate grasslands and recharge the watersheds, there will be progress for others. Simultaneously, others claim there will be no progress until the federal government relinquishes all claims to local forested landscapes. Some who focus on the deterioration of natural ecosystems say there will be only minimal success until cutting timber and cattle grazing are prohibited on public lands. Indeed, one can wonder whether, taken separately, any of these measures of success can be used.

Can a group like the Catron County Citizens' Group achieve success by building trust, being inclusive, being fair, seeking common ground, and asking everyone to share power and consider each others' perspectives? Can such diverse views of success find any common ground? How many crises can one community or one group endure with limited resources? Even with the recent successes in Catron County and elsewhere, we do not yet fully know the answers to these basic questions. However, we can note a number of reasonable and healthy parameters by which to guide community collaboration:

1. Tangible evidence of the success of collaborative processes in public land decision making must be demonstrated to build and maintain the commitments of community members.
2. Success in community ecosystem stewardship must also be tangible, as when watersheds are improved or catastrophic wildfire risks are reduced.
3. Community progress in many critical stages can still be somewhat intangible, such as the occurrence of different feelings when people who were unable to speak to each other begin to converse; when there is an initial willingness to try a new, more progressive land management approach; or when participants stay at a meeting when they had really planned on walking out and never coming back.

4. It is not feasible to rebuild a community if people in that community are not asked or are unable to take part in healing the land with which they are deeply, inherently, ecologically, and economically connected.

5. And, finally, the sustainability of natural ecosystems and the surrounding communities are often so intertwined that the ultimate outcomes and successes of each are inextricably related. They cannot be separated.

As in many collaborative processes involving communities and public lands in the West, in Catron County there are no conclusive answers, only options to be discovered in the common ground lying amidst the ambiguities of power and perspective. There is also hope, albeit moderate at times, that when people sit down together, the desire and need for community and ecosystem sustainability can outweigh the political divisions, polar positions, and administrative gridlock caused by unclear national public land policies.

Even with the uncertainties and continuing barriers, some ways of recognizing success in community-based, natural resource management processes are emerging. The act of holding together a collaborative community organization, such as the Citizens' Group, is profoundly challenging and an unmitigated success when it occurs. While communities may begin the kind of rebuilding and local healing that governments and land management agencies cannot address, these governments and natural resource agencies must be more supportive by providing some staff and financial resources and increasing their capacities to work collaboratively with and assist communities. The very presence of these supportive activities are themselves important indicators of success.

Above all, real healing on the land and in the community needs to occur. In Catron County, as elsewhere, range and watershed conditions need to improve. Overgrown stands need to be thinned. Hazardous fuels that cause catastrophic wildfires need to be removed. More natural conditions in forest ecosystems must be achieved. A long-term perspective must be adopted if older forests are to be continually regenerated. Sound, balanced ecological and economic analysis must be undertaken in a context where diverse interests can agree to reasonable and achievable ecosystem management and community sustainability goals. Small successes, such as the log-holding yard in Reserve and the proposed pine restoration in the Sheep Basin Unit of the Negrito Ecosystem, will need to become increasingly likely, with consistent and expected support of good scientific knowledge and community, environmental, and public land management leadership.

Concrete measures of success and tangible outcomes of building cooperative processes can in part assuage the economic pain of community change, sanction the rebuilding of trust, and publicly legitimize the need and benefit of ecological sustainability. Community building and healing of the land must occur in concert to encourage the redemption of divisive and broken social bounds. This will make it possible for the communities to become partners in improving the well-being and integrity of public lands. If communities are not trusted and do not perform as true partners, the challenging, long-term process of healing the lands most likely will not succeed.

A scenario for progressive change in the West has been proposed and demonstrated in numerous places over the past decade. Yet its full implementation will require balanced, integrated, and inclusive perspectives that see value in both the more traditional, communal ways of life based on extracting a living from the landscape and the new ecological principles of land management. A balanced and integrated set of perspectives is the single most important sign of success of a collaborative process and a precondition for setting an agenda for broader institutional and organizational reforms in natural resource management at the national level. The need for an integration of diverse and valued perspectives is the seminal lesson of the Catron County story. The fact that the challenge is being gradually met by the continued commitment of diverse parties is the single most important and lasting legacy of the Citizens' Group.

The standard way of operating and governing our public lands has changed from a centralized, governmental, scientific model to a new model where diverse interests, national and local, have a "seat at the table." Where local communities have been excluded from planning and decision making, they now demand inclusion along with the national conservation and commodity organizations. A new and collaborative model for community decision making holds some of the answers to long-standing resource management problems, but many incremental steps are needed. The Catron County Citizens' Group possesses an ongoing opportunity to contribute to those steps by its continued resolve to rebuild community and heal the land.

The final chapter of Catron County's and other similar western stories will depend on a complex interplay between rebuilding community and restoring the land. Many skills will be needed, along with patience, hope, and an inclusive understanding and definition of the meaning of success in each particular place and its unique time in history.

The Catron County experience demonstrates an emerging yet undeniable realization that one cannot heal the land while destroying a community. Catron County, as a representation of the broader story of the West, reveals the importance of community, its loss, and its ultimate necessity in the collaborative stewardship of public lands. About this lesson, we will continue to learn. As enlightened as we may become about collaborative processes in natural resource management, authentic and lasting success will best be achieved as we come face to face with the real challenges and experiences of rebuilding and healing in actual communities and on the public lands.

References

Baca, Ann, and Bob Moore 2002. "Big Win for Forest Service and Catron County: Corner Mountain Provides Logs for Holding Yard." *Catron County Citizen* 3, no. 1 (January): 1.

Burns, Sam. 1997. "Integrating Community Strategic Planning with Forest Planning." Field and interviews notes, U.S. Department of Agriculture National Research Initiative Project. Study conducted by the University of Arkansas and Fort Lewis College.

Burns, Sam, and Michael Preston. 1998. "Where Economy Meets Ecology." Unpublished workshop outline presentation to Catron County Citizens' Group, Reserve, New Mexico.

Catron County Citizens' Group. N.d. "Vertically Integrated Community-Based Small Diameter Forest Products Industry." Funding proposal submitted to the Four Corners Sustainable Forests Partnership, prepared by Bob Moore, executive director.

Coates, Jim. 2002. "Don Weaver—A Good Education, Hard Work, and a Lot of Trust." *Catron County Citizen* 3, no. 2 (March): 6–7.

Davis, Tony. 1996. "Catron County's Politics Heat Up as Its Land Goes Bankrupt." *High Country News* 28, no. 12: 1, 8–11.

Four Corners Sustainable Forest Partnership. 2002. "Evaluation Field Notes." Office of Community Services, Fort Lewis College, prepared by Sam Burns, Durango, Colorado.

Moore, Bob. 2001. "Forest Restoration: Not a Flagging Issue." *Catron County Citizen* 2, no. 4 (June): 1.

New Mexico Center for Dispute Resolution. 1997. "Proceedings of Communities, Land Use and Conflict: Reserve, New Mexico." Sponsored by the Catron County Citizens' Group, University of New Mexico School of Medicine, New Mexico Center for Dispute Resolution, Western Network, Albuquerque, July 18–19.

Paulson, Steven K. 1999. "Court Rules on Grazing Rights." *Durango Herald,* February 24, 2A.

Sheep Basin Restoration Project. 2001."Environmental Assessment." Gila National Forest, Reserve District, U.S. Department of Agriculture, National Forest Service, August 1.

Smith, Melinda. 1998. *Case Study: Catron Country, New Mexico.* Albuquerque: New Mexico Center for Dispute Resolution.

Tate Gallery. 1953. "Guadalupe Hidalgo—Treaty of Peace, 1848, and the Gadsden Treaty with Mexico, 1853." Reprinted from *New Mexico Statutes,* annotated vol. 1, 5th ed. Truchas, N.M.: Tate Gallery.

Yaffee, Steven L., Ali F. Phillips, Irene C. Frentz, Paul W. Hardy, Susanne M. Maleki, and Barbara E. Thorpe. 1996. "Negrito Project." In *Ecosystem Management in the United States: An Assessment of Current Experiences.* Washington, D.C.: Island Press, 205–6.

CHAPTER 5

From "Them" to "Us"

THE APPLEGATE PARTNERSHIP

Victoria E. Sturtevant and Jonathan I. Lange

After years of battling over the environment, an unlikely array of adversaries put aside differences, pinned "No They" buttons to their shirts, and rolled up their sleeves. They were ready for what they considered to be the real work ahead—figuring out how to sustainably manage the forest and watershed and learning to work more effectively together and to be better neighbors in the process.

Loggers, environmental activists, timber industry representatives, ranchers, old-timers, and newcomers to the Applegate Valley launched the Applegate Partnership as an alternative to the conflict and litigation that was defining resource management politics and community responses throughout the Pacific Northwest. In a historic departure from most environmental and wise-use rhetoric, the Applegate Partnership posited that environmental and community concerns were interrelated and must be understood and resolved together.

Weekly meetings and informal gatherings changed local vernaculars from "we–they" constructions to an extended (or, to some critics, overly simplified) "us." To the partnership, trust among stakeholders became as significant to sustainable ecosystem management efforts as mandates of the National Environmental Policy Act. A community-managed park, local riparian protection measures, community forums for civic action, local economic development, reinvestment, and land use zoning meshed environmental concerns into community projects.

Despite their "successes," however, the Applegate Partnership's efforts are continually challenged by local and regional environmental organizations over who may assume stewardship of place and make management decisions on a watershed that includes public land.

The Applegate Valley of southwest Oregon had become a battlefield for an array of stakeholders in the land management debate. The oversimplification of "jobs versus owls" set loggers against environmentalists, and "newcomers" injected new attitudes and assumptions that offended some "old-timers." But as years of contention seemed only to exacerbate community conflict and increase the degradation of their watershed, neighbors first accepted and then put aside their differences. In 1992, a group of environmentalists, loggers, mill owners, ranchers, government agency scientists, and managers formed the Applegate Partnership to assess, manage, and restore their shared watershed and to initiate ecosystem management that would link environmental and community sustainability.

Despite their profoundly different economic and cultural backgrounds, members of the group agreed on one basic set of principles: Resource management should be ecologically creditable, aesthetically acceptable, and economically viable and must be carried out in a coordinated manner across the landscape. Through countless hours of meetings and discussions, years of shared work, and a "no they" philosophy that both empowered and held accountable an array of local resource managers and residents, the Applegate Partnership shepherded community, environmental, and agency efforts from conflict to collaboration as it designed and carried out projects to improve the environmental and social health of the Applegate Valley.

The Place and the People

The Applegate River watershed encompasses just under 500,000 acres of southwest Oregon but stretches slightly into northern California as well. Its rugged terrain ranges from 1,000 to 7,000 feet in elevation and receives between twenty and one hundred inches of rain per year. Lowlands and riverbed valleys support farming, ranching, and residences, and the forested highlands support timber and other forest products, recreation, and grazing.

As a part of the Klamath Geological Province formed 150 million years ago, the watershed manifests great genetic diversity because its geological formation provided a "bridge" for plant migration between the Cascade and Coast Ranges. This bridge still functions today for scores of rare plants and sensitive vertebrates, including spotted owls. Intensive logging, extensive road building, hydraulic mining, fire suppression, and drought have dramatically changed the composition and structure of the forest watershed. The risk of catastrophic fire in the dense stands of young and old trees has increased and is compounded by insect damage and the continuous vegetation of rural residential dwellings.

Divided into residential lots, small woodland and hobby farms, industrial forests, and federal lands, the watershed is a patchwork of legal entities defining diverse individual, group, and organizational interests in a highly valued geographical area. With federal government management of 70 percent of the Applegate and timber industry ownership and management of 8 percent, many of southern Oregon's most active watershed-based environmental groups are located there. One of the most influential of the groups, Headwaters, was formed in the mid-1970s with "back to the landers" concerned about large-scale clearcutting, herbicide applications, and upstream riparian damage that, they felt, threatened their neighborhoods. By the mid-1980s, local, regional, and national environmentalists' legal protests and appeals of federal land management decisions in the Applegate Valley and surrounding region restricted the volume of timber that could be removed from the watershed. Then, in 1990, federal court injunctions pertaining to the spotted owl halted most timber sales.

The human community of approximately 12,000 residents is complex, extending throughout the valley and surrounding hillsides. No communities are incorporated, and many political and economic functions are located in two nearby cities in two different counties (Medford and Grants Pass in Jackson and Josephine Counties, respectively). Major highways convey an array of users over miles of twisty roads: resident commuters to nearby cities on weekdays, out-of-area recreational travelers on weekends, and Christian Fellowship churchgoers to their Wednesday night and Sunday morning services.

As in many rural resource-dependent communities, economic and demographic transitions are changing the content and profile of the Applegate. Traditional extractive and manufacturing employment is declining, urban retirees and equity migrants seeking rural lifestyles are moving into the area, and local youth are leaving in search of greater opportunities elsewhere. The poverty rate—but also mean household income and average property values—is higher than elsewhere in the surrounding region, and transfer payments account for a sizable portion of local personal income. Self-employment is substantially higher than the national average as increasing numbers of residents connect to markets and business centers through fax machines, computers, and mail-order catalogs.

In the region surrounding the Applegate, employment in trades, service, and construction is growing, and many residents commute to work. Although many work in agriculture and forestry, family income is subsidized with second or third jobs in nearby cities. Much of the employment in agriculture is related to the area's growing number of nurseries, pear orchards, and wineries.

Since the 1970s, urban "refugees" have come to the area for its rural quality of life; in-migration is considerable but is partially counterbalanced by out-migration. In-migrants tend to be affluent, older, retired couples or younger families who come with their own assumptions and expectations of what constitutes the "good life." Normative definitions among the newer and older residents differ, and socioeconomic and political changes provoked by the newcomers are not always supported by the longtime rural residents, especially when the newcomers' attitudes and behaviors appear judgmental or contemptuous of rural culture or when their requests for additional services increase local taxes or stress existing resources. The cultural conflict of in-migration brought to the Applegate is reported by Preister (1994) as being related to newcomers "not getting it"—not taking the time to figure out how things work. Not only do "they want to keep everything green" and "make us a park for Portland" but "they are out of touch with the land." The coup de grâce, however, is not only that they are out of touch but also that "they want to take charge," and "they stir it up too much," and "they want to change everything!" (Preister 1994, 21).

The recent waves of newcomers come with economic assets (often from the sale of property in California, hence the name "equity migrants") and human resource strengths (such as education and training). The entire community feels their impact in rising property values, competition for existing jobs and markets, and restricted access to public and private lands and natural resources. When a prime riverfront section of a farm settled by the owner's grandfather is sold in response to rising property values, for example, friends and neighbors accustomed to river access through that property feel displaced. More subtle, and perhaps more insidious, is the conflict stemming from the status differences and symbolic statements about personal worth displayed through newcomers' conspicuous consumption—the houses with walls around one-acre "front yards" and the expensive European cars navigating dirt roads.

The Applegate has experienced widespread and continuous change for decades, but the effects have not affected local residents equally. Some families have been able to take advantage of new economic opportunities and the rising values of property and services; others have not and have had to leave the valley. Many old-timers remain distrustful of the new strangers. Describing some old-timers' resentments toward newcomers, one Applegate Partnership board member said,

> I've always been what this community considers a redneck; my family has always been involved in farming and logging and the timber industry. We've always taken a real firm stand about protecting our natural resources, but that was our living, the natural resources . . . and has been for five generations . . . we felt that these outsiders who were moving in were trying to change us and take [the land] over and it's hard for us to release that feeling and . . . make room for them to live here and . . . not feel the resentments. I still know so many people that really feel the resentment of outsiders moving in and pushing their way in saying, "you're going to have to change the way you look at things." (Connie Young, personal interview, 1995)

Nevertheless, the in-migration of people with new skills and interests has not been without its social benefits. Newcomers' and "midtimers'"[1] skills, knowledge, financial resources, businesses, consumer demand, and interest in civic organizations have added social capital and economic vitality to the Applegate Valley and the partnership board. Aware of the stress of cultural and economic dislocation for those displaced by shifting resource policy, economics, and social institutions, they see the partnership as a way to re-create community by caring for people as well as ecosystems and by acknowledging the vital relationships between healthy communities, a local timber industry, and sustainable forests.

A First Step to "We"

The Applegate Partnership was initiated by two unlikely conspirators: Jack Shipley, a local resident and then vice president of Headwaters, a local environmental organization, and Jim Neal, a central Oregon logger and board member of Aerial Forest Management Foundation. After a number of discussions during which they discovered their mutual interests, Shipley and Neal began networking with a small group of associates from industry, environmental groups, and federal land management agencies. They circulated a briefing paper drafted by U.S. Forest Service scientists outlining basic ecological tenets[2] and then held a meeting for interested parties at Shipley's house in October 1992. Shipley asked the forty to fifty people who came to the meeting to introduce themselves not by affiliation but by their hopes and dreams for the Applegate, as individuals rather than "stakeholders" willing to nurture a local, cooperative approach to forest management and politics.

That first day, the group established the criteria for a working board: that members be wise, be skilled, have no previous agenda, care deeply about the place, and feel a personal stake in both the Applegate Valley and a collaborative process. One week later, nine board members and nine alternates representing different facets of the environmental, timber, agency, and community interests were selected. The ensuing five years brought resignations, replacements, and additions; yet many of the current core leadership still hail from that second gathering. A vision statement developed at the first official meeting of the board reads,

> The Applegate Partnership is a community-based project involving industry, conservation groups, natural resource agencies, and residents cooperating to encourage and facilitate the use of natural resource principles that promote ecosystem health and diversity. Through community involvement and education, this partnership supports management of all land within the watershed in a manner that sustains natural resources and will contribute to economic and community stability within the Applegate Valley. (Applegate Partnership 1992, 1)

Their vision statement had been crafted in only one and a half hours, but a list of commonly shared goals and objectives took the board members three months to complete. They stressed basic objectives, not ground-specific prohibitions or projects, and worked to identify common interests rather than opposing positions. For example, instead of writing, "no new road building"—something that the agencies by law could not "sign off" on and the timber contingent would not support—they wrote, "minimize erosion." The goals and vision have served as a "map" for a clear, articulated, shared purpose and direction, and the partnership has repeatedly turned to them when lost in disagreements or dilemmas.

In order to avoid the media and the politicians who the partnership thought would only exacerbate conflict, the partnership stayed "underground" for its first five months. It chose to "come out" in February 1993, when Secretary of the Interior Bruce Babbitt accepted its invitation to visit the Applegate on his way to then-President Clinton's Forest Conference in Portland. In anticipation of innovative solutions from Clinton's efforts but also fearing new restrictions on forest management, the partnership wanted to make public its ecological principles, vision of collaboration, and plans for restoration and monitoring. Members of the partnership met Babbitt wearing the "No They" buttons (the word "They" slashed diagonally with a red line) that have since been distributed across the country.

The criteria for ecosystem management projects that the partnership presented to Babbitt (such as how the project addressed old growth, biodiversity, riparian zones, and community concerns) were applied to an existing federal timber sale that proved to meet them. The fact that officials from both the Forest Service and the Bureau of Land Management had actively participated in criteria development and served as the partnership's board members demonstrated the agency's potential for collaboration. Agency line officers and scientists provided important encouragement and guidance throughout the early partnership meetings and acted as visionary leaders in laying the groundwork for innovation.

Both community and ecological issues were addressed in ecosystem and social assessments done by well-respected, locally connected scientists from agencies and universities. The data from both assessments were considered to be fair and neutrally derived by the partnership's participants and agencies, which avoided the "you get your science and I'll get mine" phenomenon when difficult decisions had to be negotiated.

A former county commissioner who supported the partnership effort helped facilitate a few of the early meetings, followed by two professional facilitators who volunteered their time, alternating weekly and adapting their style to the already well-established group dynamic. Though these facilitators were not Applegate residents, both knew many of the issues and players since they had previously been active in forestry and environmental issues.[3] The facilitators helped with communication, goal setting, meeting structure, group dynamics, meeting ground rules,[4] and general conflict management. When, for example, tempers would occasionally flare up during meetings, the facilitator would help the group move through the difficult moment, helping to identify what was "underneath" the outburst and channeling the conflict into a productive opportunity to increase group trust, understanding, or empathy.

These facilitators were active during all meetings and retreats until they were able to step aside once board members were comfortable sharing the task of meeting facilitation. For many years, professional facilitators were requested for meetings only when the group had to deal with particularly sensitive issues; but recently, a professional facilitator has been on contract, helping the group through daytime meetings focusing on forest issues, which are more likely to involve agency staff and draw environmental group representatives.

In their work to transform the decades-old forestry conflict, the partnership's board members developed a feeling among themselves that was reflected in their use of language; linguistic phrases such as "being on the team," "at the table," and "in the circle" represented an unusual amount of group cohesiveness given that members had so recently been adversaries. Members shared the belief that they were "making history." Early on, different board members spoke about how their work was reflective of a "new paradigm" that would help "change the world."

Through the hard work and lengthy deliberations of weekly meetings, long-held stereotypes and misconceptions gave way to common goals. The words of participants reflected the general sentiment: "We're finding that those people who [we] perceived as enemies for so long are just like us." "On Wednesdays we come together, other days we go in different directions."[5] In the process of working toward common goals, many of the relationships that had developed around the partnership's table expanded, and empathy and understanding grew on a new and solid foundation of these relationships. The love of their place held them together as members walked forest trails, flew observation planes, and held community potlucks. Some appeared together on panels, on radio shows, and in geographically distant forums. After a year or so, members could predict what subjects to avoid at the table, who would say what when, and the way a particular announcement would affect others. They learned how to lobby each other outside the meeting room, began to share their woes about constituency groups (see Lange 2002), and increasingly saw themselves as a unit. On occasion, they would "speak each other's lines," as when an environmentalist would advocate for timber or vice versa. Slowly, the "we–they" was being replaced by "us."

Challenges of Collaboration

A motto printed on an early partnership brochure reads, "Practice trust, them is us." Trust was a goal, an accomplishment, and an issue with all the partnership's endeavors. When arguments began, members reminded each other of a person's "trustworthiness." The issue of trust arose sufficiently to spark discussion of the possibility that the watchword "trust" not only was overused but also stifled dissent. Still, when various partnership members describe their experiences of the partnership's collaborative process, they stress how trust developed. One early board member said that while he still could not "tolerate" some of the others' constituencies, he trusted "each and every one of [them] to never do anything that would deliberately hurt [him]."

Trust is tenuous in partnerships, however, because "partners" represent groups whose conflict continues through the partnership collaboration. While representatives from the timber industry, environmental groups, and resource agencies were attempting to collaborate on issues in their watershed, for example, others from the industry and environmental camps were simultaneously filing lawsuits against the agencies for what they considered illegal forest management practice. Regional and national environmental and timber activists waged negative information campaigns against each other, lobbying the public, Congress, and both agencies, while at the same time local timber, environmental, and agency partnership "representatives" were looking for collaborative solutions to Applegate forest management problems.

Though many partnership constituents were supportive of the collaborative efforts, all the groups represented in the partnership included vocal opponents who undermined the collaborative process. When sale output was meager in the beginning, for example, timber industry personnel ridiculed their board representatives for the lack of payoff after their substantial investment of time and energy in the partnership. Initially, some agency personnel scorned their colleagues for spending so much time with nonagency personnel. Even local residents were suspicious, wondering what the partnership was really up to. The most difficulty came from environmental groups who continuously hindered or resisted the process because they feared that their movement's integrity could be threatened by a collaborative process that involved the timber industry. If terms like "at the table," "on the team," and "in the circle" described the goals and concerns of the partnership, "co-optation," "compromise," and "local control" were expressed by those in doubt (McCloskey 1995).

Many environmentalist concerns were related to decision making, which is never clearly defined in the partnership because of issues of trust within the group, veto power of those not at the table, and federal management of much of the landscape. When decisions are required, they have been done by consensus, and issues have been discussed until everyone at the table has aired his or her concerns and all board members could reach agreement. Decisions are seen as recursive, and members return to them with additional knowledge to readdress issues. Decisions are also incremental, with harder issues tackled after the easier ones have been resolved.

Members of the partnership and community began to see that partnerships are not exclusively win–win processes in which everyone gets what he or she wants but rather involve compromise[6] and concessions, so that some gains can be achieved or worse losses avoided. When a partnership does engage in compromise, it will invite the accusation of being "co-opted" by their less moderate constituents. And even if those constituents could eventually be satisfied, other constituents would most certainly appear to take their place on the extreme end of the political spectrum. Given the range of participation in the partnership, the potential lines of co-optation are nearly balanced (for example, industry—currently the weakest presence at the table—could co-opt environmentalists, but environmentalists could co-opt industry and local ranchers).

The "degree of difficulty" of the issues that any partnership is willing to address is also a concern.[7] Collaborative groups favor broadening areas of agreement while avoiding the most contentious issues, arguing that these require a disproportionate amount of time and increase the likelihood of failure. Early on, the partnership made the decision not to get involved in the "Sugarloaf" timber sale in an adjacent watershed, turning down some environmental constituents' request that the partnership register an official protest. The sale was deemed "too religious"; that is, a rational and useful discussion among representatives and constituents, all of whom viewed Sugarloaf as critical, was unlikely. Moreover, the sale was located just outside the Applegate watershed, and the partnership had decided to limit its scope by the geographic boundaries of the watershed unless broader policy issues were at stake. Yet residents of the neighborhood highly impacted by the sale appealed to the partnership's commitment to community; they wanted the partnership's leadership to "heal the rift" in their "torn" community by serving as "neutral ambassadors" to the agencies and monitoring environmental damage caused by the logging. After much difficult discussion and listening to stereotypes and accusations by visitors from the affected community, the partnership agreed to adopt the limited role of encouraging open dialogue and opportunities for community field trips.

Research on group process has demonstrated that avoiding disagreement is a mistake, for evasion generally results in lingering doubt, reduced trust, and/or mounting anger that eventually explodes. Smoothing over conflict may occasionally be useful but more often results in the problems returning in different forms. If managed productively, conflict can be used for learning, providing a mechanism for recognizing errors and improving the partnership process. Members of the Applegate Partnership knew this or learned it along the way.

Lessons for Success

During the early years, the partnership relied heavily on the leadership, resources, and credibility of a range of local nonprofit, nongovernmental organizations. The

Southern Oregon Timber Association (SOTIA), the Rogue Institute for Ecology and Economy (RIEE), the Farm Bureau, and Headwaters[8] brought a balance of interest groups to the original partnership table. These groups provided representatives to the board with histories of local resource and conservation activism as well as established relationships (in both collaboration and conflict) with public agencies. None of these groups is located in the Applegate Valley, but many of their constituents are local, and partnership success is important to them in any event. This plurality of organizational interests and representatives on the first partnership board brought a diversity of resources, perspectives, and insights to complex resource management and community development issues, broadening the base of support and scope of outreach and increasing the responsiveness and accountability of both the partnership and the participating government agencies.

These nonprofit organizations contributed to the beginnings of the partnership in many ways. Headwaters, SOTIA, and RIEE networked throughout the region and reached watershed groups, employers, and individuals in the valley with interests or resources relevant to partnership issues, and their regional and national meetings provided forums for sharing partnership activities and ideals. The executive directors of SOTIA and RIEE brought important organizational leadership experience and skills to the first partnership board.[9]

RIEE's work in wood product certification, special forest product inventories, and density management in the Applegate was important to the partnership's learning and efforts at economic development. Representatives of SOTIA advocate for timber interests, explaining and interpreting the impact of policies on the local industry and workforce. This group helped shape the partnership's position regarding forest health, and members have shared innovations in fire salvage, reforestation, and ecologically sensitive harvesting.

State agencies have contributed resources and expertise to the partnership, and state university faculty and students have contributed scientific research and landscape design projects. The Aerial Forest Management Foundation provided early funding and helped facilitate projects with Oregon State University researchers and the Pacific Northwest Research Station for collecting and digitizing forest canopy data gathered from ultralight planes. Southern Oregon University contributed social scientists' time, some working on economic and social assessments and another doing considerable work with a local Forest Service planner, synthesizing geographic information systems data across multiple landownerships.

In 1994, under the administrative umbrella of Oregon's State Watershed Management Group (SWMG) and with support from the state lottery, local councils were formed to restore watershed ecosystems. Seeing this opportunity to address forest and watershed health issues on private lands, the partnership successfully applied to be the Watershed Council for the Applegate River and developed a subgroup to fulfill this responsibility.

The Watershed Council's numerous projects and extensive community outreach provided much-needed concrete results to mark the partnerships' success.[10] Council staff completed a watershed assessment across private lands in cooperation with local and federal agencies, followed by implementation of a number of state-funded riparian restoration projects across private properties. It has funded and staffed the *Applegator* community newspaper, which provides a neutral forum for sharing information, local history, and diverse ideas. It has sponsored informative public meetings for community members to bring their concerns about water to representatives from state and federal agencies. It has involved local schoolchildren and residents in various projects, such as organizing their planting of over 250,000 trees. These positive activities help build community and mend previous rifts created by environmental conflict.

The Watershed Council has built new leadership capacity in the partnership. People outside the partnership's core leadership have had opportunities to develop and demonstrate their talents in watershed assessment, project planning, community outreach, newspaper editing, grant writing, and organizational networking. Outreach and discussion of common riparian issues between individual council members and local residents have lessened old-timers' suspicions that the partnership "was just a bunch of preservationists." This one-on-one outreach effort, directed at people interdependently connected by the health of a creek, has demonstrated the council's commitment to maintaining resource-based livelihoods while enhancing watershed health.

While nonprofits and universities have contributed to the partnership's early and enduring strengths, collaborative relationships have somewhat blurred their goals, which can be at odds with the partnership and the local community. For example, individuals speaking or writing about the partnership in public forums (often national) may not accurately represent the collective voice of the community or take responsibility for the consequences of the publicity they generate. In some cases, the Watershed Council feels it must defer to the agendas of others. Outside groups have even written funding proposals or initiated projects involving the partnership or the council without consultation. Indeed, members of the council, the partnership, and the community at times felt like guinea pigs or "poster children" for other people's agendas.

No federal funding goes directly to the Applegate Partnership. Indirect support comes from grants such as Northwest Economic Adjustment Initiative projects, Forest Service Pacific Northwest Research Lab cooperative agreements with the local university, positions such as an interagency liaison and community development specialist,[11] and facilities such as Provolt Nursery. Federal and state funding, as well as foundation and individual donations, support the work of the Watershed Council.[12] Private contributions and the sales of buttons and videos provide the only direct support for the partnership.

Getting Government on Board

Working with the federal agencies managing lands in the Applegate watershed is particularly complex because of multiple jurisdictions: two national forests with three ranger districts, one Bureau of Land Management district with two resource areas, and the Adaptive Management Area (AMA).[13] Managers range in their approach to land management and public participation, but key people have brought a genuine openness and commitment to organizational innovation that, in turn, has been rewarded by their engagement in the partnership process. The synergy between the various players, organizations, and policies set the scene for citizen involvement in adaptive management; the setting was ideal for the partnership to "push the envelope," encouraging the agencies to conduct business differently. Agencies shared resources with one another, combining their different strengths, values, and opportunities, and increased public involvement and transparent decision making.

Agency collaboration with the partnership has facilitated innovative landscape-level timber sales. Partnership One—the collaboratively planned sale carefully designed as a demonstration of the complex mix of interests and ecological tenets at play—became a focal point of opposition from those environmental groups who distrusted local collaboration. Delayed by the upheld appeals and mandated revision of the Environmental Analysis, the already expensive project, which prescribed helicopter logging and labor-intensive work, was no longer economically viable.[14] A later Bureau of Land Management sale more successfully went to bid, winning accolades from local citizens, the state, and federal agency directors for innovative funding for brush removal and thinning "from below."[15] Many sales in the watershed reflect this "lighter touch."

The partnership has worked in a collaborative manner with the two counties in arenas that range from road maintenance to land use zoning and resolution of conflict over aggregate mining. Their mobilization of local organizations to keep open Cantrall Buckley Park when county budget cuts had it slated for closure was highly valued by the general public. The "people's park" is still managed by the community, adding to the existing camping and picnic areas a network of nature trails and summer outdoor movies.

With the local ranger district, the partnership successfully applied for National Fire Plan funding for a comprehensive interagency and community effort at strategic hazardous fuel reduction, community outreach, and emergency preparedness.

Nineteen agencies have contributed to a document, edited by a local writer, building on previous hazard and risk assessments to develop overall priorities for fire prevention and suppression in the watershed. Community meetings and workshops have increased awareness and provided skills and resources for creating defensible space. Neighborhood gatherings have come up with emergency phone trees and evacuation plans. A recent wildfire tested a neighborhood's planning and served as testament to the value of this effort.

From "Us" to "Them"

Of course, the partnership has difficulties. Raised community expectations of the agencies resulted in frustrations when regulations could be stretched only so far, and hard-earned relationships are abandoned when agency staff are transferred or promoted. Congressional pressure to "get out the cut," funding cutbacks and increasing demands on specialists and planners, new projects that raise neighbors' and environmentalists' concerns, and repeated threats of lawsuits put agency staff back in the crossfire, returning some to their "fortress mentality."

In 1994, interpretation of the Federal Advisory Committee Act (FACA) forced agency representatives to resign from the board. Although they could continue to attend meetings, few personnel other than the interagency liaison did so on a regular basis, and the old "us–them" distance between the agencies and the public returned. As community members had to go to agency offices to talk with those no longer at the table, anger and frustration mounted. Operationally, the FACA setback was overcome through a careful reinterpretation of the law; information can be exchanged in open public forums such as partnership meetings, but the agency cannot convene a group as a recommending body. Over the ensuing years, agency representatives have returned to the partnership, and as projects have been generated, relationships have been reestablished; the early and heady sense of collaborative decision making among equals, however, has evaporated.

As staunch supporters of the National Environmental Policy Act, the partnership's members did not need to be reminded that federal land management must consider the interests of all stakeholders.[16] When FACA diminished federal agency participation and the board turned to the task of filling empty places, they were reminded of the importance of diverse local community participation. In order to encourage wider representation, the partnership has made a conscious effort to make time commitments more flexible, and now the board has shifted from being a majority outside to one inside the community. Loggers and ranchers have been actively recruited, and more representation from industry has been sought, but getting these interests to the table will continue to be a challenge.

Over the years, as the group has evolved and new people have either joined or regularly attend meetings, the collective sense of mutual trust has eroded, and old enmities have resurfaced. Respect for others' perspectives does not appear as heartfelt; group cohesion is not assured by its early "chemistry," and informal gatherings are less frequent. Jockeying for constituents' positions and political gain is more transparent, and respect is less evident. The Newcomers are asked to view the early partnership video in order to gain understanding of early struggles and accomplishments, but the care required for building trust among the first participants is difficult to communicate, comprehend, and maintain.

Nationally organized environmental groups resisting local collaboration between communities and agencies have rallied local environmentalists to resist or even undermine the success of collaborative groups such as the partnership. Individuals and groups holding strong "no commercial timber" or "zero cut" views are a particular challenge to the partnership as it attempts to be inclusive and maintain a rational discourse. After years of difficult interaction, the group has not achieved any resolution or common ground with those who hold more extreme views and decline to "buy in" to the original vision and goals of the partnership. The hard question continues to surface: "Who is the Applegate community, and who gets to speak for it?"

Conclusion

The shared vision, sense of place, and recognized successes of the Applegate Partnership has translated to other groups in the valley, creating a proliferation of community forums for civic action regarding local economic development and reinvestment, land use zoning, watershed restoration, and stewardship of public resources and facilities. Mutual respect and trust have developed between competing communities of interest and individuals. Cattlemen, ranchers, and loggers have worked with scientists and environmentalists to preserve both riparian health and traditional land uses; self-proclaimed "rednecks" and "preservationists" are admitting that they have much to learn from one another.

The partnership began as a diverse group of people representing various interests in resource management, all of whom understood that a path through the labyrinth of forest management conflict required a focus on common community interests and empowerment. While early discussions revolved around timber and forest protection, communities were always a subtext. When the partnership confronted obstacles in its work toward forest health, its focus on community helped overcome them. Some projects are incomplete, and others have only begun, but the importance of the collaborative process and community involvement is becoming increasingly apparent. Rather than providing any single approach or method for solving resource management or community problems, the partnership can be seen as a means or a process for addressing the interfaces of community and resource management issues. As one local resident said to the partnership in describing its evolution, "You started with trees; now you're getting into social issues. You are becoming an important alternative social process. You have a power."

Acknowledgment

This research was funded in part by the USDA Forest Service Northwest Research Station.

Notes

1. Many who moved to the valley as young "pioneers" in the back-to-land movement of the 1960s and 1970s have become community leaders; however, they still are not considered "old-timers."

2. For example, to restore, maintain, or enhance the diversity of plant communities and wildlife habit, particularly native plant communities; to support the use of both human-caused and natural disturbances to enhance forest health; and to maintain or re-create ecological old-growth habitat areas (compare Applegate Partnership 1992, 4–5).

3. One of these facilitators is the second author of this chapter.

4. Examples of ground rules include "check your agenda at the door," honor the diversity of opinions, and make no "zingers" (derogatory comments) or personal attacks.

5. In order to work together for the immediate and long-range goals, some members from opposite sides agreed to leave differences aside on meeting days, knowing they would return to their other constituencies.

6. Some partnership members prefer to see it not as compromise but as an innovative approach to finding solutions. They find common ground and create new outcomes by clarifying the vision of what the group desires, building on that vision, and, with patience, encouraging others to buy in. Sensitivity to the concept has grown as "compromise" and "selling out" are among the barbs hurled by the partnership's opposition.

7. Related to compromise and degree of difficulty is the issue of "lowest common denominator" where the process of finding a position all can agree on may weaken it. As with "co-optation," critics of consensus groups are more likely to raise this concern than are those involved in the process.

8. Headwaters withdrew from the board after a couple of years. This was a jolt to the partnership and of particular concern to the timber industry representatives who served as "counterpoints" at the table. Since then, the participation of Headwaters at partnership meetings has become more overtly "watchdog" in its stance, although it is involved in other capacities, including research and monitoring.

9. SOTIA still participates via a new director; RIEE also changed directors and then disbanded because of fiscal mismanagement.

10. While the partnership's early success was primarily in process and relationship development, it was unable to successfully implement many projects on the ground.

11. The community development specialist was funded by State and Private Forestry Rural Community Assistance of the Forest Service. When she left for another position, funding was not continued. The interagency liaison also left, and the pivotal position was not filled permanently for a few years.

12. Among the contributors of about a million dollars are the Bureau of Land Management, the Forest Service, the Fish and Wildlife Service, the Environmental Protection Agency, the Oregon Governor's Watershed Enhancement Board, the Oregon Land Conservation and Development Commission, Flintridge, and the Carpenter and Oregon Community Foundations.

13. In 1993, the Northwest Forest Plan designated ten AMAs as locations for innovative forestry and community involvement. While a number of ecological characteristics were considered in selection of the areas, the existence of the partnership contributed to the designation of the Applegate AMA. It encompasses most of the federal ownership within the watershed.

14. The dying pines and fir had lost value, compounded by a weak market for lumber.

15. The prescription for this sale was based on the ecological assessment of the entire watershed and reflected social values. It included fire hazard reduction and established fuel breaks, and areas were opened up to re-create oak/pine savannas. Logging was with helicopters and of trees less than thirteen inches diameter, and the net number of logging roads was reduced.

16. A shared principle of many forest community partnerships is that they recognize the right of people at a distance to have a say in resource management. Partnership members implicitly recognize the rights of nonresident public lands stakeholders; however, the partnership does not support the "no cut" view of some of their urban constituents. Instead, it returns to its belief in managing for the entire ecosystem rather than a single resource within national laws, many of which were established in response to pressure from the national constituencies.

References

Applegate Partnership. 1992. "Applegate Partnership Vision Statement." Unpublished manuscript.

Brick, P., D. Snow, and S. Van de Wetering, eds. 2001. *Across the Great Divide: Explorations in Collaborative Conservation and the American West.* Washington, D.C.: Island Press.

Lange, J. I. 2002. "Environmental Collaborations and Constituency Communication." In *Group Communication in Context: Studies of Bona Fide Groups.* 2nd ed. Edited by L. Frey. Hillsdale, N.J.: Lawrence Erlbaum Associates, 209–34.

McCloskey, M. 1995. "Report of the Chairman of the Sierra Club to the Board of Directors." Sierra Club, Washington, D.C., November 18.

Preister, K. 1994. *Words into Action: A Community Assessment of the Applegate Valley.* Ashland, Ore.: Rogue Institute for Ecology and Economy.

Rolle, S. 2002. *Measures of Progress for Collaboration: Case Study of the Applegate Partnership*. General Technical Report PNW-GTR-565. Portland, Ore.: U.S. Department of Agriculture, Forest Service, Pacific Northwest Research Station.

Spinos, C., and S. Rolle. 1995. "Applegate Adaptive Management Area: Building a Foundation for Managing Southwestern Oregon Forests." *Western Forester*, March 20–21.

Sturtevant, V. E., and J. I. Lange. 1996. Applegate Partnership Case Study: Group Dynamics and Community Context. Seattle: U.S. Forest Service, Pacific Northwest Research Station.

CHAPTER 6

Waiting and Seeing in Coos County
THE PROMISES OF LAKE UMBAGOG

Thomas Brendler

In the mid-1980s, a dam was constructed to power a sawmill and facilitate the float of logs downstream in northern New Hampshire. This industrial project led to the surface waters of the local lake increasing sevenfold as Lake Umbagog became the second-largest lake and part of the largest inland wetland system in all of New Hampshire. A century and a half after the timber industry first backed up Umbagog waters for a mill that forced locals to keep their windows shut and blinds drawn against the ash and mill dust, the lake is now prized for its recreational opportunities and its wildlife habitat.

The pristine waters of Lake Umbagog are an easy car trip from Boston, and the lake area has been targeted by developers. Local residents, who have had the lake mostly to themselves, are now chafing at the first and second home development that threatens wildlife and a local way of life. Residents also want assurances that the activities of the forest products industry, long the dominant landowner in the region and a cornerstone of the regional economy, will not degrade the landscape. At the same time, residents are resisting federally imposed regulations to reduce impacts on wetlands. Like many rural New Hampshire residents in the "Live Free or Die" state, residents of the Lake Umbagog area see their way of life threatened by outsiders and government regulation.

To cast this conflict as an insider–outsider battle is to erroneously frame development as an outsider-driven phenomena. Within this view, the forest product industry is perceived as locally based, while government action is assumed to be intrinsically negative. Finally, the solutions to community and environmental problems are seen as residing with either one group or another. In the case of the Umbagog, a government official has brought people together not with the threat of regulatory action but with a sensitivity to local ways and needs and with the objective of resolving issues. As Umbagog suggests, coming to grips with cultural and environmental issues requires transcending boundaries, real and imagined.

Context and History

On most maps of northern New Hampshire, the roads end at Errol, dodging east along Lake Umbagog and into Maine or west through the Dixville Notch toward Vermont—and with good reason. This is the heart of the Northern Forest, one of the largest contiguous forests in the United States, stretching some 26 million acres across New York, Vermont, New Hampshire, and Maine.

Lake Umbagog lies in the northeastern corner of New Hampshire and straddles the Maine border. It is fed by two dam-regulated tributaries that carry water from six other lakes in western Maine. Lake Umbagog serves as the headwaters of the Androscoggin River, which flows through the towns of Errol, Berlin, and Gorham, beyond which it cuts southeast through southern Maine before emptying into the Atlantic. For centuries, the region has been prized by the Anasagunticook, who trapped, hunted, and traded here.

The outlet of Lake Umbagog at Errol was dammed in the mid-1800s to power a local sawmill. Upgrading the dam to control water flows enabled timber companies to float logs to other mills more reliably. The construction of more dams downstream eventually harnessed the Androscoggin to power a giant pulp mill in Berlin, some forty miles downriver. Rising water levels expanded Lake Umbagog from 1,000 to 7,000 acres and enabled the creation of the plentiful wetland habitats prized by today's conservationists. While Umbagog is the second-largest lake in New Hampshire, it is also that state's largest inland wetland system. In 1979, a portion of the lake's wetlands was designated as a National Natural Landmark by the National Park Service because it is home to an abundance of diverse wildlife, including many threatened and endangered species. Lake Umbagog is, for example, the largest loon breeding area in the state. Umbagog's ecological significance was also recognized as a priority under both the North American Waterfowl Management Plan and the Emergency Wetlands Resources Act of 1986. The lake's forested shoreline is undeveloped except for a few rustic cabins used as weekend respites for the region's residents, who hunt, fish, and snowmobile there. Aside from the natural landscape and its wild inhabitants, timber interests dominate the area. The entire Northern Forest has been continuously cleared and cut since European settlement. Exploited for the virgin white pine that was used for ship masts for the British Royal Navy, it soon became the foundation of the new nation's expanding economy. By the end of the nineteenth century, much of the land that had originally been bought up by a mixture of wealthy families, timber companies, and farmers was acquired by paper companies. Although the paper companies themselves have been bought out and renamed at a dizzying pace, the land has remained in the hands of large forest products companies. As recently as the early 1990s, timber, paper, and forestland investment companies owned approximately 86 percent of the land around Lake Umbagog (U.S. Fish and Wildlife Service 1991).

The legacy of the forest products industry, the magnitude of industrial holdings, and the plenitude of forestland are three reasons why it has come to form the backbone of the region's economy. Until its recent closure, Crown Vantage paper mill in Berlin was the largest employer in a county of 35,000 people, with nearly 1,000 employees, and relationships with some 150 independent suppliers. The mill generated about $200 million in added value annually. For the towns and unincorporated townships in the Umbagog region, the forest and the forest products industry have traditionally been the primary source of work, whether through direct employment with one of the large firms or small sawmills, logging contracting, road maintenance, consulting forestry, log hauling, or truck repair. Tourism is on the rise and contributes to the region's economy but remains a distant second.

Since the mid-1900s, Berlin as a whole has lost 40 percent of its population, largely because of limited economic opportunities, and the trend is continuing. And even with Fraser Papers opening up an operation in part of the old Crown Vantage mill, in the words of one area resident, "Berlin is kind of a ghost town." Countywide, well-paying manufacturing jobs have been steadily replaced with lower-wage retail and service jobs. The forest products industry's contribution to personal incomes in the county has plummeted, falling from 27 percent in 1969 to just 4.5 percent in 1993. And, despite the fact that unemployment in Coos County is declining, the area has the highest jobless rate in the state.

Coos County accounts for 20 percent of New Hampshire's land base but is home to only 2 percent of the state's population. Many of the people who live there have made a deliberate, often defiant choice to "live close to the land" and at "arm's length" from urban culture and government centers. This northern corner of New Hampshire, which is divided from the south by the White Mountains, is in some ways a state unto itself. Those who live there see themselves as different than their neighboring southern "flatlanders." They identify more with the rural communities of western Maine and Quebec, from where many of their ancestors emigrated. Some have lived in the region for generations. Most are suspicious and often resentful of the outsiders flocking into the region or "meddling" in local affairs. These sensibilities have been galvanized by what many see as chronic under representation in the state legislature, a dynamic only compounded by Coos County's dwindling population.

People in the Umbagog region have made use of its forests, lakes, and rivers for generations, especially for boating, fishing, hunting, and, more recently, snowmobiling. Many residents of Errol, Berlin, and other nearby towns own "camps" in the woods or along the lakeshore where houses or cabins were built and are used by families for recreational use in the warmer months, although some are used year-round. While families own their camps, most have historically leased the land from large landowners like Crown Vantage. Leases have traditionally been inexpensive and accompanied by few restrictions, encouraging recreation of all kinds. These types of arrangements are characteristic of the long-standing, cordial relationship between large industrial landowners and local residents across northern New England.

The influence of companies has stemmed as much from the magnitude of their holdings as from their role as employers and guarantors of access to forest-land and hunting habitat in the logged-over tracts. For many local residents, the timber and paper companies have long been seen as guardians of a way of life. One need only walk through downtown Berlin, where the paper mill rises like a cathedral, to note its significance. The successive owners of the mill have made substantial contributions to the social and cultural institutions of the region, but, as people see companies like Crown Vantage go out of business, they are beginning to wonder what the future holds. Many conservation groups believe the region's forests cannot sustain the forest industry's demands for raw material.

The Specter of Development

The prosperity of the 1980s led speculators of all kinds to set their sights on the Northern Forest, especially in northern New Hampshire. For residents and conservationists alike, fears of detrimental and irrevocable change were validated when a land developer bought 186,000 acres of former timber company land for subdivisions. The sale was alarming because it was being offered for far more than the value of the standing timber. As Dobbs and Ober (1995) conclude, "Land was becoming a commodity beyond its value for growing wood. Real estate was a corporate asset that could be sold as needed to improve cash flow, ward off a hostile takeover, or pay off a debt" (xxi).

The "Diamond Sale," named for the match company which originally owned the land, served as a proverbial warning sign and prompted conservation groups to scramble to buy land. Rising public concern about the fate of the region attracted the interest of Congress, which commissioned the U.S. Department of Agriculture Forest Service to conduct the Northern Forest Land Study in 1988. The study was designed to look at landownership patterns and trends in the Northern Forest and propose strategies for possible congressional action. The Governor's Task Force on Northern Forest Lands, composed of four government-appointed representatives from each of the Northern Forest states (New York, Vermont, New Hampshire, and Maine) worked with the Forest Service on the study and, in 1990, issued a report to coincide with the release of the Northern Forest

Land Study. One of the recommendations of the Governor's Task Force was to create a four-state advisory, nonregulatory, nonacquisition body, the Northern Forest Land Council, to continue the work begun by the Northern Forest Land Study. The council met from 1991 to 1994, sponsoring what Dobbs and Ober (1995, xxiv) refer to as a "regional town meeting and arguably the most exhaustive debate ever held over a regional land-use issue." The group's recommendations were published in a report titled "Finding Common Ground: Conserving the Northern Forest." Among its recommendations, the report proposed basic strategies for public land acquisition in the Northern Forest, supported funding of the Land and Water Conservation Fund (a federal conservation-oriented land acquisition program) and state land acquisition programs, and emphasized the need to look beyond acquisition for other viable conservation tools.

To many people, the Diamond Sale foreshadowed the larger, imminent threat from developers eager to buy lakeshore property and subdivide it for second homes and recreation-based enterprises. Umbagog was widely considered the last unspoiled lake in New Hampshire, but with the improvement of interstate highways, travel time from Boston was cut to a few hours, and there seemed to be nothing to keep Umbagog from the fate of lakes like Winnepesaukee and Squam to the south with built-up shorelines, sprawling settlements, and swarms of watercraft. Tempted by rising land prices or, in some cases, as a consequence of corporate buyouts, some timber and paper companies were unloading their land. Other corporate landowners were realizing that they did not need to own land to secure a flow of raw material: Crown Vantage, formerly James River Corporation, the largest landowner around Lake Umbagog, had been selling most of its land since the early 1980s.

Many people, however, especially local residents, denied that a threat existed. They pointed out that despite the development frenzy, the Diamond Sale developer never subdivided the land. Some people also said that development was not bad if it led to employment and business. Other people, especially outfitters, had begun to enjoy the monetary benefits of increasing numbers of "flatlander" outdoor enthusiasts and argued that developing Umbagog's shoreline might be bad for the businesses that market the area's pristine qualities. The question that emerged was, If there was to be development, what types were desirable; how much should occur, and who should—or would—do the developing? People who agreed that development was a threat revealed varying and sometimes contradictory views of nature. The fact that much of Umbagog's biological wealth is itself indebted to development raises the question, What exactly was to be protected from development, and why? Did those that sought to "protect" the lake seek merely to stave off an influx of second homes and shorefront hotels? Or did they want to "fence off the region" as reclaimed wilderness and make it off limits to local people pursuing the local way of life?

By the late 1980s, concern for the natural wealth of the Lake Umbagog region was widespread, with one significant exception. As one Berlin native explained, the dominance of the paper industry in Berlin had created an island of industrial culture that shaped how people viewed their physical surroundings. His boyhood memories included running home from school with his eyes clenched to keep out the ash from the mill's boilers, of the river water just beyond the mill bubbling from discharge, and of housewives wiping down clotheslines before hanging the wash. He described how, despite the fact that most of the hillside homes in Berlin had a "million-dollar view" of the legendary Mt. Washington, most people kept their windows closed and shades pulled. In seeming contradiction, these same people who spent much of their time blocking out their natural surroundings spent weekends and vacations around Lake Umbagog more to escape Berlin than to "reconnect" with the forests beyond the mill. The natural wealth of the Umbagog region is proxy for the well-being of the surrounding communities.

The Roots of Response

One of the great ironies about Umbagog is that, although most people seem to want the same thing—an unchanged Umbagog or one that remains as close to its current condition as possible—individuals differed greatly about how best to achieve this goal. The differences of opinion reflect differences not only in how people envision their relationship to the forest but also in how they interpret change and their roles in the world around them.

Powerful interests and vast sums of money were involved, and one resident explained that the level of information about what changes were afoot in the region, as well as the ideas about what should or should not be done, varied greatly among local residents. Many people, even town officials, seemed altogether ambivalent about the change and what would be the best response to it. Coos County residents were already feeling overlooked by the state legislature and increasingly powerless and resentful in the face of growing outside interest in Lake Umbagog.

The question of what to do about development raised a question about necessary roles for governmental and nongovernmental organizations. Local residents were vocally distrustful of conservation groups, most of which were based outside the region, and anxious about increased government "meddling" in local affairs. Yet state conservation groups, including state chapters of national groups, saw state and federal governments as the only possible partner with the capacity to stave off development. The complexity and scale of the threat and the breadth of public opinion would require a broad assemblage of public and private institutions. The success of such an effort would rest heavily on delicate partnerships, adaptive new techniques and organizational relationships, and the integration of area residents' values and priorities.

Birth of a Refuge

In 1983, the Concord, New Hampshire–based Society for the Protection of New Hampshire Forests came up with the idea of protecting some of the Northern Forest by purchasing it for conservation. The society bought a 160-acre island in the middle of the lake. The question became how to continue this purchasing for land acquisition and conservation easements with limited money as well as the lack of a mechanism for brokering deals. An answer came in the form of a unique public–private partnership, the Trust for New Hampshire Lands, which formed in 1986 to raise private funds to negotiate land deals. The Land Conservation Investment Program was established by the New Hampshire state legislature in 1987, with nearly $50 million in state money. The prosperity of the 1980s had raised the specter of development at Umbagog, yet, ironically, it had also made public monies more plentiful in New Hampshire—a famously frugal state. Perhaps one reason for the palatability of the Trust for New Hampshire Lands and the Land Conservation Incentive Program was the fact that both were created with the explicit understanding that they would be phased out after a period of five years. In the first three years of the effort, the Land Conservation Incentive Program and the Trust for New Hampshire Lands together secured some 90,000 acres in 110 towns across the state. Maine created a similar entity, the Land for Maine's Future Board, at approximately the same time.

Amid this atmosphere of abundant state and private conservation monies, the Trust for New Hampshire Lands assembled stakeholders interested in the Umbagog region, including state agencies from Maine and New Hampshire, the Appalachian Mountain Club, the National Audubon Society, private landowners, and the U.S. Fish and Wildlife Service. This assortment of stakeholders came to be known as the Lake Umbagog Study Team. In the group's discussions, the Fish and Wildlife Service, which had been interested in Umbagog for quite some time, championed the idea of a national wildlife refuge. The Fish and Wildlife Service's long-standing interest in creating a national wildlife refuge at Umbagog was galvanized by the 1988 discovery of a nesting pair of bald eagles, the first in the state in nearly forty years.

The agency convened a series of preliminary meetings involving state agencies, conservation groups, landowners, and the Fish and Wildlife Service to discuss a refuge at Umbagog. Two years later, the Fish and Wildlife Service began preparing an environmental assessment as required by the National Environmental Policy

Act of 1969 to determine whether its refuge proposal would "significantly affect the quality of the human environment." Preparation of the Umbagog environmental assessment began in 1990. As part of this process, the Fish and Wildlife Service organized three preliminary "scoping meetings" in Errol, Berlin, and Concord in September and three more following the December release of the draft environmental assessment. At the same time, Fish and Wildlife Service officials met one on one with the county land board, hunting clubs, and other local interest groups in an effort to promote the refuge. The final environmental assessment, issued in June 1991, concluded that the creation of a refuge at Umbagog would not "adversely affect the quality of the human environment" and would "result in the preservation of existing uses [and that] land use changes [would] be minimal" (U.S. Fish and Wildlife Service 1991).

The action proposed in the final environmental assessment called for the creation of a 7,256-acre national wildlife refuge through the gradual acquisition of property by the Fish and Wildlife Service. The function of this "core" area would be to protect and manage the lake's wetland habitats for dependent species. According to the plan, this refuge would be surrounded by an 8,609-acre protective "buffer" constructed through a combination of conservation easements procured by both the Fish and Wildlife Service and the Land Conservation Incentive Program. For its part of this cooperative effort, the State of Maine proposed easement protection for nearly 13,000 acres on the eastern side of the lake.

The key to the success of the refuge and the broader collaborative effort was to involve the handful of large industrial landowners that owned most of the land in the area. According to an official from Crown Vantage, industrial owners had a number of reasons to cooperate for the creation of the refuge; much of the land that was considered to be of high conservation value (namely, wetlands) was not productive timberland, the Fish and Wildlife Service was obligated to pay market value for the land it sought, and selling off ecologically significant parcels would spare the company difficult, unwise, and perhaps controversial land deals later on, and this might ultimately spur unwanted litigation and legislation. For the time being, the landowners could enjoy the freedom to negotiate with an emerging legion of interested buyers.

Not surprisingly, Crown Vantage was the first large landowner to negotiate with the Fish and Wildlife Service and the Land Conservation Incentive Program. Boise Cascade, the second-largest landowner around the lake; the Pingree heirs, represented by Seven Islands Land Company; and Union Water Power Company followed suit. While some landowners preferred to sell their land outright—perhaps out of a concern that a clear and succinct relationship with the conservationists was the safest route—Crown Vantage negotiated easements with the Land Conservation Incentive Program, believing that land did not need to be publicly owned to be well managed and protected.

In July 1992, the Land Conservation Incentive Program purchased the first piece of the refuge complex, a nearly 450-acre waterfront tract for $2 million. The Lake Umbagog National Wildlife Refuge was officially established in November with the Fish and Wildlife Service's purchase of its first parcel. In 1999, the Clinton administration identified the Northern Forest region as one of only three "Focus Ecosystem" regions, which helped bolster a congressional effort to fund land acquisition through the Land and Water Conservation Fund, funding by which, in late 2001, enabled the Fish and Wildlife Service to purchase a 6,200-acre tract for $3.2 million. By 2002, the refuge had more than 16,300 acres under management. The State of New Hampshire, via the Land Conservation Incentive Program, now owns more than 1,000 acres, and the State of Maine now protects 1,600 acres under conservation easements.

A Precious Puzzle: Perspectives and Lessons

As is the case with many rural communities, the people who live near Lake Umbagog harbor a fundamental distrust of the federal government. For this reason, many of those who agreed with the need for a refuge expressed interest in seeing a county-based rather than a state or federal solution. Many people considered the creation of the refuge to be emblematic of a larger trend toward increased government involvement in the affairs of rural communities. One critic saw the refuge as a foothold that the state and federal governments would soon begin to use to leverage increased restrictions on land access and uses. Indeed, the environmental assessment does state that the refuge's primary purpose is habitat protection. Regarding human activities, the assessment includes malleable wording, such as "appropriate traditional wildlife-oriented public uses."

For some local residents, apprehensions were validated during the creation of the refuge. Errol residents and other participants in the process almost unanimously state that local people were involved too late and too minimally in the process. There were only six public meetings, four of which took place in rural communities near the proposed refuge. It is also clear from the environmental assessment that at the time the first public meetings took place, a proposal was already on the table. In fact, some people who were present at the first public meeting in Errol recall raising concerns about the creation of a refuge, only to be advised that the purpose of the meeting was to explain "how things were going to be." Citing the 50 percent drop in public meeting attendance following the release of the draft environmental assessment, many argue that the Fish and Wildlife Service in particular should have taken a greater role in working with local residents. Nevertheless, while the local residents interviewed faulted the refuge process, most conceded that the refuge was a hard choice and a good idea.

The final environmental assessment reports that 85 percent of all written responses to the draft environmental assessment supported the refuge proposal and that substantial support was expressed at public meetings, albeit less vocally than the opposition.

Defenders of the process maintain that communities like Errol constituted neither "interested buyers" nor "willing sellers" in a project based on sale and purchase of land. They also point out that the landowners, on whom the success of the effort rested, insisted on confidentiality, which precluded public involvement earlier in the process.

Some contend that the "unweighted" public involvement facilitated by the National Environmental Policy Act (NEPA) process is insufficient and question the Fish and Wildlife Service's determination of "no significant impact" on the human environment. Perhaps an environmental impact statement that included a finding of "significant impact" might have anticipated and resolved some of the local residents' lingering concerns. As one observer noted, "Public policy needs to account for proximity." Supporters of this concept argue that because neighboring communities stand to be most acutely affected by changes in land management and ownership, they should be afforded greater involvement and influence in public resource management. As one local resident said about the policymakers, "Those people don't live here." The question that remains is, To what extent should local communities be involved in efforts like the Umbagog refuge, and how? Can greater local involvement be compatible with the fundamental goals of the proposed project, namely, in the case of Umbagog, habitat protection?

Local complaints of inadequate involvement may be symptomatic of a larger problem—that communities are too often caught in a reactive posture. This thinking is reinforced by policy mechanisms like the NEPA process in which the public's role is largely responsive rather than proactive. One observer advocated the need to develop the capacity of rural communities to become proactive by overcoming divisiveness and aggressively pursuing a "homegrown vision." Why, he posited, did the town of Errol or Coos County not create a strategic plan for the Umbagog region or at least seek assistance in doing so rather than wait for the Fish and Wildlife Service to propose a refuge?

Local people have also been perplexed by what they see as slow progress since the refuge was designated. The refuge's hunting and management plans, both of which the environmental assessment assured would be promptly completed and involve extensive consultation with local residents, have taken much longer: The hunting plan was completed in 2000, and the process for developing a comprehensive conservation management plan began in the summer of 2002. The main reason for the delay appears to be inadequate funding that stalled acquisition for many years, limits staff, and hampers refuge activities such as ecological inventories. A new staff person was added in 2002, but the refuge still has only one recreational trail.

Some critics see Umbagog's budgetary crisis as a fundamental shortcoming of the process since first the refuge is designated and then property and/or easements are purchased to gradually "fill in the puzzle." One hindsight recommendation was to ensure that the Fish and Wildlife Service has the resources to implement its plans prior to designation. Under such an arrangement, funds for acquisition not only would be in place at the time of designation but also would be paired with management monies. Even so, the dramatic rise in large land offerings since the late 1990s—as forest companies consolidate, merge, relocate, and go out of business—has made for increasingly tough decisions about how to spend conservation dollars.

Many residents of Errol and nearby towns point to detrimental and perhaps unforeseen impacts that they believe are linked to the refuge. These impacts include higher property taxes, inadequate revenue-sharing payments, and restrictions placed on lakefront camps. While some residents argue that the Fish and Wildlife Service's willingness to "pay anything" has driven up property values and property taxes, it is more likely that the agency was trying to be a competitive bidder amid growing demand for lands around Umbagog. This, however, is curious, considering some landowners' sense that agency bids were below market value and agency regulations require offering market rate for property based on the land's "highest and best use"—in this case, development.

Residents argue that revenue-sharing payments, made by the Fish and Wildlife Service to local governments in lieu of property taxes, have not reflected the agency's original promises. While it is true that the agency's congressional appropriation can cause payments to fall short of agency calculations, data indicate that the Fish and Wildlife Service revenue-sharing payments have exceeded the amount local governments would have received had lands remained in private hands. The main reason for this disparity is that the Fish and Wildlife Service payments are based on appraisal of its property based on its development value. By contrast, at the time the refuge was created, 78 percent of the Errol lands to be included in the proposed refuge complex were taxed under New Hampshire's "current use" status, which, as an incentive to keep land in a forested condition, yields a reduced tax rate. Moreover, because much of the land that interested the Fish and Wildlife Service was wetland, which is taxed at an even lower rate, it is likely that the margin between the Fish and Wildlife Service payments and property taxes would be even greater. The agency also points out that keeping the land it acquires in a forested condition spares the local governments the cost of the additional public services, such as sewage, schools, and road maintenance, that development require.

It might have been the Fish and Wildlife Service's appraisal system that led to local residents' frustration about increases in land rents for camp leases.

Many people believe that costly leases, together with tight restrictions on repairs to existing camps, are part of an attempt by the Fish and Wildlife Service to close the refuge to an array of human uses in much the same way that rising property taxes were seen as a way to force people to sell. By one account, land rents tripled in a few years, but some of those interviewed added that rents had already been increasing under corporate ownership. Since camps embodied the local way of life—the independence, self-sufficiency, and direct interaction with nature—and because leases were originally created by large, private landowners to encourage public stewardship, their demise seems ironic in this era of heightened conservationism.

Beyond the Refuge: Emerging Efforts in the Upper Androscoggin Valley

The creation of the Umbagog National Wildlife Refuge and the crisis that led to it marked a turning point for local residents and concerned "flatlanders" and was a proverbial Rubicon over which there was no return. Although local concerns certainly linger, the ten years since the refuge was created have seen the development of a savvy, pragmatic sensibility characterized by a commitment to local capacity building, an appreciation for the interdependence of economic and ecological concerns, and an adherence to a long-term, regional perspective. A heightened sense of regional identity has been coupled with a new breed of sophisticated and intriguing partnerships. While few would credit the Umbagog refuge as the wellspring of these initiatives, most would agree that the refuge has played a crucial role by drawing valuable attention to a neglected corner of New Hampshire and illuminating the complex web of issues and stakeholders involved in balancing the region's economic development and environmental protection. These contributions, however indirect, may prove to be among the refuge's most significant.

In 1997, for example, the relationships built through the creation of the refuge have led to a collaborative effort among the Appalachian Mountain Club, Crown Vantage, and the Fish and Wildlife Service involving an extensive forest inventory and an ecologically minded forest management plan. A pilot timber sale under the collaborative management plan was carried out and judged as economically viable despite the lower softwood volume and extra staff time involved. By working cooperatively with large landowners, the Appalachian Mountain Club hoped to preserve the natural wealth in the Umbagog region while allowing forests to continue to generate income and employment.

For the Appalachian Mountain Club, this experience formed part of its Upper Androscoggin Valley Community Conservation Project, a broader effort to stimulate the long-term conservation of the region's natural resources by promoting a sustainable local economy. This effort involved opening an office in Gorham, collaborating with and participating in a variety of local groups (not to mention supporting some of their endeavors through a minigrants program), and commissioning a regional community development study. The Appalachian Mountain Club also organized a popular "source-to-sea" canoe trek and helped develop a pilot watershed curriculum for Gorham Middle School. Most significantly, perhaps, is the development of an Androscoggin River Watershed Council, which was designed to address such integral issues as river recreation access, riparian protection, and recreation-based economic development. All these activities, coupled with a heightened local presence, mark a significant transformation for the Appalachian Mountain Club, a 120-year-old conservation organization with a deep-seated local reputation as an "elitist outsider." The Appalachian Mountain Club's new role as a sympathetic, effective partner may bode well for a region wracked by long-standing tensions between outsiders and locals.

As in many areas of the United States, the Umbagog region's natural and cultural heritage is becoming increasingly recognized as a fulcrum for sustainable, locally based economic development. It is perhaps most visible in Berlin's Northern Forest Heritage Park, which includes a heritage trail highlighting Berlin's historic features and an interpretive center on the cultural, forestry, and natural history of the Upper Androscoggin Valley. In addition, Tri-County Community Action, a multipurpose social service and advocacy organization in northern New Hampshire, developed a conservation-based development ecotourism project as part of its economic development program. These initiatives have been strengthened by the governor's creation in 1998 of a new tourism district in Coos County called the Great North Woods and the establishment of a clearinghouse for information about the region to residents and visitors.

Epilogue: A Legacy of Hope

On a blustery day in June 1997, some fifty people clustered in the shade of a tent pitched on the lawn next to the new headquarters of the Lake Umbagog National Wildlife Refuge. Both the weather and the liveliness of the guests seemed at odds with the purpose of the gathering: the dedication of the refuge headquarters to the memory of Steve Breeser, Umbagog's first refuge manager, who had died a year before.

Breeser continues to be hailed by locals and nonlocals alike as an example of how things should and can be done. Although not native to the region, Breeser made an earnest and exhaustive effort to bridge the awkward and cavernous gap between the federal government and rural communities. He was interested, compassionate, and an excellent listener. Breeser's reputation and successes testify to the enormous dividends possible from the seemingly small investment of asking and listening and, more broadly, to the pivotal role of personality, a human face in natural resource management.

One of the central ironies in the Umbagog refuge's evolution was that both its proponents and its detractors wanted to preserve Umbagog's natural wealth and the ways of life associated with it. It is this sentiment that has supplied a crucial common thread for the wealth of initiatives that have emerged in the wake of the refuge's creation, projects that regard economic and ecological objectives as inextricably connected and whose strength depends on innovative partnerships. Perhaps Breeser's most significant legacy is that people who disagree can indeed be brought together around matters of common concern and sometimes make progress.

Acknowledgments

This chapter would not have been possible without the patience and generosity of the people of Berlin, Milan, Dummer, and Errol, New Hampshire, extended to this curious flatlander. In particular, I would like to thank Joan Chamberlain, Norm Charest, Dennis Cote, Luc Cote, Everett Eames, Dick Ober, Dick Pinnette, Mike Wilson, Brad Wyman, and Rick Blair at Paradise Point Cottages for lunch and the great boat ride on the lake. Thanks, too, to the Forest Community Research and the Communities Committee of the Seventh American Forest Congress for patiently supporting this project.

References

Dobbs, David, and Richard Ober. 1995. *The Northern Forest.* White River Junction, Vt.: Chelsea Green.

U.S. Fish and Wildlife Service. 1991. "Final Environmental Assessment: Proposal to Protect Wildlife Habitat, Lake Umbagog, Coos County, New Hampshire, and Oxford County, Maine." U.S. Department of the Interior, Washington, D.C.

CHAPTER 7

Collaboration for Community and Forest Well-Being in the Upper Swan Valley, Montana

Barb Cestero and Jill M. Belsky

When anxieties over diminishing employment and increasing degradation of the local forest environment became so intense that neighbors screaming at neighbors was no longer the exception but the rule in western Montana's Swan Valley, some people decided it was high time to do something about it. Armed with a love of place and the knowledge that neighborly relationships can still be a key to survival in the rural West, they formed the Swan Citizens' Ad Hoc Committee.

The Swan Valley lies between the Mission Mountains and the Swan Range. Grizzly bears, mountain lion, elk, moose, deer, coyote, and cold-water fish describe something of the ruggedness of the terrain and the reasons why a few hundred permanent and seasonal residents fight to stay there. There is wildness and a kind of territoriality that goes beyond ownership and law and seeps into the people who inhabit a place like this until they feel as rooted to it as the trees.

Corporate and administrative boundaries that overlie the physical landscape make land management and decision making not only complex but also potentially explosive between neighbors, absentee owners, and others whose decisions affect the land. The Mission Mountain and the Bob Marshall Wilderness Areas, the Flathead National Forest, the Plum Creek Timber Company, and the Montana Department of Natural Resources and Conservation dominate land management decision making in the area and in the lives of the people who live there. In the late 1980s, when harvests declined regionwide, neighbors took sides in a simplistic jobs-versus-environment debate. Loggers and others whose livelihood was related to timber wanted the allowable annual cut increased. Environmentalists, however, appealed timber sales and demanded greater environmental protections. Others felt that the clear-cuts visible from the road and the fisheries degraded by logging and road building threatened an emerging tourism industry that they wanted to see grow. And others, as a matter of principle, simply did not accept that government has any right to tell communities what to do.

In 1990, the Swan Citizens' Ad Hoc Committee called for a moratorium on the hostility and anxiety that permeated the valley and appealed to neighbors to be neighbors, saying they all needed to work together if they all wanted to live there. The committee provided a public forum for valley residents to voice their opinions. As a result of ongoing community meetings, the animosity began to give way to civil dialogue. These exchanges led to discussions that in turn led to questions and field trips. Resident volunteers spent hours studying fire ecology, logging, and U.S. Forest Service regulations, and for the first time, working relationships developed between valley residents and nonlocal corporate and federal land managers.

As residents gained some hope that they might influence the corporate and land management agencies affecting their lives, they began to treat one another in a more neighborly fashion, and the death threat to an environmentalist that came at the apex of community anxiety seemed an aberration born more of frustration than of chronic problems deeply rooted in the community. Whether or not that is true will depend on how dialogue and land management continue to develop.

To what extent community, corporate, and environmental needs can be successfully integrated into a sustainable management plan is a question as much about power, flexibility, and responsiveness to local concerns as about planning. In this effort, land management agencies will be required to open management processes, and industries will need to be more responsive to local needs.

Travelers driving Route 83 through western Montana's Swan Valley might be out of town before they realize they have reached Condon. All that marks the town's physical presence is a log community hall, a small diner, and a combination market and gas station. Yet Condon is the meeting place for the residents of the Swan Valley. For the past twelve years, loggers, environmentalists, outfitters, retirees, and businesspeople have gathered in Condon to talk about the related health of their community and environment in this relatively remote, forested valley. The town has also become a center of attention for people outside the area in search of models of communities with "social capital"—the social ties and civic dialogue that enable conflicts that accompany local community development and natural resource management to be collectively resolved.

One reason for Condon's "place on the map" are the activities of a small group of Swan Valley residents calling themselves the Swan Citizens' Ad Hoc Committee. Formed in 1990, the ad hoc committee provides a public forum for valley residents and other interest groups seeking practical and collective solutions to the valley's increasingly contentious economic and environmental problems. The story of the Swan Valley Citizens Ad Hoc Committee has only recently been documented (Cestero 1997). This study explores a part of that story: the history of the ad hoc committee's formation, its accomplishments to date, and some of the challenges it currently faces. As an environmental studies graduate student and a professor of rural and environmental sociology at the University of Montana, we attempted to document this story through the multiple perspectives of people closest to the ad hoc committee and its work. Thus, the story includes the voices of the ad hoc committee's leadership, valley residents who have not been involved in the committee's activities, the U.S. Forest Service employees familiar with the committee, and other stakeholders with an interest in the committee's decisions, such as environmental advocacy groups.[1] To construct this case study, we consulted the growing literature on collaboration and community stewardship efforts as well as local newspapers and archival material relevant to the history of the Swan community and the Forest Service in the region.

The Ecological and Social Setting

Nestled between the Mission Mountains to the west and the Swan Range to the east, the Swan Valley in northwestern Montana is a long, narrow corridor of human development through rugged and relatively pristine country. The glacially carved valley measures fifteen miles wide and seventy miles long and is separated from the Clearwater Valley to the south by a small, almost imperceptible divide (Seeley/Swan Economic Diversification Action Team 1993). Montana State Highway 83 runs the length of the valley, but it is the landscape, not the highway, that first catches the traveler's eye. Snow lingers late into summer on the steep slopes rising to the rocky summits that define the valley's borders. Alpine lakes tucked against the mountains gather melting snow and spill into the headwaters of the valley's river system. Below, the Swan River meanders through a forested valley, snaking its way around the Missions to join Flathead Lake and the larger Columbia River watershed.

A moist climate endows the valley with diverse, thick coniferous forests that include Douglas fir, Englemann spruce, lodgepole pine, western red cedar, and grand fir. In the fall, yellow on the hillsides reveals stands of western larch. Some large-diameter ponderosa pine still rise along the highway and from the remaining mature forest stands scattered throughout the valley. Cottonwood and willow mark the riparian areas that, along with the forests, provide habitat for a diversity of species.

The habitat quality of the valley's forest and aquatic ecosystems is high. Grizzly use the valley bottom to travel between the Missions and the Bob Marshall Wilderness, and black bear, mountain lion, elk, moose, mule deer, and coyote make the Swan Valley home. The river system provides habitat for cold-water fish species, most notably one of the last populations of native bull trout, an important indicator of healthy aquatic ecosystems (Frissell et al. 1995). The valley also supports the highest known concentration of rare plant populations on the Flathead National Forest, including the locally endemic plant water howellia (USDA Forest Service 1994).

The political boundaries that overlay the valley's physical landscape make land management in the Swan Valley a complex task. The rugged mountains mark the boundaries of two federally designated wilderness areas—the Mission Mountain and Bob Marshall Wilderness Areas—a designation that protects the Swan from development and resource extraction above the valley bottom and foothills. The Swan Lake Ranger District on the Flathead National Forest is responsible for the management of these wilderness areas.

Land management between the two wilderness areas is complicated in part because it is divided. The Plum Creek Timber Company, the Flathead National Forest, noncorporate private landowners, and the Montana Department of Natural Resources and Conservation own or hold management authority over alternating sections of valley (Seeley/Swan Economic Diversification Action Team 1993). The Plum Creek Timber Company owns approximately 18 percent of the land in the Swan Valley, a legacy of the 1864 land grant to Northern Pacific Railroad. The Flathead National Forest manages 73 percent of the valley, some of which is designated wilderness. Private, nonindustrial owners hold less than 10 percent of the Swan's land with their properties concentrated along the valley bottom. The Montana Department of Natural Resources and Conservation is the remaining landholder, with management authority over several sections at the northern end of the valley (Swan Valley Community Club 1996).

Approximately 550 permanent and seasonal residents call the Swan Valley home, even though most of them agree that it is a hard place to "make ends meet" (Lambrecht and Jackson 1993). "When I first moved here I did anything that was legal and moral available to make a living," declares Mary Phillips with a laugh, "That's the way it is here." Residents share a fundamental ethic of "whatever it takes" to remain in the valley. Because there are no single, large-scale employers in the Swan, earning a living requires independent initiative and an entrepreneurial spirit. A 1993 community profile study found that 25 percent of the permanent residents held more than one job and that about half the valley's employed permanent residents were self-employed (Lambrecht and Jackson 1993). Thirty percent of the valley's total population, the largest and fastest-growing segment of the community, is retired (Lambrecht and Jackson 1993). Some retirees become small-business owners or artists after leaving lifelong occupations as teachers, government employees, or loggers.

These characteristics of the Swan Valley—its relatively pristine landscape, its forest resource–dependent community, its demographic characteristics, and its large, absentee landholders—together set the stage for conflict.

The late 1980s was a contentious, volatile time in the Swan. A combination of economic uncertainty and environmental degradation pushed this quiet, neighborly community into battle over the jobs-versus-environment debate. Forces seemingly beyond the control of local residents threatened to tear the community apart. Nationally, the timber industry was in decline, and rural areas like the Swan felt the effects. More than 100,000 workers in the wood products industry had lost their jobs. In the Pacific Northwest, mill employment had declined by 2 percent each year even while production rose (Power 1996). Northwestern Montana faced a 25 percent decline in its annual timber harvest, while the western and southwestern portions of the state showed declines of 24 to 39 percent, respectively (Flowers et al. 1993).

Closer to Swan, the local newspaper, *The Seeley-Swan Pathfinder,* painted an equally gloomy picture of the timber industry's future. The volume of timber sold by the Forest Service in the region was steadily dropping (Noland 1989). Headlines announced, "More Unemployment Likely in Timber Industry," over stories with sobering statistics: 2,000 to 2,500 of the region's jobs will be lost to increasing mechanization and structural changes in the timber industry (*Seeley-Swan Pathfinder* 1987). An estimated 27 percent of the valley's permanent residents worked in timber-related jobs in 1980. By 1993, however, only 16 percent were employed as loggers, sawmill workers, log home builders, log truck drivers, Forest Service employees, and foresters, and 10 percent worked in the recreation and tourism industry (Lambrecht and Jackson 1993). This economic transition increased fear and anger among the valley residents connected to the wood products.

During this same period and as evidence of ecological degradation was mounting, valley environmentalists grew increasingly concerned about the ecological and aesthetic impacts of logging in the Swan. In 1987, the Montana Department of Fish, Wildlife, and Parks released studies showing that the native west-slope cutthroat trout had disappeared from the Swan River and as a result instituted new fishing regulations. The state agency cited sedimentation from forest roads as one factor in declining trout populations and deteriorating habitat (Vernon 1987a), as when, for example, sediment from a logging operation along Jim Creek washed into a stream, severely damaging its bull trout population (Schwennesen 1990). Large clear-cuts visible from the highway drew sharp criticism from those who cared about the valley's scenic beauty (Vernon 1987b), and other residents involved in the valley's tourism industry worried that clear-cutting would jeopardize their livelihoods (Dahl 1990).

The news in the local paper divided Swan residents. Advocates for continued timber extraction traded irate letters to the editor in the *Seeley-Swan Pathfinder* with those demanding protection for the valley's remaining forests. Between 1987 and 1990, the community grew progressively polarized. Both sides staked their positions and screamed accusations at the other. Green wooden signs appeared at the end of driveways proclaiming, "This family supported by timber dollars." Mill workers and their families went to Missoula to demonstrate against Montana congressional representative Pat Williams's Wilderness bill. In 1987, Friends of the Wild Swan, an environmental advocacy group headquartered in the town of Swan Lake, launched a fight to protect the Swan Valley. Led by Swan Lake residents, this group began to challenge logging and road building on state and federal public lands through successful administrative appeals and litigation.

Public meetings that addressed any natural resource issue drew up to two hundred people to the Condon Community Hall on several occasions (Woodruff 1987). Described by one resident as "disastrous, with lots of screaming and yelling about logging, environmental issues, and national forests decisions," these meetings are legendary. Hostility was such that one local environmentalist allegedly received a death threat from a group going by the name V.E.T.S. (Victims of Environmental Terrorism and Subversion) (Vernon 1990).

Amidst this rancor, a few residents began sowing the seeds of what would become the Swan Citizens' Ad Hoc Committee. A 1990 meeting sponsored by Scenic 83, a short-lived, local group advocating management of the highway corridor for scenic qualities, was a watershed event. Those who endured the marathon meeting, featuring speakers from Friends of the Wild Swan and candidates in an upcoming election, began calling for an end to the polarization (Dahl 1990). The *Seeley-Swan Pathfinder* carried a story about the meeting, capturing the sentiments of these battle-weary residents. "I want to appeal to neighbors to be neighbors," commented one resident. Neil Meyer, one local logger who would become active in the ad hoc committee, observed, "We need to quit drawing lines between environmentalists and loggers. I'm an environmentalist." The feelings of those weary of fighting were summed up with: "We all need to work together on these things because we all want to live here" (Dahl 1990).

When two widely respected valley residents together decided it was time to build a broad community dialogue on the natural resource issues dividing the community, they initiated several meetings and invited residents whose opinions were diverse but who were willing to talk with and listen to each other. This small group of people evolved into the leadership of the ad hoc committee. It was motivated by a desire to reduce the hostility and anxiety that permeated the valley. According to Sue Cushman, a current ad hoc participant, "It was an attempt to prevent division in the community, to come to middle ground." Ecological concerns also motivated the ad hoc committee's founders. Members of the group were concerned about road building and timber harvest in the Swan. According to Bud Moore, a founding participant who operates a small sawmill after retiring from the Forest Service, "People began to fear that we'd screw up the habitat of the Swan badly trying to keep the mills going. We were afraid that in desperation to keep the money flowing we would damage what brought us here to live." The ad hoc founders wanted to integrate environmental protection with residents' ability to earn a living in the valley. These neighbors tackled what they understood to be the immediate issue: the declining timber economy. Meeting in people's homes, this small, self-appointed group began brainstorming alternative business ideas. In the words of Bud Moore, "We needed to think through converting the economy to lesser dependence on timber. Right from the beginning we had the idea that we needed representatives from all the interests in the valley . . . so we called together the 'think group.'"

In what was perhaps their single most important action, the ad hoc founders invited individuals of widely divergent viewpoints whom they felt could together rationally and civilly discuss the valley's problems. While having their own individual interests, these individuals demonstrated concern for the greater community. Many of these original participants remain active ad hoc committee members after twelve years of monthly meetings. In the fall of 1990, after a year of informal meetings, a professional facilitator who lived in the valley volunteered his services. Alan "Pete" Taylor became the "neutral traffic cop" who kept people with diverse viewpoints talking rationally and listening to each other at meetings. He initiated a strategic planning process to help the group define its role, and the Swan Citizens' Ad Hoc Committee was born.

The Swan Citizens' Ad Hoc Committee

ORGANIZATION AND PROCESS

The mandate, mission, and goals statement that the founding participants created using Taylor's planning process still guides the ad hoc committee today. In January 1991, the group presented its vision to other Swan Valley residents during a meeting with the Community Club and in an article in the *Seeley-Swan Pathfinder*. The one-page document states that

> this ad hoc group of citizens has a self-imposed mandate to: address the economic, environmental, and cultural problems related to the decline [in the valley's natural resource base] . . . and to suggest to the full community possible remedies that maintain or enhance economic livelihood and the quality of life in the Swan Valley. (Swan Citizens' Ad Hoc Committee 1991)

According to this guiding mandate, the ad hoc committee will also "assist the community in resolving, collaboratively, the conflicts affecting the Swan Valley" (Swan Citizens' Ad Hoc Committee 1991). The group explicitly excluded "serving as a spokesman for the community" as one of its roles.

With the exception of the mandate, mission, and goals statement, the ad hoc committee has no formal structure. There are no bylaws or official members, and officers have no designated responsibilities. Membership is open to the community, requiring no dues or any explicit commitment of time. As meetings begin, Alan Taylor explains, "If you walk in the door you're a member for as long as you want. There are no permanent fixtures." This loose structure and fluid membership is intended to prevent the domination of any specific special interest and to encourage the broad-based participation of valley residents. Two simple ground rules guide the group: Each participant must listen respectfully to the others, and those present at a given meeting must reach consensus in order to advocate a specific position. Consensus is attained once everyone is comfortable with a decision.

General meetings of the ad hoc committee usually occur monthly. These meetings consist mainly of information sharing and feature presentations by land managers, public officials, or interest group representatives who serve as "resource people." Controversial topics draw the largest crowds. Grizzly bear conservation and Plum Creek's land use plan in wildlife linkage zones produced the largest turnout during the year-and-a-half period in which this study was conducted. If an issue or project emerges during these general meetings that participants believe warrants more attention, volunteers form subcommittees to work on these specific topics. For example, smaller "working" groups tackled a ponderosa pine restoration project, Forest Service road closures, an economic diversification plan, and the threatened closure of the Swan Valley Forest Service facility.

While the ad hoc committee's founders sought to include the valley's many diverse perspectives by inviting specific individuals who could speak for a particular viewpoint, the valley residents who participate in the ad hoc speak as individuals, not as representatives of formal groups or organized constituencies ("stakeholders"). Volunteers, committed to their community and landscape, are the driving force behind this collaborative group. To foster broad participation throughout the valley, they try to "talk up" their activities among neighbors using what Taylor calls the "dispersion model." The ad hoc committee is continually challenged to achieve broad public participation but has made some tangible accomplishments.

ACCOMPLISHMENTS

In 1992, the ad hoc committee initiated a communitywide survey of the Swan Valley's human resources, residents' visions for the future, and their attitudes regarding valley issues. This survey was conducted by the University of Montana's School of Forestry, and the results continue to provide the committee with an empirical foundation for understanding community demographics and attitudes (Lambrecht and Jackson 1993).

The community survey contributed directly to an economic diversification plan developed in conjunction with residents from Seeley Lake, an adjacent community. Three ad hoc committee participants and three Seeley Lake residents worked with technical advisers from the Forest Service and a Missoula-based regional economic development group to produce the plan. This sixty-page document describes the 1993 status of the area's economy, quality of life, and environment as well as its "desired future conditions" (Seeley/Swan Economic Diversification Action Team 1993). The Action Team developed a variety of potential opportunities for economic diversification in keeping with the community goals of maintaining the valley's rural character. Projects resulting from the creation of the diversification plan include a visitors' guide to the valley; an interpretive trail and exhibit at the Swan Ecosystem Center, which is committed to hiring local people rather than outside experts whenever possible; and the Swan Valley Arts and Crafts Gallery.

Also in 1992, ad hoc participants identified the Elk Creek drainage as a high priority for protection because of the pristine bull trout–spawning habitat in the creek's upper reaches. The ad hoc committee reached consensus to support public acquisition of three sections of Plum Creek Timber land along the creek, and when Plum Creek refused a direct sale of the property, the Forest Service proposed a land exchange that the ad hoc committee supported. According to committee participants, the group's ability to reach consensus on removing some forestland from the valley's timber base to preserve bull trout habitat is a major accomplishment.

Ad hoc subcommittees worked with the Flathead National Forest on a number of local, forest-related issues and gained limited flexibility with road closures on the valley's Forest Service land when it opened select roads for a fourteen-day period so that residents could gather firewood. The newly created Swan Ecosystem Center is perhaps the most far-reaching of the ad hoc committee's tangible accomplishments. In an attempt to prevent the complete closure of the Swan's remaining Forest Service facility (the Condon Work Center), an ad hoc subcommittee established the Swan Ecosystem Center in the fall of 1996 as a nonprofit organization that will, among other purposes, "represent the community in partnership with the Forest Service" (Swan Ecosystem Center 1996).[2]

Finally, another subcommittee collaborated with the Flathead National Forest on a ponderosa pine restoration project behind the Condon Work Center. This specific project and a similar one on private land, illustrate the links between community well-being and forest health in the Swan Valley. Restoration of the "open parklike conditions" that once characterized the valley's ponderosa pine forests was the goal of the thirty-acre Forest Stewardship project. In conjunction with Forest Service officials, ad hoc committee participants selected a stand of old-growth ponderosa that was choked with Douglas fir and lodgepole pine saplings for their first experiment with forest stewardship timber management and logging. Specific project goals included using commercial logging to thin the stand, returning low-intensity fire to the area, and ongoing community involvement in the long-term monitoring of the site (Harris 1995).

According to ad hoc participant and Swan resident Sue Cushman, the Swan residents involved in this project are "taking responsibility to make sure it's done right." During the actual logging, participants monitored the operation to ensure it was done well; one post and pole business, assisted by an ad hoc participant, salvaged post and pole material from the slash piles left by the logger. Residents involved in this project established study points to monitor changes in vegetation over time as well as among the bird and animal populations. These resident volunteers have spent countless hours educating themselves about fire ecology, forest stewardship logging, and Forest Service regulations in the design and implementation of the project.

FOSTERING COMMUNITY WELL-BEING: THE ENDURING ACCOMPLISHMENTS

While the tangible projects are expanding, there are also less tangible but essential outcomes that laid the foundation for the on-the-ground work that the Swan Ecosystem Center is now accomplishing. During the research for this chapter, the committee's leadership, as well as many of the nonparticipating Swan residents who were interviewed, ranked the new relationships built through the collaborative problem-solving process as the ad hoc committee's most important accomplishment. Creating a civil dialogue and building trust among former adversaries also topped the list of important outcomes. Finally, the relationships forged between valley residents and the area's nonlocal, land management decision makers were among the less quantifiable but vitally important benefits of the ad hoc committee. The valley residents interviewed during this research saw these outcomes as the first steps toward protecting the Swan's rural character and landscape. The growing list of on-the-ground accomplishments is testament to the importance of this relationship-building period.

As Anne Dahl, who has been actively involved in the committee since its inception, sees it,

> The period of animosity was making people scared. Now I see people starting to listen to each other again. The climate seems less adversarial. There's more will-

ingness to tolerate. We've learned to listen, to respect each other. Maybe it's fil-
tering into the community, or maybe people gave up the fighting when they realized it didn't get anywhere and [they went] back to being the good neighbors
they really are.

According to Tom Parker, a local outfitter and active participant, the committee has

> created an environment of positive community dialogue [and] helped to show
> people there was more common ground than people realized. It brings out bet-
> ter thinking, less judgmental, rational, caring thinking [and] listening [that]
> tends to force you to give time to think before you speak. The example of oth-
> ers who discipline themselves to [be] calm rubs off.

The connections built between Swan residents and land management decision makers are among the most important relationships fostered by the ad
hoc's collaborative efforts. The valley's checkerboard pattern of landownership
and management means that residents' livelihoods and the landscape are
greatly affected by the decisions of large, absentee stakeholders. The ad hoc
committee's general meetings provide a forum for representatives of the Flathead National Forest and Plum Creek Timber to discuss their plans affecting
the valley. In March 1996, a Plum Creek spokesperson attended a general ad
hoc committee meeting to address rumors that the company was selling some
of its land in the valley. Though he emphasized the decision-making rights of
Plum Creek as a private landowner, he indicated that the company was willing both to discuss its plans with the community and to consider alternative
options. As a result, a subcommittee formed to identify the community's priorities should Plum Creek land become available for future trades into public
ownership.

The Swan Lake District ranger now routinely brings his staff from Bigfork
to discuss projects proposed for the valley. In addition to the collaborations with
the Forest Service already discussed, ad hoc committee participants are actively
involved in a Forest Service landscape analysis of the Upper Swan Valley that will
become the foundation of future Forest Service land management activities in
the area. Many committee members are hopeful that the willingness of both the
Forest Service and Plum Creek to attend ad hoc meetings and address residents'
concerns means that residents are gaining greater influence in valley land management decisions. Rod Ash, a retired schoolteacher and founding member of
the ad hoc committee, believes that

> contacts with Plum Creek and the Forest Service might give [us] a little
> more control over our destiny that other isolated communities might not

have. We all know lots of decisions will get made outside of the valley but now we have contacts. That's important to a community whether everybody realizes it or not.

While ad hoc participants are not after local control of Flathead National Forest lands, they do want a greater voice in decisions than they previously have had.

According to many ad hoc participants, the relationships built between the ad hoc committee and Swan Lake Ranger District staff are important steps toward involving residents more meaningfully in Forest Service decision making. The public involvement processes of all federal land management agencies, including the Forest Service, are often criticized for not meaningfully involving the public. Because the agencies present what appear to be already developed plans, public participation becomes public review of decisions already made rather than meaningful public involvement in the actual decision making (U.S. Congress 1992; Wondolleck 1988). As ad hoc participants have become involved in the actual design of Forest Service projects, such as the ponderosa pine restoration effort, their perceptions of the public involvement process are changing.

Ad hoc participants are feeling empowered to affect Forest Service decision making; in turn, this fosters continued involvement. Anne Dahl, for example, participates in the ad hoc committee because "it was . . . about residents working together to decide the future before disaster brings the government in to tell us how to do it. I am uncomfortable with stone throwing. Looking for solutions versus just complaining is important to me."

The persistent efforts of ad hoc participants are building real influence with the Forest Service, in large part because of the close, positive working relationship developed with the Swan Lake District ranger. As Dahl explains, "We are actively helping the Forest Service decide what needs to be done. In the past we were only reacting to the Forest Plan."

Chuck Harris is the Swan Lake District ranger and the primary decision maker for on-the-ground operations. He regularly attends ad hoc committee meetings. For Harris, the collaboration is a welcome relief from the usual adversarial position he experiences in other public meetings. He believes that his involvement with the ad hoc committee is restoring the Forest Service's historic link to the rural communities that district rangers were once a part of. Harris's congenial personality and leadership style, as well as the support of his supervisors for his collaboration with the committee, all contribute greatly to the ongoing working relationship between district staff and Swan residents. One important motivation for his involvement, as well as his supervisors' support, is the hope that collaboration will reduce the number of appeals of Forest Service projects. This institutional motivation to collaborate, while not directly related to community well-being, is important to recognize because it affects the participation of an essential stockholder: the Forest Service.

The agency's motivations to participate are not merely self-serving, however. Agency officials also see the benefits to community well-being. Hal Salwasser, the Northern Region's former regional forester, emphasizes the role of the ad hoc committee in building community or civic capacity, an objective now touted as part of the Forest Service agenda. He defines civic capacity "as a group to leverage other groups to accomplish its projects." For Salwasser, the ponderosa pine restoration effort and the establishment of the Swan Ecosystem Center are evidence of increasing community capacity in the Swan Valley and the role that the Forest Service played in fostering it.

Committee participants also see a change in the way agencies approach public involvement. According to Rod Ash, the Forest Service (as well as Montana state agencies) is approaching the ad hoc committee "at the idea stage of the process rather than in the action stage." He sees agency personnel modifying their ideas on the basis of community input, manifesting the sense of empowerment fostered by a sense that the community can influence decision making.

Challenges

While the ad hoc committee and its collaboration with the Forest Service has produced many benefits, the committee nonetheless faces major challenges. Three "limitations" emerged from an examination of the committee:

1. Limited resident participation in the committee
2. Limits to the committee's power and authority
3. Uncertain results as far as fostering ecological well-being in the Swan Valley

Limited Resident Participation

Despite open invitations to the broader community and the committee's fluid membership, a core group of very active participants is clearly identifiable.[3] This group is recognized locally as the leadership of the ad hoc committee and the source of information about the committee's actions. Over the past years of ad hoc committee work, this group has evolved into a cohesive unit with a large level of trust and understanding. Members describe themselves as "a diverse group, one that can be friends now but couldn't for a while." However, despite continued efforts to encourage other community members to become involved in the ad hoc committee, broad, inclusive participation from the Swan community's diverse sectors remains a challenge. Committee leaders identify three issues that they believe contribute to the wider community's less active participation:

1. The informal structure that defines the ad hoc committee may contribute to the lack of participation of some of the valley stakeholders. According to facilitator Alan Taylor, "The downside of the structure is you don't have someone in charge of getting the word out and advertising meetings like we should." The creation of the Swan Ecosystem Center is helping to alleviate this problem because a paid staff person now has responsibility for mailings, and there is a budget for sending meeting announcements to every Swan resident. Another consequence of the informal structure, however, is the lack of a process to ensure that all perspectives are included. If a participant who brings a unique perspective attends meetings irregularly or drops out, the ad hoc committee has no formal means for ensuring the continued inclusion of that person's perspective. While the informal structure fosters a more participatory (rather than representative) form of public involvement, the informal structure also leaves the group open to the criticism that not all stakeholders are included in a decision.

2. Collaboration involves long hours in meetings over many months before tangible results are achieved. As Rod Ash observes, people "get tired out," and new people must be recruited as older participants "start running out of steam." But because most of the ad hoc committee's leadership is either retired or self-employed—a condition that is not representative of the valley's population—the core participants have the free time and flexible schedules that allow the thousands of volunteer hours dedicated to ad hoc projects.

3. The challenge of participation involves group dynamics among the leadership. After many years of working together, these active participants are comfortable and confident with each other and the collaborative process. Core members tend to speak more frequently during general meetings, questioning resource people two or three times more often than other participants. This dynamic is, at least in part, due to the fact that the leadership attends meetings in higher numbers and is comfortable speaking openly about issues. A downside of this natural outcome of working together to build common ground, as Anne Dahl observes, is that the leadership has "evolved to the point of working together too smoothly. We're more alike than we were at the beginning." Some nonparticipating Swan residents criticize the ad hoc committee for being a group of like-minded individuals. This perception, though not necessarily accurate, contributes to the challenges the ad hoc faces in its efforts to be inclusive.

In addition to the Swan residents who choose not to participate in ad hoc activities, another key nonlocal stakeholder does not participate in the collaboration. The Friends of the Wild Swan, a regional environmental advocacy organization, chooses to remain outside the collaborative process and has twice appealed Forest Service projects that had ad hoc committee involvement: the Elk/Squeezer Creek land exchange and the Forest Stewardship's ponderosa pine restoration project. Formed to "address the impacts to wildlife, water quality, fisheries, scenic values, and other amenities found in the Swan Valley," Friends of the Wild Swan prefers to use the existing public participation process, including administrative appeals, litigation, and public education, to advocate a biologically based ecosystem approach to land management.

Arlene Montgomery, the director of Friends of the Wild Swan, is concerned that local, place-based collaboratives do not conform to the requirements of the National Environmental Policy Act because there is no analysis of a range of alternatives within an environmental analysis. She cites the lack of analysis of ecological outcomes of committee projects as proof that the collaborative process leads, more often than not, to the lowest-common-denominator decision in land management. She also doubts that decisions made in the Upper Swan Valley, for the benefit of that particular community, will be appropriate for communities and environments downstream. As Montgomery sees it, all the projects produced by the collaborative groups she is familiar with involve some form of logging. For her, that is evidence that the process does not result in ecological health and restoration. Despite some Swan residents' impression that the ad hoc committee is environmentally oriented, Montgomery feels her ecological concerns were unwelcome during the few meetings she attended.

As a result of the challenges of fostering broad and inclusive participation, the ad hoc committee is careful to state that it does not represent the full spectrum of interests in the Swan Valley, nor does the committee speak for the community as a whole. Despite this fact, Forest Service personnel closest to the group believe that the ad hoc committee is representative of the Swan Valley community. According to Rodd Richardson, former supervisor of the Flathead National Forest, "It's broadly representative, but it doesn't include the extremes that might not choose to be a part of it." It is important to note that by viewing the ad hoc committee as representative and successful at providing a mechanism for wide public participation, the agency's role in assisting rural communities is legitimized.

The Ad Hoc Committee's Authority

Interviews with Swan Valley residents who do not participate on the committee suggest a cynicism regarding the outcomes of collaboration. Some valley residents insist that the main benefit of the committee's work is talk, with little authority or power for changing talk into action. One man employed in the valley's tourism industry put it bluntly: "I don't know what those things accomplish. As far as I'm concerned, it's people out of the valley that will make the decisions. Government, business, they will do as they please. It's just a typical scenario—out of state industry trying to force things down our throat, and they don't know a thing about living here and they don't care." Another resident said, "I see the public as having no role unless you're part of a group willing to bring lawsuits to further a political agenda or you're in with political figures." The belief that agency officials make decisions before seeking public input, which is based on past experience with agency public involvement processes, constrains broader participation in committee activities. Continued evidence of the influence of community input through the ad hoc's activities may slowly chip away at this cynicism.

The sense of community powerlessness and the perception of a lack of authority with large corporate interests and the Forest Service are not without foundation. Plum Creek Timber Company, while increasingly willing to listen to residents, has the right to act as a private landowner, and Forest Service officials have emphasized collaboration as a means to build public support for agency projects. Former regional forester Hal Salwasser, for example, told us that he hopes collaboratives will create "a high enough level of trust between the Forest Service citizen groups that the Forest Service can decrease the amount of analysis and planning it has to do to undertake a project and the citizen group doesn't have to spend as much energy on every project" (personal communication, 1997).

Thus, while committee members speak of a substantive sharing of decision-making power, Forest Service officials speak of building public support for the decisions the agency makes; the Forest Service remains the ultimate analyzer and decision maker, while the public provides input.

Agency officials interviewed for this study remain ambiguous about the decision-making power they are willing or able to yield to other parties. On a host of issues, they are unable to yield at all. Indeed, many Forest Service policies and cutting targets are political decisions crafted and legislated far from place-based initiatives. Such contradictions certainly contribute to the cynicism regarding the collaborative process. Though the form of public participation has altered with the advent of community-based collaboratives, the degree to which the public can sway agency decisions remains limited and contingent on personalities, political agendas, and a desire to minimize litigation.

Success in Fostering Ecological Well-Being

A final challenge, unrelated to issues of participation, is to what extent the ad hoc committee's collaborative process has contributed to the valley's ecological well-being. At the time of this study, systematic procedures to monitor the ecological impacts of committee projects were being developed. As Hal Salwasser observed, committee participants "believe they're in the best position to determine what concepts like 'ecosystem health' and 'sustainability' mean in an environment." Relatively little on-the-ground management has been implemented and even less evaluated over the length of time needed to understand a project's impact on ecological integrity or forest health. As a result, it is too early to evaluate whether the assumption in Salwasser's comment is in fact true.

Conclusion: An Enduring Collaboration Responds to New Challenges

Since the original research for this chapter was conducted, the Swan Citizens' Ad Hoc Committee and the nature of collaboration in the Swan Valley have evolved in response to both the challenges described here and emerging issues within the community. Beginning in 1998, the ad hoc committee actively sought to include more residents and nonresident interest groups in its collaborative process. The successful creation of the Swan Ecosystem Center, with its small staff and budget, has been critical to addressing some of the participation issues. The center, having grown out of ad hoc committee discussions, now functions in many ways at "the action arm of the ad hoc," and implementing the vision and ideas of the committee is no longer reliant solely on volunteers. As a result, the number of on-the-ground projects has expanded, providing more opportunities for volunteers to get involved, and regular meeting announcements are sent to all valley residents. Thus, participation in collaboration in the Swan Valley has been both increasing and diversifying over the years.

As of the fall of 2002, the ad hoc committee continues to play an active albeit somewhat different role in helping the Swan Valley meets its social and ecological challenges. The purpose of ad hoc committee gatherings in the Condon Community Hall has shifted somewhat, serving more as educational forums rather than focusing on community building and consensus decision making as they did in the past. "The shift in ad hoc meetings is a natural evolution," says Anne Dahl, current executive director of the Swan Ecosystem Center. "No one made a conscious decision to shift toward more informational meetings and fewer consensus-building meetings. It's just that we don't try to reach consensus much anymore. I think it's because it's not necessary. People just decide what to do after they have learned enough to make informed decision." As issues become known, the committee invites experts and other known specialists on a particular topic to meet with the committee and interested members of the valley to hear these diverse views. Decision making regarding proposed actions has tended to devolve to subcommittees. For example, the committee recently sponsored a series of meetings regarding noxious weeds. The committee organized a series of informational forums where botanists, weed specialists, and community groups presented their perspectives on the problem and proposed solutions. Smaller neighborhood groups continued to meet and work toward a solution that best met the concerns and conditions of their particular place and residents.

Additional "spin-off" groups also play a lead role in creating a forum for community members to be part of multiparty decision making across the valley. The Swan Lands Committee is one such subcommittee that has taken the lead role in addressing Plum Creek Timber Company's announcement that it will be selling a large portion of its landholdings in the valley for private residential development. Plum Creek Timber owns alternating sections of valley land, a legacy of the 1864 land grant to the Northern Rockies Pacific Railroad. The amount of land to be sold represents approximately half the productive forestland in the valley and as a result poses a significant threat to the community's forest-based activities and livelihoods as well as recreational opportunities, habitat conservation, and overall ecosystem health. A paid community member now leads the effort to keep the Swan Valley community aware of and involved in decisions regarding how this private land may be sold or otherwise allocated. The subcommittee does not claim to represent the valley, nor will it attempt to reach a consensus among its members regarding what it thinks Plum Creek ought to do. Its purpose is to use all communication tools and networks available to keep the community as significantly involved in the land sale process as possible. To fulfill this purpose, the Swan Lands Community Committee will gather community input and will eventually offer recommendations that are likely to be highly controversial. Indeed, a proposal being discussed by the subcommittee involves the Swan Valley community itself purchasing a portion of the land and managing it on a communitywide basis (as occurs in British Columbia and in many rural communities in the tropical South). Recently, this proposal, as well as the authority of the group offering it, has been strongly criticized by a Swan Valley community member in the local newspaper (*Seeley-Swan Pathfinder*). Importantly, the critic admits to never attending any of the public forums organized by either the ad hoc committee or the Swan Lands Community Committee.

Questions of authority, representation, and control over desired change continue to be directed toward the ad hoc committee, the Swan Ecosystem Center, and their many projects. In a series of random interviews conducted in the spring of 2002 in a local bar, those interviewed strongly endorsed the value of local input into land management decisions. Indeed, they argued enthusiastically for what might be called "local ecological knowledge." However, they did not see the valley's key local ecological knowledge represented by those who participate in the organizations noted previously. With a few exceptions, participants in these groups are viewed as "newcomers" unaware of the long-term ecological changes occurring in the valley (such as the causes and problems associated with fuel buildup in forests prone to wildfire). These "newcomers" are also seen as more economically well off than the group interviewed and largely insensitive to types of recreation that they favor (such as snowmobiling over cross-country skiing). Participants in the ad hoc committee and Swan Ecosystem Center are also seen as a political force interested in controlling the direction of change in the valley on the basis of their particular value systems. However, despite their strong concerns, few of those offering the critiques attend meetings or informational forums organized by the committees or the center. They say they do not attend because they recognize the deep-seated nature of their differences. These conversations, as well as the evolution of the ad hoc committee toward an educational forum rather than a communitywide consensus-seeking body, indicate a practical acceptance of differences across the valley. It is not known how these differences will affect future activities managed by the ad hoc committee and the Swan Ecosystem Center or how the latter will evolve further as a result of them. However, the story of the Swan Valley today strongly suggests the highly social and political nature of community conservation initiatives and at least one community's attempt over time to recognize and work with these differences.

Notes

1. Nine of the ad hoc committee's core leadership were interviewed for this project. This "core" was composed of the most active ad hoc participants at the time of the research for this chapter. Thirty-eight Swan Valley residents who do not participate regularly in ad hoc committee efforts were also interviewed. These individuals were identified by the ad hoc committee's leadership as residents who reflected various perspectives in the Swan and potentially would be willing to be interviewed. Though not a random sample and hence not generalizable across the valley, the interviews provide an in-depth understanding of some positions within the community. Forest Service personnel interviewed included Swan Lake District Ranger Chuck Harris, Flathead National Forest Supervisor Rodd Richardson, and former Regional Forester Hal Salwasser. Arlene Montgomery, director of the Friends of the Wild Swan, a local environmental organization, was also interviewed. In addition to interviews, one of the coauthors was a participant observer at almost all the ad hoc committee meetings between November 1995 and February 1997 (including various subcommittee meetings).

2. The majority of the research for this chapter was conducted during the creation of the Swan Ecosystem Center. This nonprofit community-based organization, with its small staff and budget, has had significant positive impact on the Swan Valley. The center functions in many ways as "the action arm of the ad hoc." Many of the challenges

pointed out in this story (such as ensuring participation and moving from dialogue to on-the-ground action) are being addressed successfully because of the efforts of the center. Implementing the vision and ideas of the ad hoc committee is no longer solely reliant on volunteers with full-time jobs. There have been significant strides in on-the-ground, community-based forest and wilderness management, and the center's ongoing projects are now too numerous to mention. This chapter offers a snapshot in time of an effort that continued to evolve; as a result, it is more history than current event.

3. It is important to note here that the creation of Swan Ecosystem Center has allowed the ad hoc committee to address this limitation in substantive ways. The expanding number of on-the-ground projects has provided more opportunities for volunteers to get involved. A staff and budget to do mailings have enabled the committee to send meeting announcements to all valley residents. Thus, participation in the many projects spawned by collaboration in the Swan Valley is both increasing and diversifying.

References

Cestero, Barb. 1997. "From Conflict to Consensus? A Social and Political History of Environmental Collaboration in the Swan Valley, Montana." M.S. thesis, University of Montana.

Dahl, Anne. 1990. "Scenic 83 Sparks Concerns from Different Camps: Loggers, Environmentalists Share Ideas." *Seeley-Swan Pathfinder*, vol. 4, issue 47, 6–7.

Flowers, Patrick J. and Roger C. Conner, David H. Jackson, Charles E. Keegan III, Brian Long, Ervin G. Schuster, and William L. Wood. 1993. An Assessment of Montana Timber Situation: Inventory, Ownership Policies, Economic Factors, Social Concerns, Legislation. Miscellaneous Publication 53, Montana Forest and Experiment Station, School of Forestry, University of Montana.

Frissell, C. A., J. Doskocil, J. T. Gangemi, and J. Stanford. 1995. "Identifying Priority Areas for Protection and Restoration of Aquatic Biodiversity: A Case Study in the Swan River Basin, Montana, USA." Open File Report No. 136-95. Flathead Lake Biological Station, University of Montana, Polson.

Harris, Chuck. 1995. Decision Memo: Condon Forest Stewardship Project. USDA Forest Service, Flathead National Forest, Swan Lake Ranger District, Bigfork, Montana.

Johnson, Kirk. 1993. "Beyond Polarization: Emerging Strategies for Reconciling Community and the Environment." Northwest Policy Center, University of Washington Graduate School of Public Affairs, Seattle.

Lambrecht, Mark R., and David H. Jackson. 1993. "Identifying the Profile of Montana's Swan Valley Community: An Inventory of Its Human Resources and a Summary of Its Preferences for the Future." Unpublished report, School of Forestry, University of Montana, Missoula.

Noland, Gary. 1989. "Timber Shortage Forces Pyramid Workforce Reduction." *Seeley-Swan Pathfinder* vol. 4, issue 10, 1.

Power, Thomas Michael. 1996. *Lost Landscapes and Failed Economies: The Search for a Value of Place*. Washington, D.C.: Island Press.

Schwennesen, Don. 1990. "Swan Squawk: State's Handling of Soiled Stream Stirs a Flap with Conservationists." *The Missoulian,* September 8.

Seeley/Swan Economic Diversification Action Team. 1993. "The Economic Diversification Action Plan for the Seeley/Swan Area." Unpublished manuscript.

Seeley-Swan Pathfinder. 1987a. "More Unemployment Likely in Timber Industry." *Seeley-Swan Pathfinder* 2 (7): 6.

Seeley-Swan Pathfinder. 1987b. "Timber Harvest Higher in 1986." *Seeley-Swan Pathfinder* 1 (37): 14.

Swan Citizens Ad Hoc Committee. 1991. "Mandate, Mission and Goals." Unpublished manuscript.

Swan Ecosystem Center. 1996. "Bylaws of the Swan Ecosystem Center, Inc." Unpublished manuscript.

Swan Valley Community Club, Comprehensive Plan Committee. 1996. "Swan Valley–Condon Comprehensive Plan Amendment, Missoula County." Draft.

U.S. Congress, Office of Technology Assessment. 1992. *Forest Service Planning: Accommodating Uses, Producing Outputs and Sustaining Ecosystems.* OTAOF-505. Washington, D.C.: U.S. Government Printing Office.

USDA Forest Service. 1994. "Wildlife Landscape Evaluation, Swan Valley." Flathead National Forest Supervisors Office, Kalispell, Montana.

Vernon, Suzanne. 1987a. "Variety of Problems Affect Swan River Cutthroat." *Seeley-Swan Pathfinder* vol. 2, issue 24, 7.

———. 1987b. "Residents Want to Have Their Say: Water Quality, Fisheries Concerns." *Seeley-Swan Pathfinder,* August 27, 5.

———. 1990. "Hate Mail? Let 'Em Eat Rhubarb." *Seeley-Swan Pathfinder* vol. 5, issue 4, 2.

Woodruff, Steve. 1987. "'Clearcut' Debate Echoes around Swan Valley." *The Missoulian,* August 21.

Wondolleck, Julia. 1988. *Public Lands Conflict and Resolution: Managing National Forest Disputes.* New York: Plenum.

CHAPTER 8

Revitalizing Baltimore
URBAN FORESTRY AT THE WATERSHED SCALE

Ann Moote

Gardens in previously trash-filled abandoned lots; trees along streets recently devoid of vegetation; cleaner, more accessible parks; educational programs for children and teens that cultivate neighborhood pride, local leadership, and environmental activism: The oldest partnership effort for urban forestry in the nation, Revitalizing Baltimore has produced some tangible successes in some of the most run-down inner-city neighborhoods of the nation. In the process, partners in the effort are learning how restoring the environment and community together requires a recipe most resource managers have not yet discovered. Far more than scientific prescriptions and goodwill, the revitalization of Baltimore, or of any urban center for that matter, requires a thorough rethinking of how people are allowed to inhabit, use, and care for their environment. In Baltimore, it is increasingly evident that success in environmental restoration depends on resolving issues of equity, ownership, and power.

When much of the middle class fled Baltimore for the suburbs twenty years ago, the city's tax base plummeted, decimating public services. By the early 1970s, high unemployment and crime rates, widespread poverty, and trash-filled abandoned lots dominated the city once renowned for a history of community organizing and an extensive park system. Outside the city, new suburban subdivisions absorbed any open space that remained of the once heavily forested Chesapeake Bay watershed. Just thirty miles north of the nation's capital, both the rural and the urban environment had become equally and alarmingly degraded.

The brainchild of a U.S. Forest Service forester and Yale professor, Revitalizing Baltimore brought together government agencies, nonprofit environmental organizations, and citizens groups who had never worked together before. In the process of doing so, they had to confront their basic, albeit sometimes unconscious, assumptions about race, class, and culpability. When, for example, a management analysis of social data seemed to infer that poor black neighborhoods degrade the environment more than rich, white ones do, tension between the scientific and community members of the partnership arose and generated a discussion about data, science, and community on the cutting edge of resource management thinking today.

Most unique about this multipartner, Forest Service–funded program is that it recognizes the human community as an integral member of the ecosystem and develops programs that simultaneously address both environmental and social degradation. Designed to teach people to respect and be proud of their local environment and see themselves as advocates and stewards of healthy, safe communities, Revitalizing Baltimore is an ambitious attempt to explore the relationship between environmental degradation and poverty, healthy environments, and social justice.

Baltimore is a city of contrasts. Neighborhoods dominated by grand Victorian homes and forested parks are interspersed with concrete jungles of abandoned row houses and vacant lots. It is a city rich in culture, history, and natural resources yet confronted with some of the country's highest crime and poverty rates and a pervasive illegal drug industry. In the early 1990s, natural resource planners introduced an experiment in social forestry into this landscape. The Revitalizing Baltimore experiment is a major effort to develop community capacity for managing an urban natural environment at the watershed scale, addressing both social and environmental needs in the process.

Baltimore's Historical, Social, and Natural Landscape

First settled by Europeans in the mid-1600s, Baltimore quickly developed into an important manufacturing center and key commercial port for the United States. The region's expansive deciduous forests and many streams provided excellent mill sites and shipbuilding materials for the growing community. By the late nineteenth century, Baltimore was a vibrant city with well-established neighborhoods and active textile manufacturing industries. African American Baltimoreans were well organized in churches and other community-based organizations and had unusual political influence: Between 1890 and 1931, six African Americans held seats on the Baltimore City Council. In the early 1900s, the Municipal Arts Society engaged the Olmsted Brothers landscaping firm to develop a comprehensive park plan for greater Baltimore, and the city began planting street trees at the citizens' behest. Baltimore was one of the great Victorian-era American cities and remained a major manufacturing center well into the mid-1900s.

Like many northeastern manufacturing centers, Baltimore was hit hard in the 1970s, when the manufacturing industry moved south and middle-class residents moved out to the suburbs. By 2000, Baltimore was a city with two-thirds of its former population, 40,000 abandoned lots (10 to 15 percent of the city's total land base), a severely lowered tax base, reduced public services, high crime and unemployment rates, and widespread poverty. City resources and infrastructure, including the parks and other natural resources managed by the pared-down Department of Recreation and Parks, were maintained only minimally or neglected entirely. Adjacent Chesapeake Bay had become notorious for its water pollution.

Still, Baltimore remained a city of great resources. The extensive system of stream valley parks designed by the Olmsted Brothers at the turn of the century left greenways along the city's three main watersheds: Gwynns Falls, Jones Falls, and Herring Run. Gwynns Falls/Leakin Park is one of the largest "urban wilderness" parks in the nation, and Baltimore's urban forest includes over 300,000 street trees. At the turn of the twenty-first century, the city of Baltimore is 20 percent forested with diverse native and introduced tree species, including ash, elm, beech, oak, hickory, birch, maple, and many other hardwood species. Wetland areas along stream channels support willow, alder, maple, and other species. Many trees in the urban park areas are over two hundred years old. Red fox, raccoons, skunks, gray squirrels, and deer are commonly sighted within the city limits, and over two hundred species of birds, as well as several species of snakes, turtles, and frogs, can be found in the city. Baltimore's strong sense of community is reflected in over 650 civic organizations that range in size from citywide groups to block clubs and hundreds of active church associations distributed throughout the city. The combination of Baltimore's rich social and environmental resources has provided fertile ground for community-based ecological restoration and stewardship efforts.

The Birth of Revitalizing Baltimore

Revitalizing Baltimore's roots can be traced to the vision of Bob Jones, director of Baltimore's Department of Recreation and Parks, and Bill Burch, a forestry professor at Yale University. Their vision was modeled after Burch's social forestry work in developing countries, where small-scale forestry projects are used to improve ecological conditions and foster the development of new social networks and community organizations to address community needs. Jones thought that urban America, and specifically Baltimore, could benefit from a similar program to address environmental and social needs in tandem—as well as from a watershed perspective.

In 1989, Yale School of Forestry students offered their services to Baltimore's Department of Recreation and Parks in exchange for practical experience. The student internship program, the Urban Resources Initiative, was institutionalized as a program within a Baltimore-based nongovernmental organization, the Parks & People Foundation.

Much of the forestry students' work was in the field, where interns focused on neighborhood street tree plantings and turning vacant lots into community gardens. Interns also created a map of all the city's parks and recreation centers, and, with their help, the Department of Recreation and Parks developed a new strategic plan and reorganized its departments. Where the departments had been arranged according to political boundaries, they are now organized around the city's three watersheds.

In 1991, the Urban Resources Initiative caught the attention of Bob Neville, the Northeast Region urban and community forestry coordinator of the U.S. Forest Service's State and Private Forestry program. Neville was interested in developing new concepts of urban forestry that looked at the urban ecosystem as a whole and linked community forestry projects within that ecosystem.

Revitalizing Baltimore emerged from the melding of the Urban Resources Initiative's social forestry programs and the Forest Service's idea for urban ecosystem management. With support from the city and state government and the entire Maryland congressional delegation as well as Forest Service endorsement, Revitalizing Baltimore was designated a Congressional Special Project in 1993 and given a separate line item in the Forest Service budget, authorizing the project for $500,000 per year for five years. The original Revitalizing Baltimore partners developed four project goals in 1993:

- Create a comprehensive and participatory process for managing urban natural resources that can be implemented in other urban areas
- Develop an institutional framework within the Baltimore region that influences public policy, planning, management, and funding to sustain and invigorate Revitalizing Baltimore initiatives
- Enhance the environmental awareness of communities and government and increase their ability to address environmental issues together in the Baltimore region
- Restore and conserve an urban natural environment that contributes to social and economic well-being and provides a more desirable place to live and work

The initial Revitalizing Baltimore partners made an effort to be inclusive, inviting nongovernmental organizations from other areas and city and county agencies to be partners on the project. The Parks & People Foundation serves as coordinator and project manager for Revitalizing Baltimore. A steering committee with representatives from over a dozen nonprofit, government, community, and educational organizations serves as the umbrella for a collection of indepen-

Current and Former Revitalizing Baltimore Partners and Participants

Parks & People Foundation
Baltimore City
   Department of Recreation and Parks
   Department of Planning
   Department of Public Works
   School System
Baltimore County
   Department of Environmental Protection and Resource Management
   Department of Recreation and Parks
State of Maryland
   Department of Health
   Department of Natural Resources
   Forest Conservation District Boards
U.S. Forest Service
Morgan State University
University of Maryland, Baltimore County
   Baltimore-Washington Collaboratory
Yale University School of Forestry and Environmental Studies
American Forests
Alliance for the Chesapeake Bay
Baltimore–Chesapeake Bay Outward Bound
Baltimore Civic Works Youth Services
Baltimore Ecosystem Study
Baltimore Urban League
Chesapeake Bay Trust
Greater Homewood Community Corporation
Gwynns Falls Watershed Association
Heritage Museum/Gwynns Falls Conservancy
Herring Run Watershed Association
Information Frontiers
Irvine Natural Science Center
Jones Falls Watershed Association
Maryland Save Our Streams
Morgan State University
Neighborhood Design Center
Operation Reach Out Southwest / Bon Secours Community Development
The Trust for Public Land
University of Maryland, Department of Geography
Washington Village/Pigtown Neighborhood Planning Council
Woodbury Urban Forest Initiative

dent projects and programs that all address a common set of goals. While the core of Revitalizing Baltimore's funding comes from the Forest Service, other project partners, notably state and county agencies, have contributed funding to Revitalizing Baltimore projects. All partners contribute in-kind support. Revitalizing Baltimore's efforts have been focused in three primary areas: developing community capacity and supporting watershed associations; data collection, data analysis, and planning; and neighborhood demonstration projects and educational programs.

Watershed Associations

Early Revitalizing Baltimore projects were focused on the Gwynns Falls watershed and included an effort to form a community-based organization that would address social and environmental well-being at the landscape scale. In addition to organizing the Gwynns Falls Watershed Association, Revitalizing Baltimore was the catalyst for the development of the Jones Falls Watershed Association. The Herring Run Watershed Association joined the partnership in 1996. Today, all three watershed associations receive significant Revitalizing Baltimore funding and technical assistance from Revitalizing Baltimore partners.

GWYNNS FALLS WATERSHED ASSOCIATION

Revitalizing Baltimore partners initially focused their efforts on the Gwynns Falls watershed, particularly the sections of the watershed within Baltimore City where environmental and social problems are the most severe. Of Baltimore's three watersheds, Gwynns Falls is considered the most significant to the health and vitality of the Chesapeake Bay ecosystem. Deforestation, paving, and stream degradation have resulted in rapid water runoff and severe erosion and contributed to pollution problems in Gwynns Falls creek and adjacent Chesapeake Bay. The pollution has destabilized forest and riparian ecosystems, changed species composition, and reduced species diversity. Introduced species have become a problem throughout the parks, with invasive vines and brambles forming impassable thickets in many areas and feral dogs roaming freely. Nevertheless, extensive clearing of Maryland's historical forest cover has made the forest type found in the Gwynns Falls/Leakin Park rare.

In 1994, Revitalizing Baltimore's steering committee contracted with the non-governmental organization, Maryland Save Our Streams, to develop a Gwynns Falls watershed association. In order to inform residents of the Gwynns Falls watershed of the Revitalizing Baltimore concept and identify residents' concerns, Save Our Streams held a community forum in early 1994. Eighty-four citizens, primarily from inner-city neighborhoods, attended the forum and identified trash, sanitation, vacant housing, crime, drugs, lack of jobs, lack of opportunities for children, lack of pride, and hopelessness as key issues. Specific environmental issues were not a primary concern, although one participant observed that the urban residents were "very aware of the interconnection between social and environmental conditions."

Some project partners, who believed that Revitalizing Baltimore's urban forestry focus necessarily excluded many issues raised by the Gwynns Falls residents, were critical of Save Our Streams for not restricting the forum to environmental issues. In the words of one steering committee member, the forum was "sort of a bait and switch," as citizens were asked to express their concerns but only offered tree planting as a possible solution. Still, thirty-five people signed up to learn more about forming a watershed association.

Over the next two years, Save Our Streams worked toward developing a watershed association, although considerable dissent remained among steering committee members about how to do it. Some partners felt that organizing a watershed association should wait until a Gwynns Falls watershed management plan had been completed, while others thought that they should be building citizen capacity and watershed association membership through on-the-ground projects first. Disputes continued over the importance of addressing issues of utmost concern to local residents versus focusing exclusively on urban forestry projects. At one point, all efforts were put on hold for several months.

Despite these delays, by the end of 1996, Save Our Streams had formed six subwatershed groups in the Gwynns Falls watershed, each of which identified issues of importance to their subwatershed and developed an action plan based on those issues. In January 1997, representatives from each of the six subwatershed groups came together to form the Gwynns Falls Watershed Association. In 1998, the watershed association began organizing stream cleanups and in 2001 held the First Annual Gwynns Falls Watershed Festival.

The Gwynns Falls Watershed Association has experienced turnovers in local leadership and has lower rates of community involvement than the other two watershed associations, in part because crime and poverty are more extreme in the Gwynns Falls watershed, making community organizing more difficult.

JONES FALLS WATERSHED ASSOCIATION

In 1997, Revitalizing Baltimore coordinators asked Michael Beer, a retired professor and community organizer, if he would help form a Jones Falls watershed association. Beer is the creator of and the spirit behind the Friends of Stony Run, a highly motivated group of neighbors and students from local schools and colleges that had spent fifteen years removing trash and invasive exotic species from the twelve-acre, mile-and-a-half Stony Run greenway and replanting it with native species. Beer and another community member, Sandy Sparks, agreed to take on the task.

To introduce Baltimore residents to the Jones Falls, Beer convinced the city to close a major urban artery that runs adjacent to the falls for an entire Sunday so that the nascent Jones Falls Watershed Association could hold a community bike ride on the expressway. Beer and Sparks organized rock-climbing demonstrations and lessons on one of the granite outcrops along the river, held concerts on its banks, and designed and distributed leaflets describing hikes along the river. They also persuaded the city to open the dam at Lake Roland, the headwaters of the Jones Falls, allowing enough water to flow for a community canoe and kayak trip along the river. Now an annual event, the Jones Falls festival includes a footrace, biking and walking, a community festival, and boating on the river and attracts thousands of people from throughout the region.

There is abundant evidence that Baltimoreans now see a treasure where they once saw an eyesore or danger zone. Many of the historic mills along the river have been restored and are now rented out as commercial and art space. Canoers, kayakers, and hikers regularly use the Jones Falls and participate in river cleanups.

Beer himself continues to explore innovative ways to restore the native ecosystems, involve local residents in the area's stewardship, and study the effectiveness of different restoration efforts. In one "research area," he has planted every species of woody plant native to Maryland and is monitoring them to see how well they do in urban Baltimore. He encourages local residents to "adopt" individual trees in replanted areas, then regularly check on "their" trees, pulling off invasive vines and monitoring their growth. In another area, Beer has mapped fourteen "maintenance parcels," developed a management plan for each, and assigned two or three local residents to maintain each parcel.

By 2000, the Jones Falls Watershed Association was holding monthly meetings with twenty very active members, had an overall membership over 1,000, and had begun publishing a quarterly newsletter. The Jones Falls Stewards, a large group of volunteers, walks the streamway each month, picking up garbage. After two years, the Stewards found that where they once filled thirty bags a month with garbage, they now come away with only eight. "What we're doing," Beer says, "is building a love affair between citizens and the river."

HERRING RUN WATERSHED ASSOCIATION

In 1993, Lynn Kramer reassessed her values and her career and decided she wanted to focus her energies on "building a sense of place and community in the city." With funding from Baltimore County and help from an environmental organization, Maryland Save Our Streams, Kramer organized a stream survey and cleanup of the Herring Run, one of the three major streams that run through Baltimore. Kramer then took her ideas to a neighborhood meeting where she urged people to take pride in the Herring Run stream valley and look at the stream both holistically and as an entity around which community and a sense of place could be built. By the end of that meeting, Kramer had recruited three people to form the Herring Run Watershed Association.

By 2000, the Herring Run Watershed Association had 240 dues-paying members, including local residents, community organizations, churches, and businesses, and a mailing list of 2,000 interested community members. About thirty core members lead educational programs, stream cleanups, and tree plantings; publish a newsletter; and manage the group's administration with a $150,000 annual budget. The association has developed a Herring Run–specific watershed curriculum for city and county elementary and middle schools, and volunteers lead educational field trips and slide shows. The core group organizes "stream teams"—groups of local concerned residents who agree to become stewards of designated sections of Herring Run or one of its tributaries. Each stream team walks its stream section monthly, armed with maps and survey forms, looking for potential problems like stream bank erosion or pollution and identifying potential restoration projects. Twenty-six sampling sites are monitored every other week for chemical and visual pollutants and quarterly for macroinvertebrates. The watershed association grows native tree and shrub seedlings in its own nursery and organizes plantings in the watershed. Spring Migration, an annual fund-raising walkathon and festival organized by the association, also educates and recruits area residents.

The Herring Run Watershed Association joined Revitalizing Baltimore in 2000 and began receiving funding through Revitalizing Baltimore in 2001, allowing Kramer to return to paid employment. Since 1999, approximately one-third of Revitalizing Baltimore's annual budget has been allocated to the three watershed associations.

Data Analysis and Planning

In its initial years, Revitalizing Baltimore focused considerable effort on acquiring baseline environmental and social data on the Gwynns Falls watershed for use in a watershed plan. For the first three years of the program, 20 to 40 percent of the annual Revitalizing Baltimore appropriation was devoted to data collection and analysis efforts; since then, partner organizations, particularly resource management agencies, have taken responsibility for the bulk of this work.

Partner organizations collected existing satellite and aerial photos and acquired data from federal, state, and municipal agencies. These data were used to develop a geographic information system (GIS) and to produce maps of the ecological, social, and economic conditions in the Gwynns Falls watershed. They also gathered and mapped data on social and economic conditions, institutions and other cultural resources, vegetative conditions, stream quality, air quality, toxic spills, and soil hydrology. On the basis of these data, a priority area index was formulated to target areas within the watershed most in need of vegetative projects, and a social index was developed to mark different social conditions in the residential areas of the Gwynns Falls watershed.

American Forests, a Revitalizing Baltimore partner in 1995, calculated dollar values for the city's vegetation. Its analysis showed that the existing tree cover saves the city over $26 million in residential energy conservation, storm-water retention and peak storm-flow reduction, carbon sequestration and storage, air quality, and forest health. American Forests also ran simulations that showed that adding trees to the watershed would significantly reduce peak storm-water flow and runoff. In 1998, Revitalizing Baltimore completed the *Gwynns Falls Watershed Natural and Cultural Resources Atlas,* which presents much of the data collected by Revitalizing Baltimore partners.

These first efforts at data collection and analysis created some controversy on the Revitalizing Baltimore steering committee. Committee members debated which data and models were most appropriate, and some questioned the salience of technical GIS work to community forestry in general. One steering committee member objected to the analysis of the social data, claiming it inferred that poor, African American, inner-city residents degrade the environment more than rich, white suburbanites. Although the report in question simply showed a positive correlation between poverty and lack of vegetative cover and did not suggest that this relationship was due to residents' actions, the steering committee eventually decided not to use some of the data on social conditions in the watershed atlas because it might offend community members.

Yet the studies and atlas have proven useful as public policy and educational tools. A city planner, noting that government officials are impressed by numbers, said, "Bringing in a scientific way of looking at things has been really useful [to securing government support for the effort]. It's very important to be able to show the economic contribution of urban forestry, for example."

The atlas also provides useful and formerly unavailable data to citizens working in the Gwynns Falls watershed. Gwynns Falls Watershed Association volunteers take the atlas and a slide show to many community meetings to explain eco-logical conditions in the watershed and to recruit new members. In addition, Revitalizing Baltimore staff have drafted a Gwynns Falls urban forest manage-ment plan. Revitalizing Baltimore and Baltimore City agency staff, with techni-cal assistance from the Forest Service and the Maryland Forest Service, are be-ginning to develop a strategic urban forest assessment of the entire city of Baltimore.

Although the Revitalizing Baltimore steering committee has reduced its funding for data collection and research, its initial efforts, along with the ongo-ing collaboration among agencies and other organizations, have spawned a num-ber of related research efforts. Parks & People Foundation staff report that Revi-talizing Baltimore contributed significantly to the National Science Foundation's decision to designate Baltimore a long-term ecological research (LTER) site, the first of two urban sites and one of twenty-four LTER sites nationwide. The LTER designation in turn has helped stimulate extensive, coordinated research on Baltimore's ecosystems and the role of humans within those ecosystems.

Teaching Environmental Stewardship

Small hands-on environmental restoration and education projects are the third focal area for Revitalizing Baltimore and have consistently received a significant portion of the partnership's funding. These neighborhood restoration programs are intended to teach people to respect and be proud of their local environment and to see themselves as key components of healthy, safe neighborhoods. The en-vironmental education programs teach children and adolescents about the ecosystems they live in, environmental protection, and ecological restoration.

NEIGHBORHOOD RESTORATION PROGRAMS

Community Forestry, a program of the Parks & People Foundation, developed out of the Urban Resources Initiative's urban forestry program. It is focused at the neighborhood level, where community foresters work with local schools and com-munity groups, planting and maintaining trees on streets, in vacant lots, and along stream banks. Community foresters also help residents plan and undertake neighborhood gardens, murals, and other environmentally sensitive community improvement projects, often in areas that residents have selected. Local residents and community foresters worked side by side to clear an abandoned lot of rubble, trash, and pavement before preparing the soil and planting a community garden or park. In the words of Patricia Pyle, an early coordinator of the Community

Forestry Program, this work "is about . . . stewardship, helping people take pride in their community. . . . Many [people] don't realize they have a resource. They feel like they have been relegated to a place that has no value. Tree planting translates into caring about where they live, caring about their neighbors. It changes people's values." It also produces tangible results: a garden in a previously trash- and rubble-filled abandoned lot, rows of trees along a street previously devoid of vegetation, and cleaner, more accessible parks.

The Community Forestry Program has evolved over the years to emphasize local residents' responsibility for the projects and to train them to organize and implement their own projects. After finding that street trees and community gardens were being neglected, for example, Community Forestry instituted new guidelines to encourage home-owner stewardship of the trees and make each tree planting a community event. Landowners requesting tree plantings had to sign a form stating, "I will plant a tree"; Community Forestry staff members will not plant them without landowner participation. Furthermore, people who want trees must also convince at least six of their neighbors to request a tree, to ensure community interest in the planting and, it is hoped, long-term maintenance. Before tree planting, staff members attend a neighborhood meeting to present the project and stress the importance of resident participation. Tree Tribe, a Community Forestry program introduced in 1996, gives interested citizens sixteen hours of training in organizing and implementing their own community greening projects. Tree Tribe participants also receive nine training manuals covering different aspects of natural resource management and community organizing developed by Revitalizing Baltimore staff in 1994.

In addition to an increasing focus on volunteer training and development, Revitalizing Baltimore now funds neighborhood organizations to organize local residents and manage community forestry projects. In 1999, the steering committee created a community grants program to facilitate transfer of funds directly to community groups who manage projects to restore and maintain the urban environment. Programs of the Gwynns Falls Conservancy, a Revitalizing Baltimore partner, further illustrate the range of environmental restoration and community education efforts funded by Revitalizing Baltimore. The Gwynns Falls Conservancy's work focuses on "the shared culture between humans and nature" in the Gwynns Falls Park and the Windsor Hills Neighborhood. To this end, the conservancy helped the local community establish a one-hundred-acre "wildlife neighborhood," a sanctuary made up of land owned by a neighborhood group, private land, and the city, linked by a conservation trail used for environmental education. In Gwynns Falls Park, the conservancy has undertaken a natural resource inventory and resource report to "find out what's left of what was there." Through their Return of the Natives program, the conservancy is reestablishing native plants and animals in the Gwynns Falls Park and adjacent areas. It also organizes community stream cleanups in the park and, with youth groups, builds habitat gardens for birds and plants on small urban lots.

YOUTH EDUCATION PROGRAMS

The Parks & People Foundation created the KidsGrow program in 1994 as a summer environmental education program for elementary school–aged children. The first year, children were introduced to the environment through outdoor activities, including canoeing, hiking, and gardening, and learned basic natural resource management and urban survival skills. KidsGrow has since been expanded to include an after-school environmental education program for elementary and middle school children that is operated through the city's recreation centers. KidsGrow activities focus on connecting children to their local environment through a variety of hands-on activities. These include building wildlife and butterfly habitat gardens, sampling insects to test local streams for water quality, and making maple syrup from city trees.

Revitalizing Baltimore also supports four separate programs for high school–aged youth. Outward Bound's Communities Organizing to Restore the Environment (CORE) program, while including wilderness expeditions, focuses activities on environmental restoration projects in the youths' own communities. CORE is designed to empower youth and to teach leadership and job skills. The State Department of Natural Resources' internship program gives minority teenagers from urban areas training that could lead to future employment in natural resource management fields. The third program, Natural Connections, is a partnership program of the Irvine Natural Science Center and the Baltimore City School System that trains high school students to teach hands-on environmental science to younger children in their own neighborhoods. Civic Works, a program of the Baltimore Youth Service Corps, trains teens and organizes them into environmental restoration work groups.

THE PROGRAMS THAT REALLY REACH OUT TO PEOPLE

These neighborhood and educational programs are frequently called Revitalizing Baltimore's most outstanding achievement: "the programs that really reach out to people." When Revitalizing Baltimore's programs were centered in the Gwynns Falls watershed, Parks & People staff reported that, in neighborhoods outside of that watershed, "people were begging for KidsGrow." Staff also found that tree plantings and community restoration projects have helped build a sense of community and neighborhood pride and discouraged drug dealing. Community

Forestry's Tree Tribe program is credited with creating "a subculture of environmental activists who are interconnected and advocate in their own neighborhoods." In 2002, Revitalizing Baltimore reported that it involves over 3,000 volunteers annually in community forestry projects and has provided education to over 9,000 students and 650 adults. A growing number of publications, including curriculum guides and close to twenty training and how-to manuals, further extend Revitalizing Baltimore's outreach potential.

Integrating Social and Environmental Goals: Challenges and Rewards

Revitalizing Baltimore partners say that networking among organizations and coordinating all these watershed association, data acquisition and analysis, and environmental restoration and education efforts is one of the initiative's most important functions. This coordinating function has been costly in terms of both time and resources, but it is paying off in increased capacity and support for environmental restoration and stewardship within neighborhood organizations, state and federal agencies, local government, and within the Revitalizing Baltimore partnership itself.

The integration of data analysis efforts and community outreach activities was a major challenge for Revitalizing Baltimore steering committee members. Community organizers were frustrated by assertions from the "science and data people" that highly technical analyses are necessary to identify the best sites for community greening projects. As community workers, they believed that they should work where they saw the most need and where community members asked them to and said that the strategic planning process limited their ability to be responsive to the community. Technical analysts retorted that the "field people" were forgetting their mandate to develop an urban watershed plan looking at landscape-level processes. Some of the technical analysts objected to the extent to which neighborhood greening and educational programs were funded, saying that this implementation work should have been deferred until a management plan was completed.

Revitalizing Baltimore was also criticized for lacking significant citizen leadership. In 1997, a community organizer, observing that most Revitalizing Baltimore steering committee members lived outside of the city, said,

> Revitalizing Baltimore should be focusing all its energies on building organizational capacity within the community while they have federal money. It's frus-

trating that Revitalizing Baltimore doesn't seem to be achieving this. Outsiders are getting salaries to do this work, and community capacity is not increasing. There's a mismatch in the level of effort [as well]: They're doing high quality [data manipulation], but not a lot at the community level.

Others pointed out that in its first few years, Revitalizing Baltimore had nearly all-white leadership in a city with a population that is only 32 percent white.

Revitalizing Baltimore's steering committee has responded to these criticisms in part by shifting funding from Parks & People's programs to community-based organizations, particularly the three watershed associations. Additionally, nonprofit organizations that work directly with community groups have joined the Revitalizing Baltimore steering committee, providing more balance between public agency and community voices. By 2001, the number of minorities involved in Revitalizing Baltimore had increased to nearly 20 percent of the project leadership.

Years of meeting and coordinating efforts have also helped break down some of the tensions between community organizers and scientists. A watershed association coordinator, noting that relationship building takes time, observed in 2000, "We may not have meshed science and community activism yet, but at least we've made the scientists and the activists pay attention to each other."

Revitalizing Baltimore partners point to subtle but significant shifts in the organizational focus and attitudes of public and private organizations as one of the positive outcomes of their work. Revitalizing Baltimore has brought together a wide variety of government agencies, nonprofit organizations, and citizens groups that had never before worked together, and the process changed the way they all do business. Ties between Parks & People and the City Department of Recreation and Parks have been strengthened by KidsGrow and Community Forestry, whose staff work closely with agency staff and which are now housed in the Department of Recreation and Parks. State Department of Natural Resources staff members who had never worked in urban Baltimore now regularly assist Baltimore Department of Forestry and Community Forestry employees with neighborhood tree plantings. Initially, Department of Natural Resources foresters accustomed to working in rural Maryland were more than a little nervous about going into inner-city neighborhoods. Now, according to one steering committee member, these same foresters openly discuss urban cultural issues. "For agency employees, this social experience is totally new," he says. "Most resource management makes no mention of people."

Agency officials say that they are more conscious of the way their work may affect other activities within the watershed as well. As one agency representative puts it,

We're slowly getting converts to looking at the urban environment as a system, and seeing people as a part of that system. We're starting to see resource professionals take a systems approach and recognize that the resources they work with are linked to other things. . . . People are starting to come out of their boxes and start working with other disciplines.

These shifts in perception are now being manifest in new government policies. In 1997, the Department of Natural Resources created a state-level urban resources coordinating council, an action directly attributed to Revitalizing Baltimore. The agency also created a new advisory council to facilitate communication between the agency, other organizations, and citizens. In 2000, the State of Maryland was planning a new initiative to focus funding on urban green infrastructure, and the City of Baltimore was deeply involved in a neighborhood planning process that, according to one city planner, "has Revitalizing Baltimore written all over it." Parks & People staff say that a growing number of community development organizations in Baltimore are buying in to addressing natural resources as part of the package that once included only social and economic services—"green investment" is now part of their lexicon. Where once community organizers traveled to neighborhood meetings to introduce the concept of community gardens and street-tree plantings, Revitalizing Baltimore is now "swamped" by community organizations seeking funds to undertake community greening programs on their own as a first step to renewing deteriorated neighborhoods.

Future Plans

In 2002, eight years after its inception, Revitalizing Baltimore is exploring ways to institutionalize and expand its efforts to integrate research, policy, and community projects addressing urban ecosystem management. The steering committee has approached the Forest Service about forming a new urban watershed cooperative—the U.S. Forest Service Baltimore Urban Watershed Forestry Research and Demonstration Cooperative—to coordinate the efforts of citizens, community organizations, local natural resource managers, state and federal researchers and resource managers, and private researchers and practitioners.

Acknowledgments

Revitalizing Baltimore annual reports and articles by Sally Loomis, Paul Jahnige, Guy Hager, Gene Piotrowski, Shawn Dalton, Morgan Grove, and William Burch provided much background information for this chapter. Several members of the

Baltimore community and Revitalizing Baltimore steering committee members and project staff agreed to be interviewed for this study, including Marion Beddingfield, Forestry Division, Baltimore Department of Recreation and Parks; Michael Beer, Friends of Stony Run; Peter Conrad, Baltimore City Department of Planning; Shawn Dalton, Baltimore-Washington Regional Collaboratory; Jim Dicker, Forestry Division, Baltimore Department of Recreation and Parks; Fran Flanagan, Alliance for the Chesapeake Bay; Terry Galloway, Treemendous Maryland; Morgan Grove, U.S. Forest Service; Guy Hager, Parks & People Foundation; Rich Hersey, Herring Run Watershed Association; Dave Hollander, Gwynns Falls Watershed Association; Jeff Horan, Maryland Department of Natural Resources; Cheryl Kollin, American Forests; Lynn Kramer, Herring Run Watershed Association; Kim Lane, Maryland Save Our Streams; Steven Lee, Gwynns Falls Conservancy; Sally Loomis, Parks & People Foundation; Bob Neville, U.S. Forest Service; Don Outen, Baltimore County Department of Environmental Protection and Resource Management; Patricia Pyle, Community Forestry, Parks & People Foundation; Chris Ryer, The Trust for Public Land; Bryant Smith, Community Forestry, Parks & People Foundation; Bill Stack, Baltimore Department of Public Works; and Gren Whitman, Parks & People Foundation.

Part III

STEWARDING THE LAND

CHAPTER 9

"Kicking Dirt Together" in Colorado

COMMUNITY–ECOSYSTEM STEWARDSHIP AND THE PONDEROSA PINE FOREST PARTNERSHIP

Tim Richard and Ellen Stein

Like most forest management in the United States throughout the past century, forestry on the Colorado Plateau has been synonymous with fire suppression and logging—with ironic, if not altogether catastrophic, results for native ecosystems and forest-dependent communities. Once, wildfire burned across the forest floor, maintaining open stands of large trees. Logging of the biggest trees, coupled with the U.S. Forest Service's policy of fire suppression, resulted in a forest devoid of the big trees prized by industry and choked with the small-diameter trees that, in addition to generating dangerous fire conditions, limited economic value.

In this context of a degraded and fire-prone forest, locals began to explore how to restore both the declining economy and the deteriorating forest ecosystem. Under the auspices of the Ponderosa Pine Forest Partnership, Montezuma County commissioners, representatives from the timber industry and the Forest Service, a forest ecologist, and a rural sociologist devised an experiment in "restoration forestry" that, they hoped, would demonstrate how community industry and stewardship could restore a small piece of the forest ecosystem through local labor and planning. The experimental project was designed to thin the small-diameter trees enough so that fire could be reintroduced as a natural tool for forest health and to rebuild a diminished forest economy based on small-scale harvesting and manufacturing.

If felling big trees has been a Western archetype where man's dominance of nature is cast in heroic dimensions, restoration forestry may be an emerging prototype cultivated as its tonic. Based on the recognition that sound forest management must be accountable to wildlife and forest values, restoration forestry extends human responsibility. In so doing, it begins to shift the Western drama from one of dominance and exploitation to another where care and collaboration are major themes.

According to the Montezuma County commissioners, the Ponderosa Pine Forest Partnership's collaborative approach to public lands resource management was mostly a matter of "common sense." But this experiment may, over time, also be one

191

of the measures of the West's capacity to reinvent itself. By acknowledging past mistakes, affirming diverse and multiple interests, and accepting accountability to local people as well as inhabited and wild places, the Ponderosa Pine experiment may be a model for other communities that are grappling with issues of environmental and social revival.

Since 1993, the Ponderosa Pine Forest Partnership (PPFP) in southwestern Colorado has been engaged in an experiment to address ecosystem health and the loss of forest-based businesses. One hundred years of fire suppression and high-grade logging in the 1920s and 1930s has resulted in small-diameter trees too dense for ecological health and of too poor quality to command real commercial value.

Montezuma County commissioners approached San Juan National Forest leaders with their concerns over these issues and found the Forest Service not only willing to listen but also offering to share decision-making power to solve problems. Taking a different approach than some county supremacy movement[1] leaders in the West, the commissioners chose a cooperative rather than adversarial approach to working with local and regional Forest Service staff. Local members of the Colorado Timber Industry Association, the Office of Community Services at Fort Lewis College in Durango, ecologist Dr. William Romme, and others eventually joined the Forest Service in addressing challenges to community and ecological well-being. As partners in the PPFP, they experimented with the use of the local timber industry as a forest restoration and management tool on the San Juan National Forest and adjacent private land.

Despite philosophical differences and diverse expectations, partners sought common ground, funding, technical expertise, and other resources to overcome obstacles to their demonstration project. They downplayed differing social, economic, and ecological views and experiences in order to try out new harvesting methods; adapted Forest Service administrative procedures; developed new silvicultural procedures adapted to current forest conditions; agreed to work to develop new wood products out of historically undesirable small-diameter timber; and, through monitoring and evaluation, documented and learned from the results of research and silvicultural prescription experimentation.

By addressing how people can preserve their identity even while participating in and adapting to inevitable change, the PPFP attempted to set a tone for the collaborative resolution of problems. Face-to-face dialogue has shown to be a positive avenue for sharing knowledge and values and for building relationships that can develop a sustainable community ecosystem stewardship process for forests and communities:

> We need to see that adversarial, winner-take-all, showdown political
> decision making is a way we defeat ourselves. Our future starts when

we begin honoring the dreams of our enemies while staying true to
our own.

—William Kittredge, 1992

Angry as one may be at what heedless men have done and still do
to a noble habitat, one cannot be pessimistic about the West. This
is the native home of hope. When it fully learns that cooperation,
not rugged individualism, is the quality that most characterizes
and preserves it, then it will have achieved itself and outlived its
origins. Then it has a chance to create a society to match its
scenery.

—Wallace Stegner, 1969

A Dialogue of Discovery

On July 17, 1998, a caravan of vans and pickup trucks arrived at a place in the
ponderosa pine forest near Dolores, Colorado, called Ormiston Point to see the
results of a demonstration restoration forestry timber harvest. The 108 acres had
been harvested in accord with a new silviculture prescription being tested by participants in a five-year, collaborative effort known as the PPFP. Many of the original "pine zone partners," as they are referred to, were present that day, along with
others who showed a mixture of support and criticism for the project. The field
trip was one of a series held since 1995 to share various project accomplishments,
explore challenges, and present new information gathered from research.

Standing in a circle in one of the newly created openings in the pine forest
canopy, the visitors heard Dr. William Romme, then professor and fire ecologist
from nearby Fort Lewis College in Durango, describe his study of the function
of fire in the ponderosa pine ecosystem. His study contributed to the development of the harvest prescription, the results of which the group was witnessing
that day.

In 1994, Romme had contracted as a consultant with the San Juan National
Forest to conduct "range of natural variability" studies in which he and core-
searchers sought to identify the kinds, number, and duration of disturbances that
have shaped ponderosa pine landscapes. His studies provided the partnership
with a fairly realistic picture of the region's pine forests before 1870 when Euro-
American settlers began grazing livestock, logging, and suppressing wildfire.

This "reference condition" contrasts sharply with ponderosa pine forest structure and function today. The landscape, or large parts of it, was meadowlike, dotted

by groves of pines of varying ages and sizes but dominated by old and large trees. Fire caused these stand arrangements to form by burning out the more vulnerable trees. An average of forty to fifty large, fire-resistant trees per acre was once common, Romme explained, but now more than three hundred small trees commonly crowd each acre. This crowding weakens stands to disease and insect infestation and puts them at risk of catastrophic wildfire that can be far more damaging than it was 150 years ago, when an area burned as often as every fifteen years. Gambel oak, more common than it was before settlement, together with an accumulation of pine needles, smothers most pine seedlings from sprouting so that little ponderosa regeneration occurs.

The goal of the demonstration harvest project was to thin small-diameter trees enough so that fire could be safely reintroduced to serve as a natural control of insects, disease, and catastrophic wildfire and to improve wildlife habitat. The prescription lay at the core of relationships that evolved between partners and others in the community, relationships that increasingly focused on the significance of a community joining land management institutions in redefining public land stewardship.

The conversation during the Ormiston Point field visit was a mixture of scholarly debate, disagreement, and reserved judgment as the value of restoration forestry was broached and the science and motivations for the new way of harvesting were scrutinized. Mike Preston, director of Montezuma County's Federal Lands Program, described the discussion that day as "creative tension, [in which] everybody got to have their say and be heard, and where ideas spurred by diverse perspectives contributed to everyone's thinking."

Romme's research provided empirical evidence of forest conditions and problems and a cause around which pine forest partners could rally. San Juan National Forest leaders desired "good objective science to apply to serious questions about forest conditions," planner Jim Powers explained (personal communication, July 23, 1998).

Dolores Ranger District forester Phil Kemp, present that day at Ormiston Point, was charged with applying Romme's recommended silvicultural prescription on the ground. Kemp spoke from an adaptive management philosophy, saying that restoration forestry is based on values distinct from those that have historically driven the timber industry and the Forest Service's timber program. "The Forest Service is responsible for more than timber economics," Kemp said. The agency must also be responsible to wildlife and other vital features of a healthy forest for which, on an ecological time scale and within a range of natural variability, benefits would outweigh the short-term costs. "The community just needs to decide which values it will choose to guide its actions and spend its money," he said.

Although Romme and Kemp were looking at the project and its issues from their distinct perspectives, they were touching on a common idea, namely, where the local community decides which values will guide its actions and comes together on a vision for both the forest ecosystem as well as the human community.

Barry Rhea, a local environmental consultant, asked, "If fire is such an essential restoration component of the pine prescription, what will happen if the Forest Service cannot introduce fire to properly treat the thinned-out lands and complete the two-part prescription?" Of the 550 acres harvested during three years, only 150 were treated with fire. In 1998, as many as 4,000 acres of restoration units could be harvested, which would push the burning crews even further behind. For various reasons, such as lack of funds, trained personnel, and climactic conditions, the Forest Service fire crews had not met the goals to burn harvest sites. Kemp later postponed offering restoration timber sales until burning could catch up with completed harvests. He explained, "I was confident at first that the burning would get done, but then I saw two years go by without burning taking place. I've got to give credit to Barry, because he saw [this backlog] coming early on" (personal communication, November 4, 1998).

Colorado Division of Wildlife biologist Scott Wait reminded partners of the need to listen to the biggest "partner" of all—the land—which can heal itself on its own terms and in its own time if allowed to do so. He feared that the initial optimism surrounding the PPFP led too many people to jump on a "bandwagon cure-all." Wait argued that wildlife issues are complex. "Does the fact that there are birds in the new Wal-Mart parking lot mean it's a good prescription?" he asked. It took a century for the forest to get the way it is, and it could take at least another century to see if habitat would improve, he concluded. The promise did not seem to be 100 percent supported by the facts, he said, and it is the facts we should base our actions on, along with "a sharing of our values."

Doug Ragland, who harvested the small-diameter timber at Ormiston Point and followed his father, Bill, a thirty-year veteran logger, in the family business, claimed that cutting more large-diameter trees does not threaten forest health. However, both he and his father still saw the partnership and the harvest of small-diameter trees as a chance to help the local economy and the forest ecology while earning a living. An early participant in the partnership, Bill also believed that the partnership was an opportunity to mend relationships with the Forest Service (Stein 1996).

Dr. Dennis Lynch of Colorado State University's College of Natural Resources also attended the field trip. Lynch led a comprehensive study of the project's harvest cost-and-profit efficiency and researched products and markets for small-diameter wood. His study, which complemented Romme's range of natural variability studies and ecological monitoring, focused on the question of making the project economically viable for the Forest Service and loggers.

Three variables would determine the future of the pine forest partnership, he explained—a consistent wood supply must be ensured at a reasonable cost with viable markets. He shared the message during an interview in 1996: "To make the economics work either the price paid by loggers for material from the Forest Service has to fall; the price paid for harvested products has to rise; the efficiencies within the system need to be achieved to reduce operating costs; or additional markets need to be found." In the final report on his economic study, Lynch wrote,

> This forest restoration project incorporated five sale units covering a total of 492.6 acres and the removal of 31,163 trees (63.3 per acre) for 6,075.8 tons of sawlogs, 7,254.71 tons of waferwood, and 1,047.15 tons of other products such as posts and poles, pulpwood and pine excelsior. This resulted in a total profit to the logger of $3,533.67. That is a profit of 0.81 percent (less than one percent) on gross revenues of $434,645.54. This approximates a break-even situation and while this is better than suffering a loss, it is hardly a model for a sustainable business venture. Usually, it is appropriate to see profit and risk allowances of 10 to 15 percent for this type of work. Break-even projects will never result in the investments necessary to improve efficiencies and develop new products. (Lynch et al. 1998, 14)

Finding markets for high-grade saw timber is not a problem, but finding markets for small-diameter material is, and hauling to mills more than fifty miles from the harvest site able to process small logs is too costly. The small logging and milling business owners associated with the project have hopes of acquiring equipment to be more efficient and to reduce costs, but they say they will not risk investing in equipment until they receive a predictable supply of timber (Stein 1996).

The historically conventional method of selective logging in which the largest and most valuable trees were removed had resulted in stands of small-diameter trees too dense for ecological health or for a steady supply of marketable timber. The San Juan National Forest timber program, affected by changing public values that placed environmental protection over commodity use of the forest, reduced its sales of large-diameter saw timber. Available supply was further reduced because the Forest Service offered timber sales that loggers did not bid for, because not enough valuable timber was included in what was increasingly unmarketable small-diameter timber. In addition, appeals from conservation activists organizations made it more difficult for the Forest Service to reach a point where they could even offer a sale for bidding.

The conversation that day at Ormiston Point showed that diverse members of the community talk about restoration forestry despite their different backgrounds, experiences, and viewpoints. When someone described the partnership as a collaboration, Dan Randolph said that he did not think it was, as collaboration to him meant equality and consensus in decision making, which he believed the partnership had yet to achieve. The great opportunity offered by the partnership is "dialogue," he said.

Indeed, the PPFP was creating a venue for dialogue where diverse views informed activities and guided interaction that reflected the visions and values of the region's inhabitants. The Ormiston Point field trip suggests that the direction such dialogue seemed to be leading participants is a far cry from what relationships looked like in 1992 before the PPFP formed.

A Historical Context

Since the early 1990s, southwestern Colorado's rural communities had struggled to absorb the increasingly worrisome effects of population growth on the economic, social, cultural, and ecological environments. The 1.8-million-acre San Juan National Forest had been at the center of debate over resource use and management as communities and the Forest Service tried to adjust to accommodate the tourism and recreation industries that increasingly were competing for access to the public lands. Communities that have historically relied on the area's public lands for natural resource extraction have resisted this change in economic development and public land use; generations of farmers, miners, ranchers, and loggers in Montezuma and all nearby counties have counted on access to the region's plentiful public land for their livelihoods.

Forty percent of Montezuma County is public land. The San Juan National Forest makes up 19 percent, the Bureau of Land Management 14 percent, and state land 7 percent. The Ute Mountain Ute tribal reservation covers 32 percent, and the remaining 28 percent is privately owned (Stein 1996). Twenty-three thousand people inhabit the county's 1.3 million acres of high desert and mesas in the south, its mountains in the northeast, and its three main population centers—Cortez, the county's largest town and governing seat, and the smaller towns of Mancos and Dolores.

Montezuma County overlaps the San Juan National Forest's southwestern corner, where Dolores nestles amidst 180,000 acres of ponderosa pine forests. Just down the hill was once the largest timber mill in Colorado, the McPhee Mill. Ponderosa pine was processed there beginning in 1917, but the area had been logged since the 1870s. The mill burned down during the 1940s and was never rebuilt.

Still, big-timber harvesting continued past midcentury (Stein 1996). In 1992, 517 people were employed directly or indirectly in the industry. Although mining, which logging supported, waned in the early 1900s, logging on the San Juan National Forest continued and increased drastically after World War II.

Although the amount of timber harvested after 1972 dropped from 76 million to 12 million board feet by 1993, that drop was not only because of fewer big trees but also because America's values were shifting toward environmental preservation rather than resource extraction from public lands. Many newcomers relocating to the area added a new spectrum of experiences, backgrounds, and values to the ranching, logging, farming, and mining perspectives that have characterized the region since European settlement. By 1996, agriculture, which includes timber industry activities, was less than 3 percent of the local economy in 1996. The service industry has become the state's largest-grossing industry. Service jobs, despite offering the lowest pay, are increasingly dominant.

The remains of the McPhee Mill now lie beneath McPhee Reservoir, a Bureau of Reclamation project constructed nearly two decades ago, primarily to satisfy water-rights treaty obligations to the nearby Ute Mountain Ute tribe. The reservoir is now a popular boating and camping attraction.

Making The Choice

In my lifetime I have seen things go from the ridiculous to the absurd . . . here's a chance where we can get reasonable.

—Charlie Mitchell, president,
Western Excelsior Corporation, Mancos, 1996

Finding common ground rests on the basic belief that ecosystem-oriented planning and decision-making, and efforts to address resource management reforms, as well as activities related to sustainability, multiple use, and local community futures, must move forward collaboratively within local social landscapes, rather than be imposed in a downward fashion by central authority.

—Sam Burns, director, Fort Lewis College,
Office of Community Services, Durango, 1995

In 1993, Montezuma County Commission Chair Tom Colbert initiated the Federal Lands Program. His motivation (and that of his fellow commissioners) was a desire to improve relationships with public land managers, reduce the risk of wildfire, and salvage the few remaining wood product businesses. The commissioners had watched the unproductive county supremacy efforts of Catron County, New Mexico, and Nye County, Nevada. They wanted to do something productive. One of the first efforts taken on by the newly formed Federal Lands

Program was a meeting in the pine-forested mountains near Dolores, Colorado, with San Juan National Forest Dolores District ranger Mike Znerold, who was concerned about forest health from the emerging perspective of ecosystem management. Mike Preston and the Colorado Timber Industry Association founder and president, Dudley Millard, were also there to "kick dirt" and talk about the declining local timber industry and forest health.

Preston had learned some of the legalities of county standing and participation in federal land issues while he assisted Tom Colbert in establishing Montezuma County's Federal Lands Program, which aims to "maximize meaningful community input into federal land planning, policy and decision making" (Preston 1993). He shared an idea with the commissioners before they met with Znerold:

> If local communities are going to affect the federal-lands process, local governments need to define the values and interests of the communities they represent, using a combination of factual analysis and open community input. This analysis and input is the basis for formulating policies and plans for protecting and enhancing community values and interests, giving the federal agencies something tangible to respond to. (Preston 1993)

Preston also helped Sam Burns, a sociologist at Fort Lewis College, found the Office of Community Services (OCS) in 1978 to help community governments and organizations find and utilize community development resources. Burns currently serves as director of research at OCS, and Preston is the organization's associate director. Their role became central to the PPFP, which Preston envisioned as having the potential for "transforming polarizing encounters between the 'Traditional West' and the 'New West' into something creative and constructive for people and the landscapes that sustain them" (Preston 1993). Colbert and fellow commissioners decided on a collaborative approach to working with the Forest Service. When asked why, Colbert, who was elected to the commission in 1984 after leading a grassroots fight to block the dumping of uranium mill tailings on his Mancos Valley ranch, replied, "Common sense" (Stein 1996).

In 1992, after deciding to take what Preston described as a "broad-based, collaborative, problem-solving approach" to public land issues, Montezuma County submitted a proposal to the U.S. Department of Agriculture's Rural Community Assistance Program. It received a $25,000 Economic Diversification grant to fund the partnership, which began as an agreement between Montezuma County, San Juan National Forest, and the Colorado Timber Industry Association. Preston, through the county's Federal Lands Program, coordinated activities for the pilot demonstration project until he turned the role of field coordinator over to Carla Garrison in 1995. Garrison, a Colorado State University graduate student, was recruited as an AmeriCorps member to research the state of the local timber industry. Describing their roles, Preston has said, "The county buying half my time was a critical step . . . and if Carla wasn't out there day-to-day, working with the partners, I don't think we would have made it" (Stein 1996).

Objectives listed in the proposal focused on "developing desired future conditions" in areas on the west side of the San Juan National Forest using an "interdisciplinary planning team and public involvement process." According to the proposal, the project would do the following:

- Demonstrate that a healthy ecosystem and healthy economy are compatible goals
- Reduce hazards of insect and disease infestation and catastrophic fire
- Create the opportunity for the reemergence of mature and old-growth pine along with enhanced variety of sizes, ages, and stand structures in what is currently a monoculture of stagnated second growth
- Increase livestock and wildlife habitat and wildlife species in the pine zone
- Provide a commercial approach to thinning second-growth pine
- Assist industry in transitioning to small-diameter logs and create the prospect of sustainable commercial pine harvests
- Demonstrate a process of scientific analysis coupled with broad-based public input
- Set the stage for collaboration between the Forest Service and community partners to link sustainable communities to healthy sustainable ecosystems

As many as thirty individuals from local, state, and federal government, as well as academic institutions, private industry, and private landowners, became involved in the partnership. But by the spring of 1995, despite the relationship building that had occurred since 1992, the partnership still had not triggered improvements in the timber sale program, forest health, or the local timber industry. When Romme was ready to present the pine prescription and began recommending reintroduction of fire, the community and potential partners were invited to discuss the possibilities in a May 1995 workshop in Durango. In this so-called Vital Links workshop—considered a turning point in the partnership's evolution—participants examined such topics as sale preparation, tree harvest methods, and small-diameter products. Most of them committed themselves to further actions, based largely on Romme's findings, which suggested possibilities for working together. Environmentalist members of the community who entered the dialogue publicly for the first time during the workshop pledged to participate in monitoring efforts associated with the demonstration project.

But a series of obstacles within the Forest Service's rules and regulations proved problematic. The $100 per thousand board feet the Forest Service offered was prohibitive for local logging businesses and in no way reflected the value of small-diameter raw materials. Loggers were paying half that for the more easily marketable saw timber that they could cut from private land.

By midsummer, it looked like the demonstration project would not proceed. Tom Thompson, then the Forest Service Region 2 deputy regional forester in Denver, pointed out the "Administrative Use Study" option in the Federal Code of Regulations, which he had recently discovered, that allowed a waiver of some regulations if the total value of a timber sale fell under $10,000.

An "Administrative Use Study" contract was soon written, allowing on-the-ground activity to begin in August 1995. Acting as broker to ensure that local loggers and millers received the work, Montezuma County purchased the timber and subcontracted the sale of 1.2 million board feet on five sites, totaling 490 acres, to three local, family-owned logging businesses—the first time that was ever done as far as anyone knew. The three-part "Administrative Use Study" required the following:

• An ecological report examining the effects of harvesting on the ecosystem, which was key to the demonstration project prescription
• A biomass study and subsequent report, conducted by the NEOS Corporation of Denver, to determine the feasibility of mixing wood from the projects with coal to fire power plants in nearby northern New Mexico
• A logging production report in which Colorado State University professor Dennis Lynch and Kathy Jones (a subcontracted Durango-based private forestry consultant) conducted a cost-efficiency analysis of the harvesting methods used by the loggers at the sites and researched potential product development and markets for small-diameter wood

Because the biomass report, done by the NEOS Corporation in Denver, showed poor returns on investment, power plant owners in New Mexico declined to participate. But the harvesting, production, and monitoring studies remained central to the PFPP's evolution. Forester Phil Kemp began developing Romme's prescription for application once the administrative study was arranged. However, when he and fellow pine forest partners tried to implement the project, it became evident that the usual timber sale procedures were going to be barriers. The problem of measuring volume during cruising operations raised questions of how to price small-diameter trees. Marking crews could not implement the pine prescription by using standard methods of cruising, marking, and measuring the amount of wood fiber and then separating the saw timber from the lower-quality, small-diameter wood fiber to assess the prices for each. No existing pricing structure dealt adequately with what had previously been unmarketable wood.

Despite a series of obstacles in Forest Service administrative procedures and pricing, developing small-diameter timber products and markets, and securing a steady supply, Kemp, and especially field coordinator Carla Garrison, continued to take a problem-solving approach. Lynch remembers a lot of "headaches and a lot of work by Carla to keep the project moving [through] some rough moments" (personal communication, fall 1998). The Forest Service was not easily motivated or enthusiastic at first, and Ragland and Sons Logging and the Stonertop Mill "did all the hard work and took all the risks," he said.

Despite the headaches, Lynch and his fellow partners can boast of many advances made through the PPFP effort. In July 1998, the Forest Service's national headquarters gave the San Juan National Forest a special allowance to reduce its appraised prices for small-diameter wood from $100 to $20 to $40 per thousand board feet. "We've finally gotten over the hurdle of pricing, since the Washington office appraisal specialist came out and gave us the go ahead to do what we've been trying to do for years," Kemp said (personal communication, November 4, 1998). Prices for small-diameter raw material, or "products other than logs," for making waferboard have also risen, making a break-even situation in restoration harvesting more feasible. Between 1997 and 2001, much of the very small, low-value material harvested in restoration efforts on the San Juan as well as neighboring forests went to produce waferboard at a Louisiana Pacific mill in Olathe, Colorado. That mill has permanently closed its doors, therefore eliminating a useful outlet for restoration by-products.

Conclusions

The PPFP has been about people struggling to overcome barriers and build relationships to care for their community and the national forest. Two crucial and complementary characteristics were integrated in the partnership in the dialogue about community and forest sustainability: a reliance on science to guide restoration activities and a respect for and ability to talk about values. As of the summer of 2002, nearly 50,000 acres of the 180,000-acre pine zone have been analyzed in terms of their health and productivity. Of those acres, only 7,700 have actually been treated with a combination of restoration-type treatments. Forester Phil Kemp has continued to choose a "go-slow" approach. He intimately knows the condition of all the acres he intends to manage. Only one mill remains in Montezuma County dedicated to the use of pine: Stonertop Mill in Dolores. Price reductions in 1998 triggered bids on restoration sales, but the small restoration program has yet to grow new businesses or even sustain more than one locally. Some may still question how beneficial restoration forestry is for forest health and community economic development. It seems reasonable to conclude, however, that the partnership has shown that cooperation, collaboration, and communication among partners is more valuable to the forest and the community than adversarial approaches to forest management.

The fact that environmental community representatives are participating in what Preston referred to as "creative tension" is, in itself, a notable accomplishment. More people have been included in a process focusing on the economic, ecological, cultural, and social features of rural, western life. Over time, even environmentalist criticism had evolved. Dan Randolph, who had described his role in 1995 as a "skeptical watchdog," advocated during the Ormiston Point field trip "cautious optimism." In 1992, even if environmentalists had been invited to meet with Znerold, Millard, and Colbert, they probably would not have accepted. Given their suspicion of the historical relationship between agency and industry, they preferred to remain critical observers and withhold judgment until they felt comfortable that the Forest Service and industry sought sustainable-harvest methods that reflected the values of the broader community. Nevertheless, the venue for sincere and open dialogue, made possible through the PPFP, eased the strained relationships between everyone with a stake in the forest and the community. Partners recognized that, because of lack of money and personnel within the Forest Service, salvaging the dying timber industry was the only available tool to thin small-diameter stands so that fire could be returned to its place in the range of natural variability.

The role of the environmental community in the partnership is still developing. The partnership has sought ways to empower skeptics to lead the way to solutions rather than placing the responsibility on the partners to fail or succeed while they look on. When community environmental activists insisted that monitoring be done, they were asked to assume a monitoring role. When Colorado Division of Wildlife biologists said that the first few harvests destroyed too much elk and turkey cover, Kemp adjusted subsequent harvests to accommodate their concerns. In addition, the PFPP raised funds to support a wildlife committee charged with identifying key research parameters. The committee, made up of representatives from the Division of Wildlife, Forest Service, and Bureau of Land Management, has identified big game, Meriam's turkey, Abert's squirrel, and migratory songbirds as indicator species. Ongoing research and monitoring has been commissioned in all areas except for turkey.

In 2001, the PPFP commissioned an outside "ecological review" of the restoration prescription. An assessment team was assembled and facilitated by Dr. Joyce Berry of the Department of Forest Sciences at Colorado State University. All members were professionals from outside the PPFP. The team made a number of adaptive recommendations. In general, they suggested that the partnership must increase the scale of activity in order to ever achieve notable landscape restoration. The team also found flaws in the previously established wildlife monitoring program. An advisory team recommended a more holistic approach to monitoring habitat diversity, not individual species. The full report, titled "An Ecological Assessment of Ponderosa Pine Forest Restoration Treatments in Southwestern Colorado," is available from Montezuma County (Berry 2002; Preston and Garrison 1999; Richard and Burns 1999).

Ecologist Romme has pointed out more than once the principles that he believes the partnership and adaptive management nurture. As he stated in a 1995 interview,

> I am keenly aware that we're doing some new things, and I know we may not get the results we want, but that's okay. We can go in and revise our approach. The good thing is that we have a mechanism to make it a success. We should act with an absence of dogma and not be afraid of showing our failures as well as our successes. (Richard 1995, 17)

By the summer of 1999, the area's local, small-business loggers had yet to see enough profit and a consistent supply of small-diameter material to consider reinvesting in restoration logging. Dennis Lynch recommended that 40 percent of restoration sales should be higher-value saw timber to encourage the local timber industry to invest in restoration forestry. However, without consistent supply, increased markets, and product diversification for small-diameter timber, affordable pricing alone cannot secure small-logging-business confidence and participation.

The challenge of broader community interest and participation remains crucial. Sam Burns and Mike Preston have used the PPFP as a springboard to broaden the discussion of community stewardship into a larger audience of community leaders and community development professionals. Organizers and cheerleaders Mike Preston and Carla Harper, along with Phil Kemp and Dennis Lynch, have perhaps focused hardest on bringing in traditional community people as credible sources of local knowledge and experience in the landscape. Vital contributors Preston, Harper, Kemp, and Lynch continue to move among partners to keep them informed, going to meetings, identifying questions, making comments, sharing concerns, encouraging honest and open communication, and "kicking dirt together."

Such partnership efforts may simply require the right set of personalities. Forest Service Planning Team leader Thurman Wilson said that "one thing I am not sure about is how much of the partnership is being able to come up with a list of principles and how much of the success is attributable to the personalities of those involved. I think it is a mix of both" (Stein 1996). As Preston said,

> Finding common ground among diverse interests is challenging. The human dynamic is [something] people need to study up on. A lot of Forest Service staff

need to abandon how they were schooled [to believe that there is] just one right answer and [they] need to think of things as an interrelated system.

Romme and Lynch often reiterate that the most significant guiding management principle is that "ecology drives economy." Restoration of the forest is the basic purpose of such projects. The PPFP story suggests that a sense of community can also be restored in the process.

While the partnership does not meet formally on a regular basis, it is still alive. Current activities involve establishing a long-term monitoring protocol for all ponderosa pine management in the San Juan National Forest.

Both a history of the PPFP written in 1999 and the "Assessment of Ecological Prescription" report are available by contacting Montezuma County at charper@co.montezuma.co.us or by calling 970-565-6061.

Note

1. The county supremacy movement, also referred to as the Sagebrush Rebellion II, is characterized primarily by government and economic leaders in a number of rural communities taking action to subsume federal control of lands managed by the U.S. Department of Agriculture Forest Service or Bureau of Land Management by passing ordinances making it illegal for federal agency staff members to do their job on federal lands that fall within county boundaries. Nye County, Nevada, and Catron County, New Mexico, gained notoriety by passing such ordinances during the early 1990s. At times, relationships among ranching and logging interests (mostly longtime residents) and agency staffers, as well as local environmental activists, became tense and even threatening the safety of some.

References

Berry, Joyce, et al. 2002. "An Ecological Assessment of Ponderosa Pine Forest Restoration Treatments in Southwestern Colorado." Cortez, Colo.: Montezuma County Federal Lands Program, January.

Garrison, Carla. 1998. "Ponderosa Pine Forest Partnership Winter 1998 Update." Cortez, Colo.: Montezuma County Federal Lands Program.

Lynch, Dennis, William K. Romme, Phil Kemp, and Carla Garrison. 1998. "Summary Report for the Ponderosa Pine Forest Partnership, Montezuma County, Colorado: Ecology and Economics of Ponderosa Pine Forest Restoration on the Mancos-Dolores District of the San Juan National Forest." Cortez, Colo.: Montezuma County Federal Lands Program.

Preston, Michael. 1993. "County Government, Federal Lands and Economic Development: A Journey of Discovery." Paper presented at the Western Interstate Regional Conference, Phoenix, May 13.

Preston, Mike, and Carla Garrison. 1999. "The Ponderosa Pine Forest Partnership: Community Stewardship in Southwestern Colorado." Cortez, Colo.: Montezuma County Federal Lands Program.

Richard, Tim. 1995. "Timber on a Tightrope: A Demonstration Project to Reshape the Future." *Inner Voice* 7, no. 4 (July/August): 16–17.

Richard, Tim, and Sam Burns. 1999. "The Ponderosa Pine Forest Partnership: Forging New Relationships to Restore a Forest: A Case Study." Durango, Colo.: Fort Lewis College Office of Community Services, April.

Stein, Ellen. 1996. "Community-Based Resource Management: Caring for the Land and Serving People." Master's thesis, Tufts University.

CHAPTER 10

Western Upper Peninsula Forest Improvement District

ADDING VALUE TO A WORKING LANDSCAPE

Mary Mitsos

A century after lumberjacks "shaved the countryside the way a razor shaves a man's chin," Michigan's landscape was a relative stubble of small-diameter northern hardwoods and conifers. In an effort to boost the flagging economic conditions through improved resource management, several private citizens and members of the Michigan state legislature traveled to Finland, an ancestral home to some that was also renowned for its use of forest resources for economic development. There they met with a consulting firm and contracted for a study of the forest resources to enhance economic opportunities in Michigan's western Upper Peninsula.

The study resulted in the Michigan state legislature passing the Forest Improvement Act in 1980 to create forest improvement districts for improved management of forest lands and better utilization and marketing of local forest resources. A number of forest product companies felt that the act put them at a disadvantage and opposed state funding, arguing that establishing special districts was akin to socialism. Nevertheless, planning for the districts progressed, and in April 1987 the Natural Resources Commission of Michigan approved the first district—the Western Upper Peninsula Forest Improvement District.

After more than a decade of operation, over 1,000 landowners have voluntarily joined the district, and despite their early disapproval, some industrial owners joined the district as well. Members agree that the district has significantly improved the forest's growing capacity on members' lands, increased the utilization of small-diameter trees, and created jobs. While providing land management services to landowners, the creation of the district has encouraged members to hold and manage rather than sell their land. But while they have created opportunities for landholders and, perhaps, staved off development, environmentalists still argue that the district focuses too much on timber management and not enough on other forest values. A broad-based regional ethic and capacity for stewardship of the mixed northern forests will take time to develop.

In the meantime, the most significant but least measurable benefit of the district is the increased potential for small forest landowners to hold on to their lands. Pressures to develop the western Upper Peninsula are increasing, and unless forest landowners can gain a living by managing and caring for trees, the pressure for selling to developers may prove too much to resist. By providing land management services to forest landowners, the district offers members a chance to steward rather than to sell their land.

> Michigan a century ago was one magnificent forest, and even as recently as the Civil War it had hardly been touched. But then the lumberjacks went to work, and they shaved the countryside the way a razor shaves a man's chin. Where there had been wilderness, boom lumber towns sprang up, with rickety railroad lines threading their way back into the hills. In the springtime, every stream was clogged with logs, with lumberjacks scampering across the treacherous shifting carpet with peavey and cant hook, mounds of sawdust rising beside the busy mills, and a mill town with 1,200 inhabitants normally supported from twelve to twenty saloons. . . . For a time Saginaw was the greatest lumber city in the world, then Muskegon had the title, and then some other place; fresh-cut boards were stacked in endless piles by the railroad sidings or the lakeside wharves . . . and then, all of a sudden, it was all over. The lumber was gone, the mills were dismantled, the booming cities and towns lapsed into drowsiness, storefronts were boarded up-and the razor which had done all of this shaving had left a stubble of stumps like a frowzy three-day beard across thousands of square miles. Some towns died entirely, some almost died, and the endless whine of the gang saws became quiet forever.[1]

Flying over the Upper Peninsula of Michigan today, the rolling forested landscape seems to go on forever, but from the ground one notices that the old-growth giants are mostly gone. Dense stands of small-diameter trees, primarily northern hardwoods with some aspen, birch, and conifers, blanket 80 percent of the landscape. Public and private industrial forests make up 70 percent of the total forest cover; the remaining 30 percent is owned by nonindustrial private forest landowners of which approximately one-quarter is in absentee ownership.

Bounded by the shores of Lake Superior north of Wisconsin, the Upper Peninsula has a long history of economic and social isolation, an isolation that is particularly pronounced in Houghton, Baraga, Iron, Ontonagon, Gogebic, and Keweenaw Counties in the western half of the peninsula. The isolation of the region has its roots in the political formation of the state. In 1835, the territory petitioned for statehood, and Congress separated the area known as the "Toledo

Strip" (the land along the shores of Lake Erie that includes the city of Toledo, Ohio, today) and added, as consolation, the land that is now known as the Upper Peninsula, a "wasteland"[2] according to Michigan's inhabitants at that time. Since Michigan gained its statehood in 1837, the Upper Peninsula has remained a sparsely populated, isolated region with limited employment despite the area's wealth of iron, copper, trees, fish, wildlife, and natural beauty. Like many rural areas rich in natural resources, poverty and unemployment in the Upper Peninsula are associated with the extraction of resources and their economic benefits to places and people outside the area.

After the early logging boom in the 1800s, mining was for decades the dominant industry in the six westernmost counties. When mining crashed in the early 1970s, no economic sector rose to take its place, leaving the Upper Peninsula with the highest unemployment rate in the state, often higher than the national average. During the nationwide recession of the 1980s, Michigan's economic decline became so extreme that the state legislature initiated a number of task forces to assess the state's economic possibilities. It was at this time that Michigan developed an economic development program based on forest resources. The program was designed to diversify local economies, improve public revenues, and enhance employment opportunities.

As part of this effort to develop a forest resource-based economy, some members of the state legislature traveled to Finland, renowned for its use of forest resources for economic development. One member of the trip was Upper Peninsula Representative Russell "Rusty" Hellman, a powerful member of the legislature. He became acquainted with the work of Jaako Poyry and contracted this Finnish consulting firm to complete a study of the forest resources and opportunities in the Upper Peninsula.

The study was completed in 1977 and suggested that the forest resources of the Upper Peninsula were economically underutilized. It suggested active management for greater productivity and future value of the resource. The study also identified as problematic the limited market for small-diameter materials. According to the Michigan Department of Natural Resources Forestry Division, the market in the late 1970s was so poor that the 2,000 acres per year of small-diameter trees thinned to increase forest growing capacity were left to rot on the ground. The Jaako Poyry study recommended that locally owned processing facilities be developed to utilize this abundant amount of low-value material.

Project Initiation

In 1980, the Michigan state legislature passed the Forest Improvement Act. The legislation was developed almost verbatim from the report submitted by Poyry and suggested the development of forest improvement districts to improve the state's forested resources. These districts were to correspond to political boundaries and, although legislatively authorized, would be developed by interested local landowners. Although the original legislation was passed in 1980, it was not implemented until a 1984 amendment allowed for forest improvement district pilot projects. According to the legislation, "Forest improvement districts are organized as an entity of state government under the Forest Improvement Act of 1984. The purpose of the Act is to stimulate improved management and utilization of forest lands . . . and to enhance economic and community development . . . by ensuring adequate future high quality timber supplies, increased employment opportunities, a diversified economy and other economic benefits, and the protection, maintenance, and enhancement of a productive and stable forest resource system for the public benefit of present and future generations."[3]

The primary goal of the act was to demonstrate that the productivity of timberlands of the Upper Peninsula would improve with proper management. The act also set objectives for better utilization of waste wood and the improvement of the forest ecosystem for fish and wildlife habitat and soil resources. In order for the districts to function, start-up money would be needed. The legislation would not be passed without controversy. The timber industry was vocal in its opposition.

Despite the fact that the legislation was meant to improve economic conditions along with forest resources, industry spokespeople said that the setup and funding of state forest improvement districts would create a competitive advantage for the districts. They also argued that the legislation was akin to Scandinavian socialism, which they did not like. Nevertheless, support came from a powerful political leader from the Upper Peninsula, State Representative Dominic Jacobetti, and an amendment was made that allowed for a forest restoration pilot project in the six westernmost counties of the Upper Peninsula. Since Representative Jacobetti was chair of the Appropriations Committee, the project was allotted $400,000 to begin operations and was dubbed the Western Upper Peninsula Forest Improvement District. With a vast territory of Baraga, Houghton, Gogebic, Iron, Ontonagon, and Keweenaw Counties, this auspicious, highly political beginning of the district was to have both negative and positive consequences.

The legislation provided the authority to begin a forest restoration pilot project that encompassed the western six counties of the Upper Peninsula. The pilot project would be called a "Forest Improvement District," established as a government subdivision of the state, once a petition signed by twenty-five or more landowners with a total combined acreage of more than 55,000 acres within the gross territorial boundary was filed with the commission.[4] Although funding for the district was available, it was not until late 1985 that a few local leaders began to organize the district. The first task was to enroll the required members to constitute a district. By hiring forestry consultants on an hourly basis and undertaking a local promotional campaign, within fourteen months local leaders signed up 202 landowners holding 74,000 acres. The establishment of the Western Upper Peninsula District became official in April 1987 when the Natural Resources Commission of Michigan approved this first Western Upper Peninsula Forest Improvement District petition.

Project Description

With more than two hundred landowners, the Western Upper Peninsula Forest Improvement District was born as a private, nonindustrial, self-governing organization of members committed to a program for forest resource development. The legislative language designated the district as a quasi state organization with exemption from taxation and the power to issue bonds, two unusual designations for cooperatives. The district was broken down into seven working forests, most of which follow county boundaries. Any person owning or leasing 20 or more acres of forest land can join the district, and up to 15,000 acres can be enrolled into the district annually. The legislation stipulated that at least 25 percent of the district's lands be made up of nonindustrial private forest lands of at least 40 acres but not larger than 640 acres—a stipulation included in the legislation to ensure that landowners typically underrepresented in forest management discussions would be involved in the project and receive quality management advice.

Decisions about district operations are made through a structure set up through the Forest Improvement Act in 1980. The district is designed to be run by an eight-member board of directors who are both participating landowners and elected by the members. One director is elected from each of the seven working forests and serves a staggered three-year term. The eighth person is a director at large and is elected by the current directors of the working forests to serve for one year. The powers and duties of the board are prescribed by the Forest Improvement Act[5] and include the election of officers, the establishment of the forms and requirements for membership agreements, and the establishment of a contract with a Michigan for-profit corporation as its agent (this was established but not used).

As members of a governing board, the directors are responsible for ensuring that the work done by the district fulfills the legal responsibilities set forth in the authorizing act. They are also charged with representing the interests of members by bringing their concerns and issues to the board's attention. Directors are required to attend regular and special board meetings and to represent the district at meetings with cooperating agencies and the general public. They are not compensated for their time but are entitled to reimbursement of expenses incurred while working on district matters.

Although the start-up funding provided by the State of Michigan made the development of the district possible, local leadership by the board of directors was essential. Some members were concerned that the majority of the board members were large landowners and did not represent small-landowner objectives, which were not primarily economic. As the district has hired its own employees and the quality of member contact has improved, concern about board management orientation seems to have diminished.

Many landowners feel that the board provides them with some security when a problem with land management activity on their land arises. District members can take problems to the board for redress. If a landowner voices concern about a management activity that the staff of the district has been unable to satisfactorily address, the board chairman visits the member to discuss the problem. According to current members, there have been very few times that a problem could not be corrected to the member's satisfaction with board assistance. Many landowners feel that the level of assurance of quality work the board provides is one of the more important benefits of membership.

Because the Western Upper Peninsula Forest Improvement District was designed as a pilot project, the legislature agreed to fund it through state appropriations for five years to test its feasibility. Success of the project was to be judged by an improvement in forest growing capacity, an increase in economic possibilities for the Upper Peninsula forest industry, and the district's ability to become financially independent. After the initial five years of district operations, an independent forestry consulting entity from Maine, the Irland Group, was hired in 1990 to evaluate the success of these parameters.[6] The Irland Group evaluation found that the forest management activities performed by the district were thorough and reaching the desired audience. In addition, forestry-related jobs had been created, and additional wood fiber was making its way to markets. The study also stated that the district had not become financially independent and judged that it was not likely to meet that goal in the near future. However, the Michigan state legislature continued to fund the pilot after the initial five years.

During the project's pilot years, landowners were actively recruited for membership. Consulting foresters, hired by the district and given incentives for recruitment, would approach a landowner and, if the owner was interested, inventory the land, discuss economic and aesthetic objectives, and develop a long-term management plan. A completed land management plan was returned to the landowner for review and adjustment. If the landowner accepted the plan, a management agreement was made, and the landowner became a member of the district. As a member, the landowner's primary obligation was to manage the land in accordance with the plan, although adjustments could be made.

While the district paid the consulting foresters, service to the landowner was free. The district continues to assist members in managing forest land for long-term forest resource productivity and marketing and provides services including management plan and inventory updates, timber harvest, wildlife planning, recreational planning, advice and assistance in entering land in the Commercial Forest Reserve, assistance in obtaining Forestry Incentives Practices funding, consultations, inspections, and marking for firewood.

District members can request forestry services from the district, and district employees may recommend certain services for certain members. Each year, the district checks the timber database of member lands and notifies landowners if their lands are scheduled for harvest. Although a member is not obligated to cut the timber as scheduled, landowners are encouraged to follow the management recommendations. The district offers a preharvest inspection and can delineate cutting boundaries, mark timber to be harvested, prepare an evaluation of the timber, request bids, advertise the sale, receive bids and negotiate the sale, prepare a contract, administer the sale, collect payments, oversee remittance to the landowner, and close the sale. The landowner can request full or any portion of district service and can sell the timber to any interested buyer.

Despite their receiving state funding longer than set forth in the original legislation, the district's finances began to run into trouble in 1992. Michigan was experiencing severe budgetary problems, and the retirement of Representative Jacobetti left the district without a powerful advocate. Although the intention of the district was to gain financial independence, the project needed some level of state appropriations for an additional time until a financial base could be secured. When district efforts to secure additional state funding failed, it began to look for alternative funding, and the board of directors developed a marketing proposal, "Economic Well-Being through Forestry." In addition to charging member fees for previously free services, the proposal called for the establishment of a log yard that would concentrate and market wood products from member's lands.[7] By concentrating material, the district hoped to capture increased profits for the landowners and produce an increased amount of high-quality timber to support regional wood-using industries. The district also hoped to capture a percentage of the profits from the concentration yard to fund the administrative functions of the Forest Improvement District and to create additional opportunities for regional "value-added" industries, thereby creating long-term job opportunities to strengthen the region's economic well-being. The board's proposal projected start-up costs of $120,000 with the district contributing $70,000 and requesting the U.S. Forest Service to contribute $50,000. The proposal for the development of the log yard was approved, and operations began in 1993. For the first two years, the log yard received reduced state funding.

The concentration yard operates as a joint venture with a small, local sawmill. The sawmill provides a portion of its yard for the exclusive use of the district and provides the equipment to run the yard. The sorter, however, is a district employee.

In exchange for sawmill support, the district markets sawlogs to the sawmill and sells veneer and other material to the highest bidder. The district is responsible for cut, skid, haul, and related logging costs; office overhead (computed on an average of cost per million board feet) and yard rental; machine rental; and yard manager costs. The landowner is responsible for all other associated consulting forester service costs, which are deducted from the landowner's portion of the gross receipts—costs that would have to be paid by any landowner requesting forestry services.

Since 1995, the district has been a self-funded enterprise, evolving from its initial reliance on consulting foresters to employing its own. It employs one financial manager, one office assistant, and two foresters, each responsible for half the district and the recruitment of new members. Nine to ten logging firms contract almost exclusively with the district.

Participation

From its 202 member beginning, the district has grown to 904 landowners and 147,544 acres by the end of 2001. The original legislation stipulating that at least 25 percent of the district's lands must consist of nonindustrial private forest lands of at least 40-acre tracts and not more than 640-acre tracts has remained intact.

After seventeen years of operation, the district had assisted over 1,300 landowners. Because of the large number of nonindustrial private forest landowners in the western Upper Peninsula, an enormous growth potential for the district still remains. In the early years, members were actively recruited by consulting foresters, and, although membership grew rapidly, some members were concerned that the district was not providing personal service. A number of members stated, for example, that no one from the district had ever been on their lands. Initially, there was the feeling that district foresters were not as concerned with landowner desires as they should be and that the management plans provided the landowners were generic and too focused on timber management. A large number of local landowners felt that the district was almost exclusively a timber management organization and did not represent concerns for wildlife, water, and recreation. These complaints diminished after the district employed foresters whose objectives were different than those of the independent consulting foresters who may have seemed more concerned about timber values.

Most of the landowners who were approached by the district but chose not to join said that they did not want to be a part of an organization that prescribed management practices. They were leery of losing management flexibility and believed that they knew how to manage the land. Some did not want to enroll with a quasi-governmental organization either for fear of future restrictions or because they preferred independence.

Now that the organization is economically self-sufficient, it relies almost solely on district staff for new recruitment, but most new members join because a friend or a neighbor who is a member of the district has urged them to. Fifteen to twenty-five new members join each year and get more personalized attention than was common in the project's early years.

The Forestry Division of the Michigan Department of Natural Resources has been involved in the district since project initiation. In the beginning, its function was to provide project oversight for financial and resource management. For the first six years, the appropriations received from the state were administered by the Department of Natural Resources, which also provided technical assistance with respect to the development of forest practices guidelines, development and implementation of forest management plans, and other matters in which the department has special expertise, such as working with other federal and state agencies. Since the district has become financially independent, the level of involvement by the Forestry Division has decreased. It still provides the district with technical assistance, helps members obtain funding from state-administered programs such as the Stewardship Incentives Program, and helps keep the district office informed of changes in Michigan's forestry practices laws.

Now that funds are no longer administered through the Department of Natural Resources, the working relationship between the district and the department is not as close as it once was. In many ways, the Department of Natural Resources now treats the district like any other forestry contractor rather than the enabling organization it is intended to be.

Relationships with the Wildlife Division of the Department of Natural Resources have never been strong. While some wildlife may benefit from timber management, one employee of the Wildlife Division criticized the district for not providing the landowner with sufficient management advice about how wildlife benefit from no harvest.

Throughout the length of the project, a number of federal agencies have been involved with the district. The Natural Resource Conservation Service has cooperated with the district by providing information on soil surveys and other assistance to landowners. The Cooperative Extension Service has assisted the district in demonstrations, information, and education programs that promote interest in and understanding of forest management needs, problems, and solutions. The U.S. Agricultural Stabilization and Conservation Service has cooperated with the district and its members by providing funding for Forestry Incentives Practices. In addition to providing a portion of the start-up funds for the development of the concentration yard, the Forest Service has vocally supported district efforts. Michigan Technological University has continually provided the district with technical advice and assistance. Participation from the nonprofit sector, however, in particular environmental and conservation groups, has been almost nonexistent, perhaps because of the perception that the district is a timber management organization.

Problems and Barriers

Perhaps one of the most significant problems for the district has been its political, as opposed to its grassroots, beginning. Even though it is a landowner cooperative, legislatively it is an entity of state government. Controversy surrounded the start-up of the project because forest industry interests were concerned that a state-subsidized forestry organization in the Upper Peninsula would create unfair competition. The initial Forest Improvement Act was passed in 1980, but it was another six years before the district began to function. During the early years, a number of the most contentious provisions, including the construction of a commercial wood processing plant using state funds and the permanent funding of the district through state appropriations, were removed from the act. Nevertheless, the timber industry, loggers, and independent consulting foresters still lobbied against the district, fearful of competing against a state-subsidized forestry operation that appeared to lean toward socialism.

While they were not outspoken during the discussions surrounding the passage of the act, environmental groups were concerned that the district would be too heavily focused on the production of timber at the expense of the forest ecosystem. Even after the act passed, many people felt that the legislation was not passed by its own merits but because Representative Jacobetti was a powerful politician who was owed political favors. While the district is no longer supported by state appropriations, the fact that the district is a state entity turns many potential members away because they do not want to enroll their lands in a government organization, fearful that restrictions may be placed on their property. Although never studied as an option, the start-up of the district would have been difficult if not impossible without some level of sustained funding; start-up costs were large, and asking potential members with small landholdings to pay a fee for untried services may have proved fruitless. Had the district been able to begin without state support, political opposition may have been less.

In 1990, the district ran into an operational problem that hurt its reputation. When the legislation was passed that approved the district, it was given authority to purchase land and equipment and run a for-profit business to create economic development in the Upper Peninsula. In an effort to create markets for the abundance of low-value material, the district used its authority to purchase land in Arnheim, Michigan, to develop a business fed by products from member lands. The James River Company was interested in developing a pulp mill at the site, but environmental impacts, especially on the shore of Lake Superior, made the pulp mill controversial. Because the land was owned by the district and because the district became an active and vocal advocate for the mill, a large segment of the population believed that the district was not interested in the sustainability of the local economy but instead focused on harvesting timber. In addition to negative environmental impacts, the pulp mill would have substantially increased harvesting without a significant increase in local employment or profits for the Upper Peninsula.

Because of midwestern cultural backgrounds, vocal public disagreement is rare. The majority of local residents hail from Native American and/or Scandinavian heritage, which, combined with a rural perspective and experience where material wealth is scarce and the local environment harsh, has resulted in a culture where residents tend to keep their disagreements to themselves and value stoic independence. Local opposition to the pulp mill was so high, however, that a local advocacy group, an uncommon occurrence in the Upper Peninsula, formed to fight it. Friends of the Land of Keweenaw (FOLK) developed its own proposal for value-added jobs in the timber industry as an alternative to the pulp mill. In response to the FOLK proposal, supporters of the pulp mill formed People Unopposed to Local Progress (PULP). The district supported PULP, with some district board members serving as leaders in that organization. Many local residents charged that the district did not consider the FOLK proposal for value-added jobs because it was focused on the mill. Local confidence in the district dropped. Because of the high level of local opposition, the James River Company eventually withdrew its proposal, and the controversy over the district's involvement with the pulp mill subsided. Many locals still view the district as exclusively a timber management organization, however, and the most often heard complaint among nonmembers is that the district does not pay attention to the nontimber values of a forest. As previously stated, two of the main functions of the district are to improve the growing capacity of the forest and to increase economic opportunities.

Outcomes and Successes

Although the recruitment of new members has slowed from the early years in part because membership now involves some up-front costs for landowners, membership increases steadily. The members who joined the district early in the project, even those with relatively small tracts of land, can see the effects of management on their landscape. The services performed by the district provide landowner education at a time when the Department of Natural Resources is undergoing funding cutbacks and can no longer perform significant levels of outreach. The district now produces an occasional newsletter to keep members informed of district happenings and other related information. Members have a greater sense of belonging to a local organization, and with the switch from a reliance on outside consultants to full-time district staff, members say that they feel they receive personalized, quality service. By providing additional levels of quality assurance, the quality of timber management has steadily increased. Some of the benefits of district membership expressed by small and large landowners include the following:

- A large group of members with a relatively large land base, helping the economy by supplying a sizable and consistent supply of wood to the local forest industry and helping the landowner receive a better price for timber
- Assistance in the development of land use plans
- Assistance in hiring quality loggers
- Assistance and information on the use of stewardship funds and other related programs that may allow landowners to achieve goals, such as wildlife improvement
- Supervision of the logging operations to ensure quality management
- Help in timber sale contract development
- Help for absentee landowners
- Awareness of the economic value of forested land
- Financial rewards to the landowner without sacrificing aesthetic values
- A structured organization specifically looking out for landowner interests
- Personalized long-term land management services with a dedicated staff

By 2001, the district was averaging an annual harvest of approximately 25,000 cords and 2.1 million feet of saw timber and veneer from its member lands.[8] Since 2001, landowners have received almost $6 million as stumpage payments from harvests facilitated by the district, and the total economic value from wood produced from member lands exceeds $152.9 million. The effects on the local Upper Peninsula economy have been significant, given that the district manages only about 4 percent of the commercial forestland within the six counties. In 1995, the board of directors estimated that the district provided full-time employment for up to forty-five people.

Another district achievement is its financial independence from the State of Michigan. The log concentration yard has made this independence possible while providing members with increased financial returns. By combining material harvested from member lands in the concentration yard, the district is able to receive a higher return for a larger, more consistent supply. The log yard enables the district to secure the best price for high-value logs, such as veneer-quality material. The premium received from the log yard has enabled the district to fund most of its operations while still passing on a higher dollar value to members. To achieve financial independence, landowners now have to pay for services they formerly received free, but fees are generally less than they would be without district membership. The district believes that it has significantly improved the forest's growing capacity on member lands. For members ready for a second harvest, their financial return has also increased from a higher-quality timber.

The Link between Community Well-Being and Healthy Forests

One of the legislative objectives for establishing the district was to enhance the economic condition of the area. Therefore, during the district's first few years, discussions regarding community stability were frequent. Since the project's early years, the economic situation in the majority of the six counties in the district has improved, and discussions regarding community stability have diminished, although the six counties involved in the district are still below the state average in most economic statistics. Additionally, markets for timber products in the area have remained strong for a number of years. It is impossible to know whether this improvement in economic well-being can be attributed to the district without an in-depth economic analysis. It is clear, however, that the district has had a notable impact on the local economy.

The traditional environmental community, which is not particularly strong in the local area, had been disappointed that the district has not gone further in addressing the social and environmental elements of community-based forestry. While the district is doing an admirable job of managing member's forestlands, some environmentalists say it is not using its legislative authority to improve community and environmental well-being. Two often-mentioned examples of how the district could enhance community well-being are helping to create local, value-added businesses and providing more guidance to members on nontimber forest products.

Future of the Project

The district is now a well-established organization, with the number of members and acres enrolled increasing and over 150,000 acres of nonindustrial private forestland under a long-term management plan. District members believe that the health of the land has improved, and although community well-being is difficult to measure, the district has created a number of jobs and supplied timber that would not have been available without its services. Unemployment in the Upper Peninsula has decreased since the formation of the district, but it is impossible to know to what extent its activities were a factor.

Many participants, especially district employees, feel that they are ready to go to "the next level," although no one is sure what that is. Many people claim that the district remains too focused on timber production and are concerned that a large quantity of the resource is shipped out of state for processing since the idea motivating the project was to take a long-term view of forest wealth for the benefit of the local area. More could be done to create value-added jobs that would increase the local value of the resource. District staff are considering ways to retain additional value from the resource and are discussing ways to broaden partnerships and increase involvement with nonprofit and business organizations.

Considering the number of private landowners in the six counties, the growth potential of the district is sizable. There has been talk of expanding services to additional counties in the Upper Peninsula. While financial independence has brought an additional level of respectability to its operations, this independence may also slow the ability for the district to expand.

There is little doubt that the Western Upper Peninsula Forest Improvement District has come a long way in accomplishing its initial goals. Although obstacles remain, a dedicated staff, strong local leadership, and support from its members give the project an opportunity for continued activity. Development pressures are beginning to affect the Upper Peninsula, but at the moment most of the pressure is on shoreline property. It may not be long, however, before the forested landscape is affected. By providing personalized, quality land management services at a reasonable price, members can realize a greater financial return on their land than they previously expected, a gain that may contain development pressures and allow local communities a chance to steward the landscape that has given the local culture its unique character.

Notes

1. Bruce Cotton, "The Real Michigan," in *Michigan Reader: 1865 to the Present,* ed. R. M. Warner and C. Vander Hill (Grand Rapids, Mich: William B. Eerdmans), 1974.
2. Martin Hintz and Franklin Watts, "Michigan," 1987.
3. Forest Improvement Act, 1980, Sec. 204.
4. Forest Improvement Act, 1980, Sec. 204.
5. Forest Improvement Act, 1980, Sec. 205.
6. L. C. Irland and D. I. Maass, "The Western Upper Peninsula Forest Improvement District's First Five Years," *National Journal of American Forestry* 8 (1991): 107–11.
7. J. A. Burchfield, "Grassroots Forest Landowner Organizations in the Eastern United States: A Comparative Study of Structure and Function" (Unpublished Ph.D. dissertation: University of Michigan, 1991).
8. Western U. P. Forest Improvement District Newsletter, Issue No. 1, May 1995.

CHAPTER 11

The Integration of Community Well-Being and Forest Health in the Pacific Northwest

Kimberly McDonald and Rebecca McLain

The Pacific Northwest has long been known for its fog, rugged coastline, and giant trees. More recently, the Northwest's working communities, where jobs, hope, and prosperity have eroded along with the slopes of the landscape, have drawn national attention and galvanized local efforts for restoration.

The Columbia-Pacific Resource Conservation and Development Council was established in 1972 under the authority of the 1962 Agricultural Act, which provided funding for resource conservation and development districts throughout rural America. During its more than twenty years of existence, the council has coordinated a growing number and variety of projects designed to sustain the relationships between the people and the working landscapes on which their rural identities and livelihoods depend.

An array of private and public council member organizations provide technical services, labor, equipment, supplies, funds, and in-kind support for a variety of programs and projects. Programs in worker training, unionized habitat restoration, and microlending funds in addition to grantsmanship workshops, a special forest products brokerage, park, interpretive center, fishing access for the disabled, and placement of habitat restoration structures throughout the region have earned the council a regionwide reputation for "getting things done." A number of "outsiders" have charged that council projects threaten a "free market" by reducing incentives for private business. But the council insists that subsidies are necessary to counter the area's chronic unemployment and "jump-start" local industries.

Part economic development council, part social service agency, part resource conservation and watershed rehabilitation agency, and part information and grants broker, the council can generate projects and programs around social, economic, and ecological concerns and in so doing link environmental with community well-being. Some people say that as significant as the economic development opportunities the council has developed, it is the "culture of collaboration" between local communities, private business, and government agencies that is most important. Success in both organizational areas has been attributed to the dynamic leadership of a strong executive director willing to take risks and guided by a principled commitment to inclusivity, diversity, and equality in program development for improved relationships and opportunities between land and labor.

Traveling the southwestern Washington coastline along the narrow black ribbon of Highway 101 as the fog rolls over the logging scars on the Willapa Hills is like stepping into a Ken Kesey landscape. Here, men cut timber, mills spew smoke, and fishing fleets head out early and return late. Work, risk, and danger are everyday life in this country.

The area's deep forests and vast tidal flats provided Salish-speaking tribes sustenance, shelter, clothing, and transportation for millennia. In the nineteenth century, traders from Britain and the eastern seaboard brought news from the West and precipitated the radical transformation of the land and seascape. Within decades, farmers had occupied the land and were clearing the forests and river bottoms. Feeding the industrializing economy's insatiable demand for wood, logging crews felled the Douglas firs, cedars, and hemlocks. Canneries, built along the rivers and tidal flats, processed and shipped vast quantities of salmon and shellfish harvested from the region's waters.

Over the past century, logging and fishing towns with names like Aberdeen, Hoquiam, Raymond, and Ilwaco boomed and busted. Town murals memorialize the relationship between humans, land, and sea. However, human and forest environments bear the toll of the boom-and-bust work style.

A decade of angry debate over the effects of clear-cutting on the spotted owl and salmon has made the conflict between people as mythic in proportion as the earlier New World encounter with the region's great forest. Abandoned mills, clear-cut scars on declining forests, streams choked with sediment, and confrontations between angry loggers and antilogging protesters have become part of this fabric of place.

In this landscape of people and nature, change seeps in like fog rising from the tidal flats of Willapa Bay—in increments and slowly. New ways of logging, collaborative efforts to restore the ravaged streams and eroded slopes, and businesses based on special forest products such as ferns, salal, huckleberry brush, mushrooms, and barks are emerging with public and private land managers. People of southwestern Washington are developing new leadership that focuses on the question, "How can we change?" rather than on the lament, "Why did this bust happen to us?" People are beginning to look at the landscape and themselves differently.

One of the important indicators of change is the Columbia-Pacific Resource Conservation and Development Council, a quasi-public organization that, with the help of professional and volunteer leadership, has developed programs and projects for the people and the landscape of this part of the American West.

Initiation of a Project

The council was established in 1972 under the authority of the 1962 Agricultural Act, which provided funding for quasi-governmental resource conservation and development districts throughout rural America. Council members consisted of county and municipal governments and conservation and port districts.

The grange movement in Grays Harbor, Pacific, and Wahkiakum Counties was pivotal in the genesis of the council, whose initial goal to "improve the economic and social well-being of the people in the project area" (U.S. Soil Conservation Service 1972, 3), reflected the grange's holistic view of rural life. Habitat restoration, including regeneration of logged-off lands and erosion control on poorly constructed logging roads, was a key objective in the council's first work plan, which also proposed rural and municipal water delivery and sewage disposal systems.

When federal funding dwindled to a trickle during the mid-1980s, the council became inactive until 1989, when it reemerged as a force of social change in southwestern Washington after a variety of government, quasi-government, and nongovernmental entities met to develop a new mission, goals, and bylaws.

A series of events that took place over the late 1980s contributed to the reactivation of the council. Leadership was stabilized in 1986, when the Natural Resource Conservation Service, formerly the Soil Conservation Service, agreed to provide funding for a full-time executive director in charge of acquiring funds and coordinating council activities. A downturn in the economy from the late 1970s through the 1980s resulted in mill shutdowns and massive layoffs. A series of federal court decisions regarding salmon allocation and forest management during this same time led to increased restrictions on salmon and timber harvesting.

The resurgence of the council was bolstered in the early 1990s through the activities of the Chehalis Basin Fisheries Task Force, which evolved from the Grays Harbor Fisheries Enhancement Task Force, founded in 1980 as a volunteer nonprofit coalition composed of federal and state agencies, local municipalities, businesses, tribal councils, and commercial and sport fishing groups. The task force was initially charged with enhancing salmon runs but broadened to include fish resources enhancement. In the early 1990s, the task force successfully advocated for Washington State's Jobs for the Environment, a bill to fund displaced timber workers retraining in habitat restoration. In 1993, the task force became the chief fiscal agent, responsible for habitat restoration projects in southwestern Washington. The success of the task force is due in large part to council member Diane Ellison's dynamic leadership and ability to corral resources needed to accomplish regional goals.

The Region

The council operates in Wahkiakum, Pacific, Grays Harbor, and Mason Counties, an area whose rivers provide habitat and spawning grounds for a variety of anadromous fish species, including chum, coho, and king salmon. Willapa Bay, located in the southwestern corner of the region, is the nation's most productive coastal ecosystem and provides critical habitat for shellfish and over seventy species of migratory birds (Wolf 1993). The area is located within the range of the spotted owl, a symbol of forest controversy in the Pacific Northwest. A large percentage of lowland temperate rain forest produces Douglas fir, western hemlock, sitka spruce, and western red cedar, trees that all bring a high market value.

Farming, fishing, and forestry (including special forest products industries) have been the region's economic mainstay for most of the twentieth century. Since the turn of the century, natural resource–based tourism has also been significant along the coast and in the Olympics. However, the quality of the region's natural resource base has deteriorated over the past one hundred years. A combination of overfishing, dam construction, erosive logging, and road building has decreased fish runs to a fraction of their former size and threatened the viability of certain salmon spawns. Industrial timber companies have changed most of the region's old-growth stands on private and state lands to monocrop tree plantations. Farmers have converted large areas of forests to fields and pastures, and the housing industry has begun to convert significant portions of the region's forests to residential development.

About 70 percent of the land in the region is privately owned (see tables 11.1 and 11.2). The 30 percent under public ownership includes a portion of the Olympic National Forest and some large blocks of state land in Pacific and Wahkiakum Counties. Several Indian reservations, the largest one encompassing nearly 200,000 acres belonging to the Quinault Nation, enforce treaty rights to fish and shellfish and wild plant gathering.

Table 11.1.   Public and Private Ownership by County

County	Area in Private Ownership (acres)	Area in Public Ownership (acres)	Total Land Area
Grays Harbor	842,531 (68.8%)	379,869 (31.1%)	1,222,400
Mason	378,766 (61.5%)	236,914 (38.5%)	615,680
Pacific	473,572 (81.5%)	107,548 (18.5%)	581,120
Wahkiakum	122,505 (73.3)	44,535 (26.7%)	167,040
CPRCD region	1,817,374 (70.3)	768,866 (29.7%)	2,586,240

Source: Washington State Atlas and Databook (1995).

Table 11.2.   Area and Percentage of Total Land Area by Public Ownership Type

Region	Grays Harbor (acres/%)	Mason County (acres/%)	Pacific County (acres/%)	Wahkiakum County (acres/%)	CPRCD County (acres/%)
Federal	161,063	164,940	10,953	2,632	768.866
	(13.2%)	(26.8%)	(1.9%)	(1.6%)	(13.1%)
State	81,939	62,598	93,482	41,036	279,055
	(6.7%)	(10.2%)	(16.1)	(24.6%)	(10.8%)
Indian	129,468	3,906	337	n/a	133,711
	(10.6%)	(0.6%)	(0.1)		(5.2%)
County	7,423	5,470	2,776	867	16,536
	(0.6%)	(0.9%)	(0.5%)	(0.5%)	(0.6%)

Source: *Washington State Atlas and Databook* (1995).

The region has a limited transportation and educational infrastructure. One four-lane freeway connects the area to the Interstate 5 corridor, which links the major cities of the West Coast. Grays Harbor Community College is the only institute of higher education in the region.

In 1996, the region's population was 139,800 with a population growth rate of about 2 percent per year since 1990. The percentage of nonwhites is low (6.3 percent); Native American groups include the Quinault Nation (comprising descendants of the Quinault, Queets, Quileute, Hoh, Chehalis, Chinook, and Cowlitz tribes) and the Chehalis, Squaxin, and Shoalwater Bay tribes. Asian and Hispanic workers, disproportionately concentrated in farming, shellfishing, and special forest products harvesting, are mostly concentrated in the coastal towns and Shelton.

The percentage of households with incomes below the poverty level in 1995 ranged from 10.4 percent in Wahkiakum County (slightly less than the state average of 10.9 percent) to 17.2 percent in Pacific County (see table 11.3). Approximately 44 percent of adults in the region have no education beyond high school, substantially below the state average of 60 percent with a high school education.

Table 11.3.   Median Household Incomes and Percentage of Households below Poverty Level

County	Median Income 1980 ($)	Median Income 1995 ($)	% Below Poverty Level
Grays Harbor	17,080	28,047	16.4
Mason	16,137	32,345	13.2
Pacific	14,103	24,718	17.2
Wahkiakum	19,452	33,300	10.4
Washington State	18,367	40,398	10.9

Source: Washington State Office of Financial Management, *1995 Population Trends*.

The population of seasonal residents is high (18 percent compared with 2.7 percent statewide). Unemployment in 1995 averaged 8.7 percent, down from a high of 12.3 percent in 1993 but slightly higher than the state average of 6.3 percent. Since the 1980 census, the area has experienced a net loss of 1,218 jobs.

Key features of the region's changing economy include a shift toward service-based employment, such as prisons, schools, health care, information services, and tourism; an influx of relatively well-off retirees into areas along the coast; and transformation of the state's eastern towns into bedroom communities for Olympia.

Mission and Programs

In 1989, the council's mission was to be a "visible, grass roots, participatory four-county organization dedicated to fostering cooperation on natural resources issues and economic development" for regional planning and implementation activities that "achieve quality of life and economic health." Within this broad mandate, the council focuses on economic development in natural resources industries, especially forest product enterprises.

Projects undertaken with council support range from watershed restoration to special forest products training to the development of a grants library at the

CPRCD Projects (1989–1996)1

Feasibility and Marketing Studies
   Timber Bridge Grant
   Laminated Wood Products
   Pacific Link Business Assistance
   Harbormill Feasibility Study
   Wood Waste Utilization Marketing Study
   Agroforestry Cooperative
   Alternative Wastewater Treatment Study
Fish Enhancement and Hatchery Improvement
   Chinook Fish Enhancement
   Humptulips Conditioning Pond
   Chehalis Fish Hatchery Improvement
   Delazene Boy Scout Fish Enhancement
   Wynochee River Fish Enhancement
   ASCS Fish Enhancement Cost Sharing
   Loomis Pond Improvements

Tourism
  Friends Landing
  Ocean Shores Boardwalk
  Grays Harbor Discovery Project
  Pacific County Park and Recreation Plan
  West Bend Rest Area
Interpretive Centers and Parks
  Julia Butler Hansen Elk Interpretive Center
  Coastal Resource Science Center
  Skamokawa Vista Park
Education and Training
  Habitat Restoration Training
  Special Forest Products Management Training
  Grant Library
  Grantsmanship Workshops
  Area Forestry Extension Agent Support
  Forest TV Film
  Heart in the Woods (theatrical play)
Restoration
  Displaced Timber Workers Watershed Restoration Program
  Displaced Fishers Watershed Restoration Program
Cooperative/Association Development
  North Shore Timber Cooperative
  Agroforestry Cooperative (became RainKist marketing brokerage)
  Cottonwood Growers Association
Water Quality and Erosion Control
  City of Hoquiam Water Quality
  Brooks Slough Critical Area Treatment
  Riverdale Creek Emergency
Economic Development and Lending
  Pacific Coastal Economic Recovery Plan
  Economic Development District
  Entrepreneurial Revolving Loan Fund
Workshops/Dialogue Sessions
  Forest Contract/Marketing Workshop
  Sludge Application Workshop
  Cottonwood Marketing Workshop
  Forest Base Protection Meeting
Committees
  US/Canada Salmon Treaty Committee
  Burrowing Shrimp Committee
  50th Tree Farm Anniversary Committee
      Chehalis River Basin Fishing Restoration Steering Committee
      Chehalis River Basin Planning Committee

CPRCD Roles

- Provider of technical advice for activities such as grant writing, restoration plans, market feasibility studies, and industry development
- Employer (direct and indirect hires)
- Facilitator of meetings and workshops
- Information and services broker (that is, connecting council members with expertise and funding from outside agencies and organizations)
- Advocate for legislation supportive of the council's goals
- Funder and channeler of funds for projects
- Developer of training and educational materials on topics related to timber and special forest products industries and watershed restoration
- Representative on local and regional committees that address economic development and environmental issues (that is, Chehalis River Basin Planning Committee, Burrowing Shrimp Committee, and U.S./Canada Salmon Treaty Committee)

organization's headquarters in Aberdeen (see the sidebar "CPRC&D Projects"). Council roles are diverse and range from providing technical advice to facilitating meetings, advocating legislation, and retraining displaced workers (see the sidebar "CPRC&D Roles"). Habitat restoration, special forest products, wood fiber production, and marketing programs address both forest health and community well-being.

Habitat Restoration

The Habitat Restoration program emerged in 1993 from a coalition between labor, environmental groups, small and large private landowners, and church groups to enact state legislation to train displaced timber workers in habitat restoration. In 1993, these efforts culminated in passage of the Jobs for the Environment Bill, which together with the federal Jobs in the Woods program provided funds for groups like the council to train and hire former timber workers for habitat restoration. The program is the first example of a unionized habitat restoration project in the United States. The council later helped the Pacific Conservation District acquire funds to implement a displaced fishers habitat restoration program that employs nonunion workers. Since 1993, the council has leveraged more than $4 million to fund restoration activities, employed more than sixty displaced timber workers, and completed more than thirty-five restoration projects for public and private landholders. The council is working with a local union to develop an apprenticeship program to train and certify journeyman habitat restoration crew workers.

Special Forest Products

The Special Forest Products program grew out of the council's attempts in the early 1990s to establish an agroforestry cooperative on the Olympic Peninsula. It has developed more slowly than the Habitat Restoration program because of lower funding and a lack of agreement in the special forest products community about what kind of support is needed. Like the Habitat Restoration program, the Special Forest Products program was initiated to provide local residents with training, skills, and resources; however, for special forest products, the council seeks to transform an existing industry rather than to create a new one.

In 1990, the council received $80,000 from the Washington State Department of Community Development to conduct a market feasibility study and develop a business plan for a special forest products cooperative. The cooperative was to encourage special forest products businesses to pool resources for equipment and marketing. In 1995, the program was strengthened by a full-time staff person whose duties included developing the special forest products program. RainKist Agroforestry Cooperative was incorporated in June 1995. With council support, RainKist worked with Grays Harbor Community College to set up a yearlong special forest products management training course.

Forty people, including welfare recipients, local business owners, displaced timber workers, and members of the Quinault Nation, have received training in special forest products harvesting and marketing since 1995. New businesses have formed. In 1996, the council entered discussions with ShoreTrust Trading Group, a for-profit "green" bank based in southwestern Washington, to develop RainKist into a viable organization. RainKist was transformed from a cooperative into a for-profit marketing brokerage owned by ShoreTrust. Aside from making a profit from the sale of special forest products, the Shore Trust-RainKist alliance promotes social equity in the workforce by paying premium prices for high-quality and sustainably harvested products.

Wood Products Production and Marketing Activities

A third set of activities that address community well-being and forest health are the council's efforts to assist public and private landowners and businesses in producing and marketing wood products. The hybrid cottonwood program, which is the most visible, has two aspects: 1) feasibility studies and formation of a cottonwood growers association to promote the conversion of farmlands to cottonwood plantations (1990–1995) and 2) the use of hybrid cottonwood plantations by municipalities to treat wastewater in rural locations (1996). Under its wood products program, the council has helped support a feasibility study of a woodworkers' flexible manufacturing facility (1993), a business plan for an oriented strand board plant (1995), a laminated woods product study (1991), a wood waste utilization study (1991), and a business plan to reopen the ITT/Rayonnier paper mill in Hoquiam.

Participation in Council Programs

Participants in council activities fall into three general categories: council members, staff, and nonmembers. The thirty-six-member council includes representatives from counties, cities, ports, tribes, conservation districts, economic development councils, and other nonprofit organizations (see the sidebar "Council Member Organizations"). The staff and council work with local and nonlocal businesses, volunteer organizations, and state and federal agencies.

Missing from formal council membership are the Skokomish tribe, representatives from community groups (granges, churches, and Boy Scouts), social service organizations, businesses, unions, and several of the region's cities and towns. Many of these groups, however, are active in council activities. There appears to be relatively little incentive for such groups to join as formal members since any group can approach the council for help in getting funds or other types of support for projects. The council does not try to recruit new members; with the recent expansion to include Mason County in the council region, there is some concern that the council has become too large.

As a member of the regional and national associations of resource conservation and development districts, the council has strong links to outside organizations (for a partial list of outside partners, see the sidebar "Some CPRC&D Partners"). It receives the majority of its funding from federal and state government, and the staff executive director is an employee of the Natural Resource Conservation Service. The council has also obtained private foundation grant monies. The council seeks technical, financial and marketing expertise from private firms such as Weyerhaeuser, Cascadia Bank, and ShoreTrust Trading Group and brings in outside consultants to help with feasibility studies and business plans. It has links to outside academic institutions; Washington State University cooperative extension, for example, was crucial to getting the Special Forest Products program off the ground. The council's links

Council Member Organizations

Economic Development Districts and Councils
- Columbia-Pacific Economic Development District
- Mason County Economic Development Council
- Lower Columbia Economic Development Council
- Pacific County Economic Development Council

Counties
- Grays Harbor County
- Mason County
- Pacific County
- Wahkiakum County

Conservation Districts
- Grays Harbor Conservation District
- Pacific Conservation District
- Wahkiakum Conservation District

Transportation Agencies
- Pacific Transit System
- Port of Ilwaco
- Port of Peninsula
- Port of Willapa Harbor
- Wahkiakum Port District No. 2

Native American Tribes/Nations
- Chehalis Indian Tribe
- Quinault Nation
- Shoalwater Bay Indian Tribe

Cities
- City of Aberdeen
- City of Cathlamet
- City of Hoquiam
- City of Ilwaco
- City of Long Beach
- City of McCleary
- City of Oakville
- City of Ocean Shores
- City of Raymond
- City of South Bend
- City of Westport

Community Groups
- Coastal Community Action
- Grays Harbor Trout Unlimited
- Grays Harbor Historical Seaport
- Willapa Alliance

to the University of Washington's College of Forestry will enhance the council's ability to attract funding from the private and academic spheres.

Most of the organization's funding comes through state or federal agencies, and government involvement has been an essential factor in the organization's ability to carry out activities. The executive director's salary is paid through the federal government. Representatives from municipal and county governments, including elected officials, and representatives from quasi-governmental entities, such as conservation districts and economic development districts, comprise a large percentage of the board's membership and are

Some CPRC&D Partners[2]

Chehalis Basin Fisheries Task Force
Harbor Churches Community Outreach
Seattle Catholic Archdiocese
Washington Association of Churches
Central Labor Council (Grays Harbor)
IAM Woodworkers Local No. W-2
Washington State Labor Council
Washington Environmental Council
The Nature Conservancy
Rayonnier Timberlands
John Hancock/Campbell Group
Weyerhaeuser
Simpson Timber Company
Mason Timber Company
Cascadia Revolving Fund
Mason Conservation District
Lewis Conservation District
Thurston Conservation District
U.S. Forest Service
U.S. Fish and Wildlife
Washington State Department of Natural Resources
Washington State Department of Ecology
Washington State Department of Community, Trade and Economic Development
Washington State Department of Fish and Wildlife
Grays Harbor Community College
Many private landowners

instrumental in the organization's policy direction as well as in the implementation of project activities.

Resources and Incentives

The council draws on a variety of resources within and outside the community. Council member organizations provide technical services, labor, equipment and supplies, access to land, and funds. Other organizations based in the region, including the Natural Resource Conservation Service, chambers of commerce, and private timber companies also provide cash and in-kind support. Private support extends beyond technical and financial help. Companies such as Simpson Timber and Weyerhauser have provided support in the form of agreements to allow the council to carry out restoration activities on company lands.

The mix of private and public resources used to carry out council activities has shifted from about 50 percent public in the early 1990s to over 80 percent public in 1996. The increase in public funding is due largely to the restoration program that has received substantial monetary support from the state Jobs for the Environment and the federal Jobs in the Woods programs.

How Decisions Are Made

Decisions about the activities undertaken by or with the help of the council are made through the district's local governing council. Council member organizations pay dues, with a sliding scale ranging from $75 for nonprofit groups and small-government entities to $6,000 for Grays Harbor County. Dues are waived in cases of financial hardship.

Council decisions are made by majority vote with input from the executive director. The executive director plays a major role in helping members and prospective partners develop specific projects and identify funding sources and exercises considerable discretion over program implementation.

The council is composed of an executive board and council members. The executive board consists of officers and past presidents for continuity and institutional memory. Board positions are voluntary. Presidents are restricted to two one-year terms.

The council is composed of a representative from each of the sponsoring organizations, an alternate from each group, and a member at large from each county. Full council meetings are held every other month, with the executive board meeting in alternate months. New officers are elected annually. Council meetings are open to the public. A mailing list of members and nonmembers is used to inform people of upcoming meetings. Nonmembers can participate in council discussions and project activities but cannot vote or serve as officers. Judging from the diversity of projects implemented by the council, any project that falls within the broad rubric of economic development or natural resources is potentially acceptable. The key selection criteria appear to be whether the funding and labor needed to accomplish the project can be identified. Identification and administration of resources and projects is carried out either by the administrative staff, with member organizations taking the lead on a particular project, or by outside groups with a subcontract to administer programs.

Over the past seven years, paid staff has increased from one full-time executive director and a secretary to a full-time executive director, a full-time development director, two part-time habitat restoration crew coordinators, a special forest products course coordinator, a full-time economic development officer, and a full-time secretary.

Problems and Barriers

One difficulty in evaluating the council is that it is neither a discrete project nor a project with subelements but rather an organization that carries out many projects, often only tenuously linked. Two related visions seem to drive the selection and implementation of projects. One is the vision articulated in the group's mission statement of "fostering cooperation on natural resources and economic development." The other is the vision implicitly assumed by many participants of "linking economic development and resource conservation."

Barriers or problems associated with the council fall into four categories: insufficient communications, philosophical differences about subsidizing industries, concerns about the long-term sustainability of activities, and cultural differences between the council and potential or existing partners.

INSUFFICIENT COMMUNICATION

Council communication with the community travels largely by word of mouth, and interviewees stated that few people outside the organizations that participate in council activities are aware of its existence or mission. Council obscurity is partly intentional. The executive director and the board have made a policy of keeping activities relatively quiet and giving partners most of the credit for successful projects in order to create a sense of participant ownership and to avoid exposing the group to potential conflicts.

There is little evidence that a systematic effort has been made to include all interested parties when developing projects. Watershed restoration work is carried out with individual landowners without consulting with all members of the communities who live or work within the watersheds. Moreover, council efforts to work with groups has been more successful with organized groups than with unorganized groups, so certain segments of the population, notably Hispanics and Asians, have had little contact with council programs.

Internal communications are also weak. Most council members are unaware of the linkages between projects. Although most people are well informed about the specific projects they work with, they tend to have only a limited knowledge about the council's other projects and how they fit together. This lack of connection across projects is reflected in the organization's internal documentation, which sets out projects in ways to highlight neither their cross connections nor their connection to the organization's overall vision.

The staff is taking action to resolve these internal and external communication problems. A newsletter was initiated in the fall of 1996 to help disseminate information about activities, a web page created, and a special series for the local newspapers planned as part of the council's twenty-fifth-anniversary celebration.

To address the issue of reaching communities rather than individuals, the council is seeking funding to form watershed councils to develop coordinated watershed plans. The staff is also developing a strategy for reaching out to Hispanic and Asian harvesters of special forest products.

PHILOSOPHICAL DIFFERENCES
ABOUT INDUSTRY SUBSIDIES

Another problem that the council has encountered relates to philosophical differences about the role public subsidies should play in industry development. A number of "outsiders" charged that council projects thwart a "free market," citing as an example the Jobs for the Environment program, in which incentives for private businesses involvement in restoration work are decreased by a nongovernmental organization carrying out restoration with government funds.

The Satsop Nuclear Reservation, which is being deassessioned by the Washington Public Power Supply, was also given by interviewees as an example of how public subsidies thwart private incentives. The council is working in conjunction with the Grays Harbor Economic Development Council to convert the site's large land base into a demonstration forest and business park and seeking substantial federal and state dollars to fund the conversion. Given the early regeneration phase condition of the forest, no private industry could acquire the entire property and profit. However, the subsidies are also being used to compete with a business park that is a viable private opportunity. Using the forest as an opportunity to acquire the reservation, the council wants to convert the buildings into a business park, thereby eliminating the possibility of a private conversion of that part of the site. The council sees both of these subsidies as necessary to cope with the area's chronic unemployment and as a critical "jump start" for encouraging viable local industries.

Questions regarding the merits of subsidies and their duration have practical implications for the long-term sustainability of council projects. The Jobs for the Environment program is already in jeopardy because legislators are increasingly unwilling to continue subsidies. Moreover, if community entrepreneurs begin to believe that council activities inhibit their access to potential business opportunities, opposition to activities could develop.

To address these issues, the council is taking several approaches. One has been to create opportunities for crew workers to develop contracting businesses for a network of firms that would eventually take over the kind of work that the council crews perform. Thus far, however, these businesses have experienced only limited success. Another approach is to seek private sector funds to decrease reliance on public subsidies for restoration. Yet another is a campaign to encourage private timber company investment in watershed restoration to create demand for a private restoration industry. Engagement of private landowners is crucial given that most of the region's forest is privately owned. An alternative that has not yet been proposed is to work with existing businesses (rather than create new ones) interested in expanding into restoration. Finally, the council has taken steps toward creating an endowed community foundation to serve as a future funding source.

SUSTAINABILITY OR LONGEVITY OF IMPACT

Because the work of the council is project based and funded primarily by public grants, the sustainability of the work may be problematic. The habitat restoration program exemplifies the potential pitfalls of this organizational structure. A finite number of restoration projects are possible on a finite amount of land, and a finite number of workers are available for training. In effect, restoration of resources has become a new resource. Once the resources are restored, will the projects change what they retrain workers in? And, if restoration is now the resource, is that a resource that is as dependent on government regulation as harvesting has been? While interest in salmon protection has been in the public dialogue for almost ten years, the threat of endangered species listing is relatively new. However, as a selling point for the council's watershed restoration work, the possibility of listing certain salmon spawns as threatened or endangered under the Endangered Species Act is viable. If that act is changed or the listing of species altered, the work—and the newly retrained workers—could become irrelevant.

Some interviewees question the long-term viability of the council's worker retraining program on the grounds that training methodology is not aimed at creating a workforce adaptable to long-term, sustainable employment. Some people commented that the program focuses on providing workers with knowledge about specific types of restoration methods but not with the skills to keep abreast of changing ecological theory and the ability to develop new methods that reflect those changes. They argue that this approach is similar to training workers to cut only trees of a certain age. When the system or the science changes, these same workers may need to be retrained.

Some people felt that the Special Forest Products certification program might be unsustainable in the long run because of its heavy reliance on grants. Given the scarcity of public funds, it is unclear how long program funding will be available.

The council does not appear to be taking any measures to address either the "regulation dependency" or worker adaptability issues associated with the habitat restoration program. It has taken steps, however, to decrease its dependence on public grants through proposals for substantial funding from a variety of private foundations. The council is also in the process of establishing an endowed foundation that would fund long-term community development programs. Staff members are exploring ways to make programs self-supporting—working with Shore Trust, for example, on a strategy for generating revenue from a Special Forest Products training course.

Additionally, the council is considering how to integrate its approach at the program level. In a recent proposal for a watershed reinvestment campaign, it outlined a series of activities that would be linked under the habitat restoration program, including funding partnerships, workshops, watershed councils, restoration apprenticeship, restoration projects, small-business development, and coordinated monitoring.

CULTURAL DIFFERENCES

Since the council is a vast organization with diverse members and cultural issues, members vary in the ways they perceive their roles and contributions. Economic development organizations see the council as a tool for natural resource–based economic development. Government agencies see it as a channel for funds and a tool for completing projects. Private industry sees the council as a way to accomplish restoration. Nonprofits see it as a way to network and fulfill community-based missions. By providing forums and on-the-ground projects for these different groups, the council bridges different organizational and group cultures more effectively at the local than at larger-scale levels. Without clear links between projects to the overall mission, however, differences in objectives sometimes impede the organization's ability to achieve far-reaching regional impact.

While council projects affect the region's many ethnic- and economic-based cultures, there is little assessment of how to incorporate different values into the design of programs and projects. In the Special Forest Products program, for instance, the council trained new harvesters and helped them develop new Special Forest Products businesses rather than working with existing harvesters and buyers to develop training programs that would fit their existing needs. While the council has been able to get funding for its retraining program, it has also elicited resentment from some established harvesters and buyers.

Another problem associated with cultural differences surfaced in the Special Forest Products program when the council brought in ShoreTrust to help with the cooperative. Over the previous five years, the council had developed a culture of sharing information and emphasizing the need to get away from the secrecy that many potential cooperative members felt was hampering the development of the industry. People began to see the cooperative as a way to open up lines of communication among existing businesses. ShoreTrust, however, felt that in order for the cooperative to be competitive, it would have to adopt principles of secrecy and limited information sharing. A number of cooperative members who opposed these principles subsequently withdrew from the meetings.

The council adapted to this situation by ceding to ShoreTrust, at least insofar as the operation of RainKist was concerned, which appears to have undermined support from some segments of the Special Forest Products industry. The council is seeking to reestablish that trust by developing a Special Forest Products inventory and monitoring program to engage harvesters and buyers with scientists to establish harvesting guidelines and standards.

Outcomes and Successes

One comment that repeatedly emerged in interviews about the council was that it "gets things done." Some of the more widely known accomplishments since 1989 are as follows (see the sidebar "CPRC&D Projects" for a more exhaustive list of council projects):

- Development of a grants library and grantsmanship workshops
- Creation of a unionized habitat restoration program
- Development of training programs in habitat restoration and special forest products
- Creation of a microlending fund program
- Creation of RainKist, a special forest products marketing brokerage
- Construction of fish enhancement facilities around the region
- Construction of habitat restoration structures around the region
- Construction of the Julia Butler Hansen Elk Interpretive Center
- Construction of Skamokawa Vista Park
- Construction of Friends Landing (a fishing access site for the disabled)

Interviewees commented that council activities have played an important role in creating new alliances and changing relationships among local and non-local organizations. They also noted that involvement with the council and access to its resources have increased the capacities of local groups to obtain funds and to gain access to technical expertise from outside organizations. Key examples of these new relationships and capacity building efforts follow:

- *Emergence of the council as a successful political advocate.* At the state level, the council has carried out successful advocacy efforts to increase legislative support for the Pacific Coastal Economic Recovery Plan and the passage of the Jobs for the Environment bill. At the federal level, it has played a role in getting congressional authorization for the transfer of the Satsop nuclear site to a locally managed entity.
- *Stronger links among local groups.* Collaborative work with the displaced fishers habitat restoration program encouraged greater sharing of information and resources between conservation districts. The council's work as a facilitator for the Grays River Watershed Committee fostered communication among three previously insular settlements. The construction of Friend's Landing brought a variety of previously unconnected community groups together to raise money and to provide labor for project completion.
- *Increased local capacity to obtain funds.* Access to council staff for materials and funding advice has increased local groups' success rates at obtaining funds. The council helped local groups obtain approximately $1 million in grants in 1996 in addition to the roughly $1 million that it administered itself. Income reports provide a clear indication of this rise in capacity to obtain funds: Total income rose from $55,281 in 1991 to $1,359,967 in 1996.
- *Creation of new links with neighboring communities.* The council has sought to connect groups in the district's original three counties with groups in neighboring Mason County through the creation of an economic development district

and by expanding its jurisdiction to include Mason County. The Mason County Economic Development District has already profited from this alliance through the opportunity to learn more about alternative wastewater treatment systems, such as using hybrid cottonwood plantations to treat wastewater. The Habitat Restoration program has now extended its activities to include Mason County. Most people interviewed considered the council and many of its activities successful. Chief among the successful projects cited were Friend's Landing, the Skomakowa Interpretive Center, the Habitat Restoration program, and the Special Forest Products training program. Success was defined as the council's ability to "gets things done," bring money and jobs to the area, and engage diverse and contentious stakeholders in common projects.

Keys to Success

Factors people cited as contributing to success can be grouped into the following categories: strong and stable leadership, effectiveness in acquiring and sharing resources, insistence on collaboration, and application of principles of inclusivity, diversity, and equality.

STRONG AND STABLE LEADERSHIP

Interviewees were unanimous in the belief that much of the council's success is due to the presence of an executive director with superb networking and facilitation skills. Equally important was that the director had a vision and was willing to take risks and incorporate new elements into old projects, all of which are important factors in the organization's ability to adapt to changing circumstances. Many interviewees stressed the importance of having a permanent full-time coordinator. Finally, interviewees noted that the director's and the board's long-term commitments to the region and to the council promoted continuity and increased the chances of project follow-through.

EFFECTIVENESS IN ACQUIRING AND SHARING RESOURCES

With few exceptions, the interviewees commented that success was linked to the director's ability to acquire and share resources, particularly funding from state and federal agencies. They also noted that an important part of success in this regard was creating the conditions, such as the grants library and the grantsmanship workshops, for local groups to acquire their own funds.

INSISTENCE ON COLLABORATION

A third factor cited as contributing to success was the director and the council's insistence on creating a culture of collaboration and sharing. They thought that this culture resulted in a cooperative mind-set, incentives for mutual aid, and the ingredients needed for social cohesion. They noted that the spirit of cooperation was aided by the fact that funding agencies were more likely to award grants to groups working in partnerships.

PRINCIPLES OF INCLUSIVITY, DIVERSITY, AND EQUALITY

The council's adherence to principles of inclusivity, diversity, and equality was often listed as a key element in its success. An example of the inclusivity principle is the director's policy of letting other partners take credit for successful projects, thereby creating a feeling of ownership on the part of council members and partners. Many interviewees cited the group's apparent willingness to include all stakeholders interested in taking part in projects as a factor in success. Others noted that the council members and partner organizations are drawn from a fairly diverse spectrum of organizations. Although they acknowledged that diversity could create difficulties at times, they also felt that bringing in a wide array of groups encouraged the development of the broad support base needed for sustained collective action. Representatives of the smaller organizations noted that an important element in success was that all members are treated equally when it comes to getting advice or resources for projects.

The council is successful with individual projects and programs, but it is unclear how successful it is in terms of addressing its visions. In our conversations with council members and nonmembers alike, few were aware how the various activities of the council are linked. More important, the organization has not yet developed any measurable criteria or systematic evaluation system for determining whether its projects actually have a significant impact on what the council professes to be about—fostering cooperation around natural resources and linking economic development and natural resource conservation. Without such a system, it is impossible to judge the organization's success with respect to achieving that vision.

The Integration of Community Well-Being and Forest Health

The geographic region encompassed within the council's jurisdiction is "resource dependent." From coastal fishing to the areas of agriculture and timber, the region has a long history of labor linked to the sea and the land. The council recognizes this vital link and seeks to create and sustain employment in natural resources and maintain individual and community self-esteem. Many council projects, such as the restoration worker training program, the Special Forest Products program, and the efforts to develop markets for agroforestry products, are designed to sustain this link between land and labor.

Community well-being is a way of measuring or understanding how well communities are able to address change as well as the status quo. In traditional methodology, community health was assessed using an aggregate of measures of per capita income, availability of social infrastructures, and migration patterns. Community well-being evaluates those measures in addition to other attributes, such as indicators of "quality of life." The link between community well-being and forest health is particularly important in rural communities where economic prosperity has been dependent on resource extraction. Developing strategies for sustaining communities rather than letting them go through boom-and-bust swings may require new ways of thinking about forest health and its long-term effects on community well-being. Additionally, environmental conditions, such as clean water, flood protection, the presence of diverse species, and clean air, greatly affect the quality of life and are linked to community well-being.

The council does not explicitly discuss its projects in relation to community well-being. In fact, various members of the organization have different definitions of community well-being. For some, community well-being is equated primarily with "family wage" job opportunities, relatively high or rising per capita incomes, and the influx of new businesses. For these people, economic indicators are the measure of community well-being. For others, well-being is linked to jobs but also equated with low rates of "antisocial" behavior, such as divorce, drug use, and crime, and includes a community's sense of its own worth.

For yet other people, community well-being goes beyond an assessment of what happens to individuals to encompass the relationships between individuals and groups. Their definitions include the ability of the community to come to consensus, the ability of the community to work for common purpose, the existence of a sense of community, and the willingness of corporations and individuals to invest time, energy, and money in their community. One person expanded a definition of community well-being to include natural resources and aesthetics, linking natural beauty with high morale and community pride. While all its projects address at least some of these aspects of community well-being, the council has no system for assessing the impacts of projects on those factors.

As with the definition of community well-being, definitions of forest health also differed considerably. Four different perspectives of forest health were identified:

COMMUNITY WELL-BEING AND FOREST HEALTH   243

- *A natural character.* Some of the interviewees believe that a healthy forest is one that has not been "managed" or one that is restored to a previous condition in a previous time. An old-growth or ancient forest is the primary measure of forest health. Indicators of whether a "natural forest" is healthy would be a lack of intrusive management, the absence of forest products extraction, and the absence of thinnings, cuts, or roads.
- *Sustained yield.* Other interviewees, primarily those with forestry backgrounds, believe that a healthy forest is one that provides a sustained yield of forest products. This belief focuses on timber, but a sustained yield of special forest products is becoming important. A measure of forest health would be whether the forests provide timber and other products over time.
- *Landscape management.* Others defined forest health in terms of landscape management theory, citing a diversity of age classes and stand structure. According to this theory, age and stand structure diversity are important factors in sustainability and are linked to forest health. The four age classes are stand initiation, stem exclusion, understory reinitiation, and old growth. A healthy forest is a forest in which these four stages are present. From an economic and human use standpoint, the advantage of having all four stages present simultaneously is access to a wide range of products. A measure of forest health for these people is the relative distribution of different age classes in space and time.
- *Species diversity.* Some people claim that variation in vegetation and fauna is the indicator of forest health and that a variety of species as well as age variation and structural diversity is indicative. A measure of forest health according to this definition is the diversity of age, structure, flora, and fauna.

Since the council region has always been dependent on natural resources, it is no surprise that nearly everyone interviewed recognized links between community well-being and forest health. However, the existence of differing perceptions and understandings of community well-being and forest health make it difficult to evaluate how projects address them. It is difficult for council members and partners to arrive at a common understanding or evaluation criteria for these concepts. Community people's commitment to work with the land while striving for economic prosperity makes vital the need for explicitly linking projects with the overall goal of community well-being and forest health.

Arriving at a definition of "community" is difficult when community consists of hundreds of geographic communities, thousands of communities of interest, and dozens of economic communities. Perhaps that is why many people consider the council's project-based work successful; since these projects fulfill individual communities' needs, individual communities are satisfied. What this approach does not address well, however, is the needs of the larger community made up of smaller individual communities. This approach assumes that maximizing the well-being of each individual community maximizes the well-being of the larger community. Without more effective internal communication between individual communities, this strategy could potentially undermine the council's ability to function effectively in the long term.

Whether the men and women involved in stream restoration understand the link between their project and community well-being is also unclear. For the council to assist those participants in understanding a larger picture would require the organization to clearly articulate a goal that links forest health to community well-being. It would also need to think through how individual projects are related to forest health and community well-being, and how they integrate both.

Future of the Project

The council has the potential to evolve in a variety of directions. It could, for example, become more like an economic development council or a social service agency. Given its past record, the likelihood is that it will continue to grow in its hybrid mod—part economic development council, social service agency, information and grants broker, and resource conservation and watershed rehabilitation agency. This hybrid character—with the flexibility and the potential it creates to address a number of social, economic, and ecological concerns—is one of the council's strengths. To the extent that it can maintain this hybridity, its success is likely to continue.

But the council is at the point where its success could become its downfall. The addition of a new county to the list of member organizations has brought new ideas and possibilities for new projects. Unless the council can develop its currently weak internal communications network, the "glue" that holds the organization together may prove inadequate for keeping the larger, more complex organization running. One possibility that may need to be examined is the feasibility and desirability of creating "subregional boards" with some autonomy to make decisions for geographically localized areas within parameters established by the existing regional board structure.

In the nonprofit world, there is a saying that as long as there is money, there will be programs. This is likely to be true with the council, whose excellent track record for completing projects has demonstrated the "can-do" attitude that allows it to change strategies in accordance with new demands and circumstances. The need for the kinds of projects that the council is undertaking, such as watershed restoration, rehabilitation and marketing of the Satsop nuclear site, and special forest products training and business development, will continue in the foreseeable future in southwestern Washington.

A question that remains unanswered, however, is the degree to which these projects individually maintain and enhance community well-being and forest health. The forest-related council projects are not "community forestry projects" in the sense that the forests being affected by Council activities are not community owned, nor are management decisions about them made through a communal decision-making process. However, the restoration work, the Special Forest Products program, and the restoration of Satsop certainly involve the community or, more accurately, an agglomeration of many communities and fulfill certain community needs in the region. These programs also explicitly seek to enhance or restore the area's forests. However, one of the council's weaknesses is that it lacks provisions for assessing whether it is actually achieving its goals for either community well-being or forest health improvement. Until the organization is able to develop baseline data for community well-being and forest health and establish a monitoring and assessment system for determining the links between specific kinds of actions and community well-being and forest health, it will remain impossible to evaluate the success of the council's activities in those realms.

Epilogue: Five Years Later

In 1997, when the initial work for this case study took place, the council had accomplished much but was still in the midst of defining itself. Tangible accomplishments included 1) the creation of a unionized habitat restoration program and associated restoration projects throughout the region; 2) development of a grants library and a series of grantsmanship training workshops for use by local communities, organizations, and individuals; and 3) construction of several popular tourist facilities, including Skamokawa Vista Park, Friends Landing, and the Julia Butler Hansen Elk Interpretive Center. In addition, the council had gained a reputation as a successful advocate for state and federal support for economic development programs within its boundaries. It had also made a positive contribution toward creating and strengthening links among and between council member organizations.

The 1997 interviews indicated that the council's overall effectiveness as a regional development entity was hampered by a tendency to focus on individual projects rather than on an overall vision, weak internal and external communication about the council's activities, and inadequate project and program evaluation mechanisms. Although several of the council's forest-related activities clearly sought to simultaneously enhance community well-being and forest health, the lack of a monitoring and assessment system made it difficult to tell whether those goals had been accomplished. Moreover, the council's ability to develop and maintain successful programs depended heavily on the leadership of one individual: the organization's executive director.

Five years later, what conclusions can we draw about the effectiveness of the council to develop and implement an economic development agenda that seeks to link forest health and community well-being? Before embarking on a synopsis of the council's activities between 1997 and 2002, we first provide a brief overview of key changes that have taken place in the region's social, political, and economic context since 1997.

Demographic Changes

Several key demographic and economic changes took place in the Columbia-Pacific Resource Conservation District (CPRCD) region in the late 1990s. Although the overall population of the CPRCD region remained fairly stable during the 1990s, some areas within the region experienced very rapid rates of growth (Columbia-Pacific Resource Conservation and Economic Development District [CPRCEDD] 2002, 64). Major growth areas included communities close to Olympia, on the Pacific coast, and along the Columbia River. Many of these newcomers have urban origins and tend to value forests more for their recreational, aesthetic, and ecological values than as production sites. The region also experienced a significant increase in the percentage of Hispanic residents (CPRCEDD 2002, 67). Many incoming Hispanics found work in the area's paper and pulp mills, floral greens harvesting and processing industry, and shellfishing industry. Consequently, the ethnic composition of the natural resource workforce in the CPRCD region has changed substantially in the past decade.

Employment and Income Changes

The region's overall unemployment levels also changed dramatically between 1995 and 2000. In 1995, the region had experienced a net loss of 1,218 jobs since 1980, with most of the losses occurring in the manufacturing and construction sectors. By 2000, the region had experienced a net gain of 1,915 jobs since 1980. However, the job gains were concentrated in services, government, and retail trade (CPRCEDD 2002, 69). In short, the region's transition from a natural resource–based manufacturing economy to a services- and retail-based economy continued apace. At the same time, unemployment rates dropped nearly in half, from roughly 8 percent in 1995 to just over 4 percent in 2000.

During the same period, median household incomes within the region increased substantially, although they remained well below the state average (see table 11.4). The rate of households categorized as living in poverty also dropped dramatically in all four counties, with the most dramatic declines in Pacific and Wahkiakum Counties. With the exception of Wahkiakum County,

Table 11.4   Median Household Income, CPRCD Region

County	Median Income 1995 ($)	Median Income 2000 ($)	% Below Poverty Level 1995	% Below Poverty Level 2000*
Grays Harbor	28,047	34,160	16.4	11.9
Mason	32,345	39,586	13.2	8.8
Pacific	24,718	31,206	17.2	9.1
Wahkiakum	33,300	39,444	10.4	5.9
Washington State	40,398	45,776	10.9	7.3

Note: Poverty rates for female-headed households with no husband present were substantially higher, ranging from a low of 25.2 percent in Wahkiakum County to a high of 36.9 percent in Grays Harbor County.
Sources: Washington State Office of Financial Management, 1995 Population Trends; U.S. Census 2000, table DP-3.

however, poverty rates in the CPRCD region remained substantially above the state average.

In short, while the region remained poorer than much of the rest of the state, the late 1990s brought some measure of prosperity back to the region's economy, particularly in the service and retail sectors.

Natural Resource Policy Changes

During the period from 1997 to 2002, several important changes took place in resource policy arenas relevant to the CPRCD region, including endangered species policy, state lands forest management, the Washington State Growth Management Act, and special forest products policy.

ENDANGERED SPECIES ACT DESIGNATIONS

In 1998, the National Marine Fisheries Service (NMFS), which has jurisdiction over anadromous fish (fish that spawn inland and migrate to oceans) such as salmon, designated a series of spawns and types of salmon as threatened or "of concern." These designations, along with the listing of the northern spotted owl and the marbled murrelet, have affected the area that CPRCEED covers. While the salmon listings did not specifically curtail forestry activities in the area, they have had negative impacts on the sport fishing industry off the coast from Westport, Washington. Recently, the NMFS has also proposed a listing for bottom fish. The effect of this listing is unknown but could also impact the sport fishing fleet.

Overall, the continuing listings of fauna in this region have a psychological impact on the residents. While the listings could act as an indication that forest health must continue to be an ongoing concern, typically residents believe that the listings are causing further negative impacts to the economy. As a result, little reflection has taken place over what the root causes are of the declines in forest health.

STATE LANDS MANAGEMENT

Currently, state trust lands and other land managed by the Department of Natural Resources (DNR) are undergoing a statutorily mandated ten-year review on management practices. This review will result in the development of a revised plan for levels of cutting and other management activities. Constituents of the state trust land, as well as beneficiaries of timber sales taking place on state lands, have placed pressure on the DNR to increase the harvest targets. With recent changes in the state land commissioner and members of the state forest practices board, these increases are likely to be included in the revised plan.

GROWTH MANAGEMENT ACT

Two of the four counties involved in the CPRCD have "opted" out of Washington's Growth Management Act. The statute authorizing the act permits counties with certain population levels that remain historically at low levels to not engage in growth management. The two counties are Wahkiakum and Grays Harbor. The advantage to not participating in state-mandated growth management is that limits to growth can be locally controlled and mandated. In the case of both Wahkiakum County and Grays Harbor County, this means that development can be permitted in a less structured manner. The counties throughout the state that have opted out of growth management have traditionally been areas of high unemployment where development is viewed as a means of job creation and property rights issues are prevalent.

CHANGES IN THE SPECIAL FOREST
PRODUCTS INDUSTRY CONTEXT

Since 1997, several important changes have taken place in the special forest products industry (Lynch and McLain, in press). Changes include a shift in the ethnic composition of the harvester and processing workforce, increased regulation of the special forest products industry, and a rise in global competition within special forest products markets. Prior to the 1990s, rural-based Euroamericans and members of various tribes in western Washington constituted the majority of the harvesting population. By 1996, when the CPRCD initiated its Special Forest Products program, Southeast Asians (mostly from Cambodia and Laos) and Latinos from the United States, Mexico, and various countries in Central America had entered the profession in large numbers. By 2002, Latinos dominated the commercial harvester and processing workforce on the Olympic Peninsula, although Native Americans, Southeast Asians, and Euroamericans continued to harvest special forest products commercially and for personal and ceremonial uses. Euroamericans, however, continued to dominate in buying and management positions related to nontimber forest product industries.

Labor relations between the buying sheds and harvesters also changed dramatically during the 1990s. Many Latino harvesters are undocumented workers from Mexico and various countries in Central America and thus are unable to bargain effectively in the labor market. A recent study of floral greens policy on the Olympic Peninsula indicates that the availability of a cheap and ready supply of workers has contributed to a dramatic decline in the wages that harvesters can earn in the floral greens industry. In response to the worsening labor conditions, some harvesters, buyers, a few landowners, and local social justice advocates have requested that state and federal labor agencies do a better job of enforcing the labor laws regarding farm and forest contracting. This effort seeks to provide workers with higher wages and benefits, such as unemployment and workers' compensation. Although well intentioned, the movement to obtain better working conditions for harvesters prompted a group of the larger and economically more powerful buying sheds to file a lawsuit in opposition to the move to categorize them as employers of special forest product harvests.

Since the mid-1990s, the special forest products industry on the Olympic Peninsula has experienced significant changes in how access to resources is allocated. Most landowners have shifted from a nonexclusive permit system to exclusive leases open to bid. Landowners have also imposed increasingly strict harvesting requirements with respect to quantities that can be removed and areas where harvesting can take place.

Increasingly globalized markets for special forest products constitute a fourth important change in the special forest products industry since the mid-1990s. Wages in the special forest products sector have remained low or fallen in the face of increased competition from low-wage countries, such as Russia and China, for products similar to those harvested in the CPRCD region.

Changes within the CPRCD

In 1997, the CPRCD was shifting from defining itself as a resource conservation district covering three, primarily rural counties to a combination resource conservation and economic development district operating in four counties, including one county with a strong and growing bedroom community component. In 1998, this change was formalized with the creation of the CPRCEED, with the economic development district functioning semi-independently as a subcommittee of the larger organization (www.colpac.org). In January 2002, a second key change occurred when the longtime executive director left the organization. The CPRCEDD hired a former Natural Resource and Conservation Service employee to serve as a part-time director between January and June 2002. The new director became a full-time employee beginning in June 2002.

The composition of the CPRCEDD's members has not changed significantly, although the actual sitting elected board officials have. The change in board leadership does not seem to have had a significant impact on the organization. Despite concerns voiced in the mid- and late 1990s about the CPRCEDD's reliance on public sector funding, the organization continues to rely primarily on public sector funds for its projects and operational costs. However, the elimination of the legislatively mandated Jobs for the Environment program and the funds that the CPRCEDD used to fund restoration work has forced the CPRCEDD to diversify its sources of funding for watershed restoration projects. According to the new director, the internal and external communication challenges identified during the initial fieldwork remain the same. Although the CPRCEDD created a website, the organization lacks the resources to maintain the site on a frequent and regular basis.

The CPRCEDD has not yet developed or implemented a formal evaluation process for its projects and programs. The lack of an evaluation mechanism continues to inhibit the organization's ability to understand its mistakes and adapt to changes and challenges from external sources. Similarly, strategic planning or visioning efforts that could foster greater connectivity between projects and other efforts within the jurisdiction have not been carried out. The CPRCEDD has played a key role in the development of a comprehensive economic development strategy for the region. However, an analysis of the most recent version of this strategy indicates that visioning is done largely on a piecemeal basis, county by county and project by project. It is unclear from the document what connections exist between the different projects. While the leadership may have the contacts and means to connect projects, because the connective mechanisms are not formalized, when connections are made, it appears they are done so on an ad hoc basis.

Fate of Key Forest-Related Projects

FOREST RESTORATION PROGRAM

The Forest Restoration program has become dormant, primarily because of the elimination of funding through the Jobs for the Environment programs. However, with the recent national focus on forest fire prevention, funding for federal forest restoration work related to fire prevention may be a catalyst for the development of state funding on similar efforts. Work for restoration crews could be developed in thinning, small pole timber removal, and other efforts for fuel prevention. Additionally, money is available for restoration of salmon habitat. Replacing and enlarging culverts, planting native riparian species, and other restoration activities may also provide avenues for continuing the restoration projects.

SATSOP RESTORATION

The Satsop restoration is still in the planning stages. In the late 1990s, CPRCEDD contracted with the University of Washington Rural Technologies program, which is funded through federal grants, to assist in developing a plan for the Satsop forest. Researchers developed twenty-one management options through the use of landscape management models. The researchers have presented the information to the community. One possible economic development option is for the site manager to sell carbon sequestration rights to the forest. Several large energy companies have expressed an interest in purchasing such rights as a means for developing community goodwill. Local wildlife advocates have expressed reservations about other landscape models that include harvesting of timber.

SFP PROGRAM

During the late 1990s, the Northwest Natural Resource Group (NNRG) took on the work initiated by the CPRCEDD in the special forest products arena (www.nnrg.org). The CPRCEDD program focused primarily on training harvesters and buyers how to run a business. The CPRCEDD dropped its support for the special forest products program in the late 1990s, when it encountered strong opposition on the part of several of the region's large floral greens companies. The NNRG is based in Port Townsend but operates training programs in Mason County within the CPRCEDD region. The original program was a four-month certification program run through the Grays Harbor Community College. The college experienced difficulty recruiting students for such a long period. The NNRG has restructured the training program so that it fits better with participants' schedules. It has also developed a training guide and curriculum of best harvest practices for floral greens (salal, sword fern, and huckleberry).

Harvesters are taught core competencies, including landowner relationships, first aid and safety, permit systems, and map reading. The NNRG provides the training over a one- to two-day period and does so at the request of groups of harvesters. The goal is to produce a certified workforce that will make it possible for companies to market their products as sustainably harvested. The NNRG works in conjunction with Shorebank Pacific Enterprises, which provides microentrepreneurs with access to microloans and marketing services (www.sbpac.com). The NNRG has not yet succeeded in accomplishing its goal of getting certified harvesters exclusive access on private or DNR land because of strong and concerted opposition from several of the region's large floral greens companies.

WOOD PRODUCTS PRODUCTION AND MARKETING ACTIVITIES

The CPRCEDD has funded a variety of studies related to the development of the hybrid poplar industry. Hybrid poplars produce fiber and lumber. Hybrid poplar forests also can help restore contaminated soils and clean wastewater in areas lacking conventional wastewater treatment facilities. Between 1990 and 1995, the CPRCEDD conducted feasibility studies and supported efforts to form a hybrid poplar growers association to promote the conversion of farmland to hybrid poplar plantations. Because of a lack of adequate markets for products, the CPRCEDD's efforts to support a hybrid poplar wood products industry have been unsuccessful.

In 1999, the CPRCEDD commissioned a cedar waste processing feasibility study with funds from the Washington Department of Community, Trade, and Economic Development; the U.S. Forest Service; and Grays Harbor County (Cascadia Consulting Group and Re-Sourcing Associates 1999). The study identified potential business ventures that could utilize cedar waste from the region's many cedar mills to create value-added products. The researchers identified nine products with high market potential, including pulp chips, biomass fuel, dog bed filler, landscaping mulch, activated charcoal, cedar wood oil, road fill, wood composite, and cedar siding. They concluded that a central processing facility that could produce a range of products would be the most likely to be a viable industry. According to a Grays Harbor Economic Development Council staff member, however, the benefits of establishing such a facility at current market conditions are insufficient to cover the investment and operating costs.

Another hybrid poplar project supported by the CPRCEDD holds the potential to link forest health and community well-being. In 1996, the CPRCEDD received funding from the Economic Development Administration to commission a study examining whether hybrid poplar stands could help address wastewater disposal problems (www.colpac.org/hybrid.html). On the basis of the study's results, the CPRCEDD obtained additional funding to set up a demonstration site at a shellfish farm in Mason County in 1997. The shellfish farm added a five-acre hybrid poplar stand to its existing wastewater reuse site, planted in fir and alder. The shellfish operator will irrigate the hybrid poplar stand, as well as the fir and alder stand, with wastewater from the farm's processing plant. The CPRCEDD also used a portion of the grant to develop a report of five other projects in which hybrid poplars have served as the basis for rural economic development and environmental protection efforts. It is too early in the life of the demonstration project to gauge how successful this effort will be.

Conclusion

Since 1997, global and national forces of change have continued to affect Pacific Northwest communities. Changes in how forest resources are valued and whose values dominate in local and national forest policy arenas have contributed to the emergence of a regional economy that is increasingly dominated by the service and retail sectors rather than forest-related manufacturing and processing. The idea that it is possible to stabilize the region's economy by linking economic development to the creation and maintenance of healthy forest ecosystems, however, remains an abstract concept rather than a concrete reality.

The CPRCEDD's efforts to transform this concept into tangible on-the-ground programs have fallen far short of the hopes expressed by the region's leaders in the early and mid-1990s. The CPRCEDD's inability to attain this goal is due in part to the organization's lack of overall vision and connections among the diverse set of projects and programs that fall within its umbrella. In the forestry sector, the CPRCEDD's activities have been further hampered by an overabundance of studies and the lack of follow-through and resources needed to develop and implement long-term on-the-ground projects. The CPRCEDD's inability to develop workable long-term forest-related projects is exacerbated by its philosophical inconsistencies. On the one hand, the CPRCEDD advocates for projects aimed at linking economic well-being and forest health. On the other hand, many of its member organizations insist that resource regulation by outsiders is the key factor preventing the community from achieving economic well-being. Until the CPRCEDD community can acknowledge that factors other than outside regulation have contributed to the declines in local forest health and community well-being, the economy of this region will always remain tied to resources that are controlled or managed by so-called outside agents. Until organizations like the CPRCEDD can establish a larger vision and put into place the necessary mechanisms for monitoring the progress made toward that vision, development that ties together community well-being and forest health is likely to remain an unrealized dream.

Notes

Any opinions, findings, conclusions, or recommendations expressed in this publication are those of the authors and do not necessarily reflect the views of the Pacific West Community Forestry Center.

A Comment on Methodology: The information for this study was gathered by two social scientists. The researchers worked part time over a five-week period between March and April 1997. Interviews were conducted with thirty-four people, including CPRCD staff, CPRCD board members, CPRCD council members, founders, project partners, and others with some knowledge of or involvement with CPRCD activities. Eight of the interviews were conducted in person, and the remaining interviews were conducted by telephone. Interview data were supplemented with data from CPRCD documents, census reports, and land use documents.

1. This list serves to illustrate the range of projects and activities the CPRCD is engaged in. It is not meant to be an exhaustive list of all projects and activities.

2. This list is meant to illustrate the range of partners that the CPRCD works with. It is by no means complete, and inclusion or omission is not indicative of the relative importance of partner groups' contributions.

References

Appelo, Carlton. 1986. *A Pioneer Scrapbook of the Columbia River North-Shore Communities: Wahkiakum and Pacific Counties, Washington.* Ilwaco, Wash.: Pacific Printing Company.

Associated Forest Products Consultants, Inc. N.d. *A Study of Marketing Prospects for Hybrid Cottonwood Grown in Southwest Washington by Private Landowners.* Aberdeen, Wash.: Columbia-Pacific Resource Conservation District.

Coleman, James S. 1988. "Social Capital in the Creation of Human Capital." *American Journal of Sociology* 94 (Suppl.): 95–120.

Costanza, Robert, Bryan G. Norton, and Benjamin D. Haskell. 1992. *Ecosystem Health: New Goals for Environmental Management.* Washington, D.C.: Island Press.

Columbia-Pacific Resource Conservation District. N.d. *Agroforestry Resource Guide.*

———. 1989, 1990, 1991, 1992, 1993, 1995, 1996. *Work Accomplishment Reports.*

———. Bylaws of the Columbia-Pacific Resource Conservation and Development Council as amended December 7, 1990.

———. 1991. "Financial Report."

———. 1995. *Overall Economic Development Plan for the Columbia-Pacific Region: Grays Harbor, Mason, Pacific, and Wahkiakum Counties.*

———. 1996. "Columbia Pacific RC&D Profit and Loss Statement," January–December.

———. 1996. *Forest, Farms, and Fish* 1, no. 1 (Autumn). Newsletter.

————. 1996. "Special Forest Products Management Training Program: Summary Report," October 15.

————. 1996. "The Campaign for Watershed Reinvestment through Restoration: A Grant Proposal to the Lazar Foundation," November 8.

————. 1997. *Floral Products and Self-Employment.* Course Description and Student Policies Handbook.

————. 1997. *Forest, Farms, and Fish* 1, no. 2 (Winter). Newsletter.

Fox, James R. 1996. *Washington State Almanac: An Economic and Demographic Overview of Counties and Cities.* 10th ed. Eugene, Ore.: Public Sector Information, Inc.

Hunt, Ed. 1995. "ShoreTrust Brings Innovation to Funding on the Bay." *The Daily Astorian.* Special Edition: "Willapa, Banking on the Bay," 12.

————. 1995. "Solutions for Bay Mix Capitalism, Conservation: Lenders Focus on 'Green' Loans." *The Daily Astorian.* Special Edition: "Willapa, Banking on the Bay," 11–12.

Kirk, Ruth, and Carmela Alexander. 1990. *Exploring Washington's Past: A Road Guide to History.* Seattle: University of Washington Press.

Kusel, Jonathan. 1996. "Well-Being in Forest-Dependent Communities, Part I: A New Approach." In *Sierra Nevada Ecosystem Project: Final Report to Congress, vol. II. Assessments and Scientific Basis for Management Options.* Davis: University of California at Davis Centers for Water and Wildland Resources.

McKetta, Charley, Keith A. Blatner, Russell T. Graham, John R. Erickson, and Stanley S. Hamilton. 1994. "Human Dimensions of Forest Health Choices." *Journal of Sustainable Forestry* 2, no. 1/2: 135–49.

Nord, Mark. 1994. "Natural Resources and Persistent Rural Poverty: In Search of the Nexus." *Society and Natural Resources* 7: 205–20.

O'Laughlin, Jay, R. Ladd Livingston, Ralph Thier, John Thornton, Dale E. Toweill, and Lyn Morelan. 1994. "Defining and Measuring Forest Health." *Journal of Sustainable Forestry* 2, no. 1/2: 65–85.

Putnam, Robert D. 1993. "The Prosperous Community: Social Capital and Public Life." *The American Prospect* 2: 35–42.

Quinault Indian Nation. N.d. *The Quinault Indian Reservation.* Brochure.

Ross, Thomas D. 1995. "Jobs for the Environment, Chehalis Basin Habitat Restoration." Final Report.

————. 1996. "Washington State Watershed Restoration Grants Program: A CPRC&D Project."

ShoreTrust. N.d. *The First Environmental Bancorporation.* Brochure.

U.S. Soil Conservation Service. 1972. "1972 Annual Work Plan, Columbia-Pacific Resource Conservation and Development Project, State of Washington."

Washington State University Cooperative Extension, Mason County. 1991. "Business Plan for the Establishment of an Agroforestry Cooperative in Western Washington."

Wolf, Edward C. 1993. *Notes on a Tidewater Place: Portrait of the Willapa Ecosystem.* Long Beach, Wash.: Willapa Alliance.Yates, Richard, and Charity Yates. 1995. *Washington State Atlas and Datebook.* 4th ed. Eugene, Ore.: Public Sector Information, Inc.

WEBSITES

www.colpac.org
www.colpac.org/hybrid.html
www.nnrg.org
http://ocd.wa.gov./info/lgd/growth
www.sbpac.com
http://sivae.cfr.washington.edu/satsop-plan
http://wa.gov.wdfw/do/jul02

REPORTS

Cascadia Consulting Group and Re-Sourcing Associates. 1999. "Cedar Waste Venture Feasibility Study: Final Report," December.
Columbia-Pacific Resource Conservation and Economic Development District. 2002. "Comprehensive Economic Development Strategy."
Lynch, Kathryn, and Rebecca McLain. In press. "Land, Labor and Sustainable Forest Management: Floral Greens Policy on the Western Olympic Peninsula 1994–2002." General Technical Report. U.S. Forest Service Pacific Northwest Research Station, Portland, Oregon.
Tobe, Lisa. 2002. "Hoquiam Case Study." Northwest Economic Adjustment Initiative Assessment. Forest Community Research. Draft report.
U.S. Soil Conservation Service. 1972. "Annual Work Plan, Columbia-Pacific Resource Conservation and Development Project, State of Washington." Portland, Oregon.

ADDITIONAL INTERVIEWS/E-MAIL CONTACTS

Jim Freed, WSU Cooperative Extension
Elaine Corets and Larry Nussbaum, Northwest Natural Resource Group
Michael Tracy, Grays Harbor Economic Development Council
Jerry Smith, CPRCEDD
Jim Walls, formerly of CPRCEDD (notes from an interview by Lisa Tobe)

CHAPTER 12

Community Forestry at the Urban–Rural Interface

THE BEAVER BROOK ASSOCIATION AND THE MERRIMACK RIVER WATERSHED

Peter Lavigne

Managing the forest and watershed in a remnant forest surrounded by suburban sprawl is the goal of the Beaver Brook Association (BBA), a thirty-four-year-old non-profit organization in New England. Beaver Brook forestry at the urban–rural interface is a model for how farming, forestry, and recreation can complement rather than threaten each other, a model that is increasingly important as rural landscapes are overcome by bedroom commuter communities and urbanization. This remnant Beaver Brook forest, in a landscape that in three hundred years was transformed from forest to farmland to bedroom community, is being revalued as forest again.

Two cousins who had grown up in the watershed and were saddened by the devalued land, rural poverty, and depleted soils they now found there decided to act on their nostalgia for rural ways, their belief in outdoor education, and their savvy about tax write-offs. They undertook a land-buying venture in the watershed and established the BBA, a conservation organization with an educational mission and endowment. Because of these two men, their use of money for conservation, and the associates they attracted to the BBA Board, 2,200 acres of the Merrimack River watershed is held as open space for nearby residents and visitors, creating land valuations considerably higher than the original real estate.

The BBA forest management has developed over the years to emphasize a watershed perspective. Management includes the selective logging of trees to produce income for the association's activities, for recreation, and for wildlife preservation. To demonstrate how forestry can coexist with recreation and wildlife, the association offers the growing suburban and urban populations that surround the conservancy programs for schoolchildren, public festivals, summer residential programs, nature trails, horticulture classes, and a model working farm on association lands. In 1996, almost 20,000 people attended the association's various programs.

A challenge for the BBA in the years to come will involve maintaining its integrity in the context of its growing use. The fate of these 2,200 watershed acres surrounded by housing developments and a growing human population with a propensity to either abandon or use a place to death is uncertain. Whether this forest "island" in suburban America can support the life within it will ultimately depend on how well its lessons are learned and on the will of its neighbors and others in the rapidly suburbanizing watershed.

Back to the Future

In a once out-of-the-way corner of the 5,010-square-mile Merrimack River watershed, the Beaver Brook Association (BBA), a thirty-four-year-old nonprofit educational corporation, manages an "island" of forest within a rapidly suburbanizing landscape. For the previous three hundred years, this island was a small segment of a large rural area comprising forest, farm, and swampland in southern New Hampshire and northern Massachusetts. Now this "island" of forest reverberates far beyond its limited acreage—providing a lingering educational opportunity to learn about forests, forestry, farming, and recreation for the bi-state region where farming and forestry lifestyles have mostly disappeared.

The BBA was founded through the efforts of two cousins in the early 1960s. Their initial gift of seventeen acres of land to the community of Hollis, New Hampshire, "dedicated to the advancement of knowledge and appreciation of the natural world among people of all ages," formed what has become a diverse and active institution. The volunteers and staff of the association manage a certified tree farm, a series of educational programs for schoolchildren and adults, and an increasingly important wildlife and human recreational refuge from the surrounding urban and suburban areas.

The philanthropic vision of "two unlikely partners," Hollis P. Nichols, a Boston banker, and his country farmer cousin, town official, and horticulturalist Jeffrey P. Smith, made possible the acquisition of a loosely adjacent series of played-out farms, fields, forests, and swamps at a time when prices were low and demand for the land was nearly nonexistent. The land was obtained with money from the various funds and trusts established by Nichols and his wife, Ellen, in addition to the efforts of Smith, who contributed a substantial amount of his own land.

Since its founding in 1964, the BBA's property has grown through purchases, gifts, and exchanges to encompass approximately 2,000 acres of land and several old homesteads in three towns. Much of the Beaver Brook land is managed as a productive, certified tree farm with related wildlife management practices and goals. Substantial portions of various habitats are preserved in their natural states. These include mature second-growth forests with magnificent trees, mixed-age forests, and several types of wetlands. Beaver Brook, one of two streams crossing the main set of properties in Hollis, New Hampshire, is a tributary of the Nissitissit River, which flows into the Nashua River in Massachusetts. One of the nation's great success stories in watershed restoration,[1] the Nashua River flows north back into New Hampshire, where it joins with the Merrimack River at the "Thoreau's Landing" condominium development in Nashua.

The Regional Context

The Merrimack River watershed presents a twentieth-century study in contrasts: a watershed of 1.7 million people with land uses ranging from federally designated wilderness to national forest managed primarily for recreation to heavily industrialized urban/suburban corridors along one hundred miles of the Merrimack River itself. This previously agricultural watershed is now 83 percent forested with generally poor-quality, small ownership units of slowly reestablishing forest. High-graded harvests resulted in increasingly poor regrowth since the 1860s, when less than 40 percent of the watershed was forested. The Merrimack watershed is a microcosm of eastern North America: an increasingly fragmented island of forest and wildlife habitat surrounded by the pressures of over 80 million people living within one day's drive.

The Merrimack River watershed rises in the White Mountains of New Hampshire at the southern edge of the Great Northern Forest. The 180-mile-long watershed drains two-thirds of New Hampshire (3,800 square miles) and 1,210 square miles of northern Massachusetts. Formed by the confluence of the Pemigewasset River (draining from Echo Lake and the Old Man of the Mountain and from the East Branch Wilderness of the White Mountain National Forest) and the Winnipesaukee River (draining the Sandwich Range and Lake Winnipesaukee) in Franklin, New Hampshire, the 116-mile-long Merrimack's major drainages include the north-flowing Contoocook, Nashua, and Concord Rivers, along with the Suncook, the Souhegan, and the Piscataquog, before reaching the Gulf of Maine and the Atlantic Ocean in Newburyport, Massachusetts.

Cradle of the industrial revolution in America, the Merrimack is storied in literature (Henry David Thoreau), poetry (John Greenleaf Whittier), and song (Tom Rush). The mills of the Merrimack in Concord, Manchester, Nashua, Lowell, Lawrence, Haverhill, and Newburyport provided power, textiles, shoes, machinery, and cash for a young nation. By the beginning of the twentieth century, the Amoskeag mill complex in Manchester, New Hampshire, would be the largest textile mill in the world, employing 17,000 workers.

The Merrimack's first major products after white settlement, however, were beaver and the four-to-six-foot-diameter white pines favored as mast trees for England's Royal Navy. By the time of Thoreau's trip on the Concord and Merrimack in 1839, the vast forests of white pine, white oak, hickory, chestnut, cedar, ash, maple, and beech were largely eradicated throughout the Merrimack watershed except for its northern mountain reaches. Forest cover statewide reached a low of 48 percent in 1850 with a population of approximately 300,000 people in the watershed. One hundred and fifty-seven years later, approximately 83 percent of the watershed is again forested, and 1.7 million people call the Merrimack basin home.

The people of New Hampshire have a long and distinguished history of concern for forests. New Hampshire is home to one of the oldest private land trusts/environmental advocacy groups in the country, the Society for the Protection of New Hampshire's Forests (the Forest Society). Founded in 1901 "to protect the state's most important landscapes and promote wise use of its renewable resources," the Forest Society was, in part, responsible for the 1911 passage of the Weeks Act, which established the White Mountain National Forest and laid the basis for the entire eastern national forest system.

Hollis Nichols, Jeff Smith, and Beaver Brook

One common factor for many of the land protection projects throughout the Merrimack watershed is the initiating presence of an individual or a small group of individuals who, for a variety of reasons, want to protect a body of land.[2] The origin of the BBA embodies this pattern. According to Tom Mullin, executive director from 1995 to 1998, "Jeff Smith was a farmer, forester, logger, and horticulturist, born and raised in Hollis. For years he had been involved in a variety of conservation practices and in fact had been recognized over the years for his agricultural and forestry practices by the state and other entities. Hollis Nichols was a manager of a mutual fund outside of Boston . . . he's a cousin who went into Boston and made a fortune."

According to those who knew him, Hollis (who died in 1997; Jeff died in 1987) had a deep appreciation and love of the outdoors, land, and nature. He was also deeply involved with the prestigious Roxbury Latin School in Boston. He was on its board of directors, served as treasurer, at one time served as president, and had been a student there as a boy as he grew up in West Roxbury, which, says Mullin, "at that time was a very exclusive part of Boston." According to Mullin, Hollis thought it would be a good idea and a great opportunity to set up a space near enough to the city but far enough away that the urban boys of Roxbury Latin (and eventually other organizations and people) could learn more about the outdoors. In the early 1960s, Hollis got together with Jeff to work on the idea. They were, says Mullin, "quite frankly an unlikely pair—though they had known each other for life, I'm not quite sure that without this venture they would have been anything other than distant cousins."

Ralph Andrews, a prone-to-laughter, silver-haired former president of the Beaver Brook Board of Trustees, identified a richly ironic set of factors that played into Nichols's vision for outdoor learning and preservation. He said, "It all started when he [Hollis] bought a farm to build a house for his mother with seventeen acres and his mother didn't like the house." In the early 1930s, Nichols had purchased a seventeen-acre farm on top of a hill, and he and his sister and brother built an elaborate "summer cottage" for their mother. Tom Mullin added, "Though she did go there, she didn't really like it because he had it built exactly the way he would have liked it. It looks like an Englishman's club (dark paneling); it fits Hollis perfectly, but his mother didn't like it." In 1964, when Nichols and Smith formed the BBA, the seventeen acres surrounding his mother's unwanted "summer cottage" formed the first donation.

Nichols was also motivated in part by his aversion to the Internal Revenue Service. "He began looking for ways he could use the property and found he could donate the land for conservation and get around the IRS—it motivated much of his giving! We can thank the IRS for steering him in the right direction," said Andrews. Mullin adds, "He had a vision, and after, he saw tax benefits to it."

In fact, the New Hampshire Department of Revenue Administration reports that 52 percent of all land statewide is in the Current Use Program, which provides tax breaks to landowners. Eighty-five percent of that land is forested, followed by farmland, unproductive land, and wetlands.[3] Until the tax "reform" act of 1986, land donations like those of Hollis Nichols were much more common and advantageous.

Nichols connected with his cousin Jeff Smith because while Nichols had the vision and idea for creating an educational forest conservation reserve, he did not know where to start looking for properties and forest parcels. Jeff Smith had been on the Conservation Commission, had been a selectman,[4] and knew all about the ins and outs of small-town life, so he knew which properties had been abandoned and had tax liens and which families were interested in selling. Tom Mullin remarked that "of course, this was 1964 when this major purchasing commenced—for the first ten or fifteen years I'm sure that when people heard that this new nonprofit was buying up swampland and fields reverting to forest, people probably thought Hollis and Jeff were crazy."

According to Andrews, who, in addition to his volunteer work with the BBA, the Audubon Society of New Hampshire, and other organizations, is a wildlife biologist retired from forty years at the U.S. Fish and Wildlife Service,

That was still a time when people were glad to get any money they could out of this lousy New Hampshire land and move to the city somewhere. Land was cheap, and much of it was already in the process of converting back to forest—though of very poor quality. I think people were glad to get rid of it. They weren't about to go back and try to clear and put it back into farmland because that's what they wanted to escape, and they couldn't make much out of it for forests.

The Merrimack River Watershed Initiative: Restoring an Industrial and Recreational Resource

As a kid in the 1960s growing up in New Hampshire, I knew the Merrimack as the river "too thin to plow and too thick to drink." The early 1970s knew it as one of the ten most polluted rivers in America. Its major tributaries, including the Pemigewasset and the Nashua, stunk of sulfur and dyes from the pulp and paper mills, and the Nashua would change color daily, depending on the daily run of paper colors at the Fitchburg/Leominster mills. In the 1980s, state environmental agencies in Massachusetts and New Hampshire did not cooperate on cleanup plans or action, and environmental advocacy groups were filing lawsuits against the major municipalities and industrial dischargers for gross violations of the Clean Water Act. Even the then-ten-year-old Merrimack River Watershed Council (MRWC), while advocating a watershed approach to restoring the Merrimack River, focused almost exclusively in its program on the Massachusetts stretch of the river from Lowell to Newburyport. At the urging of the MRWC and others, Mike Deland, then regional administrator for Environmental Protection Agency (EPA) Region 1, recognizing the progress that had been made with the investment of over $500 million in federal and state expenditures for sewage treatment, stepped into the breach with $150,000 carved out of his budget in 1987 and created the Merrimack River Watershed Protection Initiative.

Using $50,000 for each state and an additional $50,000 for his own staff, Deland, at the MRWC's 1987 annual meeting, called for "an action-oriented watershed protection initiative [that] will allow us to step back and examine the Merrimack watershed not as a collection of discharge permits or a list of construction grants but as a single ecological system. This precedent-setting, holistic approach will expand our understanding of the watershed and allow us to more intelligently focus our pollution control efforts." Fourteen years later, the Beaver Brook Association is the beneficiary of much of the work arising from the EPA Merrimack Watershed Initiative. Among other issues focusing the Beaver Brook's work is the availability of an interstate geographic information system created by the initiative which includes sophisticated population growth maps and other useful parameters along with a baseline geographic capability.

Through the efforts of Smith and Nichols along with the first BBA director, zo-ologist, and forester Tudor Richards and forester Peter Smith (no relation to Jeff), the BBA is composed of over ninety separate parcels totaling 1,729 acres clustered in the town of Hollis with an additional 200 acres in the nearby town of Milford.

The BBA holdings maintain Hollis's original connection with educating schoolchildren by supporting a range of programs for children of the greater Nashua area, along with public festivals, summer residential programs, nature trails, horticulture classes, a new model working farm, and various special events. A small professional staff of ten was supplemented with a part-time teaching staff of twelve to fifteen and 9,850 hours of labor from nearly two hundred regular and part-time volunteers in 1996. About 16,700 people attended various pro-grams on association property in 1996 with total estimated visitor hours at 52,000.

Land Management at the Urban–Rural Interface

At the time of Beaver Brook's incorporation, few people in the area foresaw the importance for the area of the open space Smith and Nichols were protecting. In the larger context of a 5,010-square-mile watershed, 2,000 acres may seem in-consequential. Yet an analysis of changes in population and land use of the area over the past fifty years illustrates the importance of those 2,000 acres today. This southern tier of New Hampshire has been transformed from a largely rural series of small farm towns in the 1960s to a largely suburban/urban land use base with very few farms in the 1990s. According to Tom Mullin, in 1997 there was one dairy farm left in Hollis, compared to approximately sixty dairy farms fifty years ago. Ralph Andrews reports that in 2002 the last dairy farm has closed and that the two or three farms left in the area plant only farm-stand crops like pump-kins, corn, and strawberries. There are only three large orchards left, and the market for apples is shaky, along with scattered estate hay farming, most of which is harvested for hobby horse farms in Massachusetts.

Andrews says that since 2002, all three towns surrounding BBA holdings have been scrambling to protect the look of rural agriculture in the area, as nearly all functional farms have shut down and subdivided "for nearly total high end exurbia."

Population figures for the three towns with BBA lands are instructive. The town of Hollis grew from 5,700 people in 1990 to 6,600 in 1996[5] and is pro-jected to grow another 25 percent by 2010. Respective figures for Brookline are

As everyone is aware, on Beaver Brook's land there is much more to the forest than the trees. In 1986, 2,187 registered visitors used Beaver Brook.[8] . . . As the surrounding area becomes more developed, Beaver Brook will become more important as a wildlife refuge and for passive recreation. Beaver Brook Association will have a great challenge and obligation to educate visitors about the wise use of New Hampshire's forests.

Birch's report noted that Beaver Brook's forest generally contained even-aged stands sixty years or older, with some stands ninety years old, and others, "like the Howe pasture on Ridge Road, are forested by trees which grew after the 1938 hurricane." Birch also noted the high-quality stands of white pine on the lands managed and formerly owned by Jeff Smith and projected eventual species successions based on soil types and current dominant species if the forest was left unmanaged. Birch's report took the major policy recommendations from the earlier Bennett report and suggested several key modifications:

• Maximize the utilization of all harvested products within economic bounds
• Prevent site deterioration and improve the productivity and health of the forest
• Create a demonstration forest showing ideal and commercial management practices
• Create and maintain a diverse, multi-aged forest

With those modifications, Birch proposed four basic management units on the Beaver Brook properties, recommending management plans for each unit "prescribing treatments on a stand-by-stand basis." To ensure future "old-growth forests and to protect aesthetic interests," Birch also recommended more areas be designated as natural or wild areas. Birch's report completed the transformation of the BBA's holdings from its past working rural agricultural landscape to its future as a showpiece forest oasis. His recommendations focused on the integration of people with forest and wildlife management amidst the surrounding suburban development.

In 1982 Mark Lapping forecast Beaver Brook's fate in his essay "Toward a Working Rural Landscape."[9] This carefully documented work showed the progressive loss of farms and farm acreage in New England to forest and potentially to suburbanization[10] and concluded that "the problems of New England agriculture are numerous. . . . A rejection of the business-as-usual scenario is required though warmed-over Jeffersonianism is not enough." Lapping's recommendations included this critical and largely ignored point: "Capital investment strategies that do not place growth-inducing elements like sewer systems and highways in farming areas are required, lest the land squeeze on farmers be further exacerbated."[11] The consequences of the lack of action on Lapping's recommendations have led to the near elimination of farming from southern New Hampshire.

Watershed Management for the Next Century

Lee Kantar, natural resources manager from 1997 to 2000, headed the effort to update and manage plans for Beaver Brook's lands. He worked with an advisory group of foresters, including Jonathan Nute of the Hillsborough County Cooperative Extension; John Ferguson, a retired county forester who is now consulting; and Karen Bennett and Craig Birch, consulting foresters with the New England Forestry Foundation's wholly owned subsidiary New England Forestry Consulting. Birch and Ferguson, also Beaver Brook trustees, still mark and arrange for cuts with a local logger with whom they have a long-term relationship and whose extraction practices they trust.

Kantar's long-term management goals included a shift from individual resource management to a more comprehensive view of management for the Nissitissit watershed. Kantar's partially realized goal was to complete a comprehensive resources inventory so that the BBA can more clearly understand what needs to be done to protect the ecosystems of their properties. He said, "We want to make sort of a shift to watershed management, to a more comprehensive view of how things affect the whole—how doing 'a' will affect 'b', etcetera." The shift to "watershed management" represents a series of new challenges for the BBA. Wildlife management, user conflicts, timber harvest, riparian area and stream management, and education programs around land use practices will all experience growing pains as the task of knitting a comprehensive whole for association lands continues.

In many ways, Kantar's effort to manage BBA lands from a watershed perspective mirrors the difficulties of ecosystem protection within the current system of environmental law. Thirty years of a system of environmental law that manages air quality separately from land use and land use separately from water quality have shown the inadequacy of the current law's ability to protect ecosystems from the cumulative effects of permitted discharges, developments, and diversions.[12] In like manner, the association's laudable past efforts are not enough, in Kantar's view, to adequately address the management challenges facing the association's landscape today.

Forest Management Practices and Timber Harvests

Completing the initial natural resources inventory for the Beaver Brook watershed will require a huge investment of finances and time. As programs and acreage have grown and with the backlog of a previously unfilled positions, Kantar's time initially was consumed with trail maintenance, program planning, improving signage, and managing the annual harvest. His time eventually shifted

In 1899, an Episcopal missionary for northern New Hampshire found the critical human angle that started to turn the tide. The Rev. John E. Johnson wrote an incendiary pamphlet that accused the New Hampshire Land Company—a Hartford-based concern that, along with other investors, was buying up and consolidating large tracts to sell to the timber companies—of genocide. An article in the December 1900 issue of *New England Homestead*, a farm newsletter, followed this pamphlet. "The people are a unit in behalf of New England Farms, homes and industries!" the newsletter thundered. "The wanton destruction of forests in northern New England has aroused universal indignation . . . which simply needs to be organized to accomplish the desired reform."

Three months later, former New Hampshire Governor Frank West Rollins convened a meeting of nine friends from a range of backgrounds. They called themselves the Society for the Protection of New Hampshire Forests. "The early Society was an amalgam of New Hampshire's political power with Boston's social and financial elite, plus a seasoning of pioneer conservationists and outdoorsmen and hardy Yankee townsmen and farmers," historian Paul Bruns tells us. Interests ranged from the altruistic (the Appalachian Mountain Club) to the commercial (the American Pulp and Paper Association). United with advocates for a southern Appalachian reserve, the coalition decided that the only adequate response was federal ownership. . . . Leisure, timber, and scenery were all factors, but it was water that turned the tide. In a booklet titled *Reasons for a National Forest Reservation in the White Mountains*, Amoskeag Manufacturing Company President T. Jefferson Coolidge blamed clear-cutting upstream for the alternating floods and droughts that were damaging his mills in Manchester. Soon, more than one hundred mill owners joined the fray.

Finally, in 1911, with the support of Progressives in Washington and sponsored by Representative John Weeks of Massachusetts, a native of Lancaster, New Hampshire, an Eastern forest reserve bill passed both houses and was signed by President Taft. The legislation enabled the federal government to purchase privately owned land to protect the headwaters of "navigable streams." No region of the country was specifically named, but within a year of passage, land acquisition had begun in the White Mountain National Forest. Eventually, the Weeks Act would enable the creation of fifty national forests in the East.

Adapted from Richard Ober, "The Weeks Act of 1911, *At What Cost? Shaping the Land We Call New Hampshire* (Concord, N.H.: Society for the Protection of New Hampshire's Forests, 1992)

Wildlife Management

The suburbanization of the lands surrounding Beaver Brook is beginning to raise complaints about "nuisances." Andrews chuckles, saying that "people want wildlife, but when they find out what wildlife is, beaver, deer, etcetera, they become 'nuisances.'" He calls it the "conservation land syndrome," saying that the real estate industry emphasizes lots that back up to protected conservation lands, leading to increased fragmentation on the edges of the conservation land and home-owner opposition to tree cutting and new recreational trails.

Most of the conflicts at Beaver Brook about forestry and wildlife operations have to do with the timber cuts around the wildlife pond and adjacent land the BBA does not control. The most controversial issue is the increased use of mountain bikes, but motorized vehicle use has been banned, and there is very little problem with all-terrain vehicles, motorcycles, or snowmobiles. Andrews adds, "We've had some controversy with Trustees who were upset about ruts on their favorite trails and other damage from forestry operations, but never to the point where the trustees have said we don't want further cuts. In a sense, in the eyes of the public, we are a nature preserve because we do have regulations against hunting and trapping, and you can't pick the flowers, you can't remove vegetation." With irony in his tone, Andrews notes, "It's all right if we do forestry, but you can't pick the flowers. Fortunately, it hasn't come up into a big controversy that you can cut the trees but you can't pick the flowers."

In 1968, Beaver Brook received Public Law 566 funds to build and maintain a dam for a wildlife pond and swamp. Beavers were long extirpated from the area, and there was no standing water for migratory waterfowl or other creatures. The wildlife pond is now one of the most popular spots on the trail system, and fishing is allowed. In keeping with the spirit of the BBA's name, wildlife management practices actively encourage beavers for maintaining wetland habitat for other species, and education programs are focused on their role. Andrews notes, "This at a time when ex-urban home owners, road supervisors, and sawlog foresters want to get rid of them." But beaver have recolonized the association properties, and the pond is no longer an isolated water body.

Management of aquatic species, however, is one of the gaps in the history of the BBA. According to Mullin, "We really don't know what kinds of fish we have." Though the land comprises a large part of the Nissitissit watershed and both Rocky Pond Brook and Beaver Brook are in relatively untouched condition, there has been no study or inventory of aquatic species other than an annual beaver census. There was an effort in conjunction with the Audubon Society of New Hampshire in the late 1980s to use Beaver Brook as a long-term monitoring station of environmental quality. But the effort became mired in conflict about methodology and expense and eventually faded away after only one report.

Education

The original mission of serving kids from the Boston-area Roxbury Latin School waned over the years. According to Mullin, the school's philosophy changed about twenty years ago with the arrival of a new headmaster and Hollis Nichols's

departure from the Roxbury Latin board. The school's new leadership deempha-
sized natural science and the importance of outdoor recreation, and the close ties
to Beaver Brook faded away. The mixture of students that Roxbury Latin serves
has also changed over the years from a diverse group of rich, working-class kids
to primarily rich kids. Andrews says, "The original intent of bringing kids from
the city became not so special . . . coming here was no longer coming to the
farms and fields of New Hampshire, and so it changed at both ends."

One tie remains between the school and Beaver Brook. Seventh graders
from Roxbury Latin attend a two-night, three-day orientation program and
camping experience each year. Andrews adds, "From the standpoint of what
Beaver Brook is about—that being the educational opportunities, with the land
being the workshop for these opportunities—education is always the focus of
what we do here at Beaver Brook. Kids are now bused in locally from the Greater
Nashua area and neighboring Massachusetts schools and organizations."

Management Concerns and Growth

Growth put pressure on the board to fund programs from endowment and develop a professional staff. Ralph Andrews relates how

> originally we were very fortunate here, thanks to Mr. Nichols's foresight and
> antipathy toward the IRS. He made sure he set up tax-exempt funds so that
> we could keep our entire staff and maintain these buildings and facilities
> without need for any membership money. But there came a time when we
> were outgrowing that, and also we found we had to put some of our money
> in more conservative investments—we were getting into a lot of junk bonds
> (which in the heyday were paying us quite a bit of revenue, but fortunately
> we got out in time)—and put our investments in more conservative sources
> of revenue that didn't bring us as much. So, we really had to focus. There
> were some years where we cut back on staff, and for a long time we were with-
> out a professional director . . . the president of the board was pretty much the
> person who ran things.

For many years, Beaver Brook was managed primarily by the all-volunteer
Board of Trustees who were elected by a small group of members. Hollis Nichols,
informed by his banking experience, held a traditional viewpoint of how the
board should be operated and how they were morally as well as legally obligated
to be well informed and to go deeply into operations. Over time, the hands-on
nature of the volunteers willing to be trustees changed with the growth of pro-

grams and in particular the growing sophistication of the education programs. "The nature of the operation was changing so that it was more complicated, and a person with another job could not keep up with the day-to-day operation," says Andrews. Eventually, the management structure had to grow with the programs. Tom Mullin adds,

> And then . . . we went pretty much from a rural community to an urban community; [we] had much more demand by the community, desires by the community about what you could provide. We saw this overwhelming demand; we were turning things away, while for many years, up until about five or six years ago, the board was running the organization. The committees at the time, about six or seven different standing committees, Executive, Finance, Library, Horticulture, Publications, Forestry, Trails—all those indications of a board-run organization.

According to Andrews, "This was an extension of Jeff Smith's personality, and he looked a little bit askance at some of the things that developed in education of horticulture operations here, but we all did eventually realize we did need to have a full-time director."

Beaver Brook's operating budget is about 40 percent endowment income, with the rest coming from a variety of sources, including educational revenues, grants, and approximately six hundred members in the "Friends of Beaver Brook Association" effort. Most of the education programs are provided on a fee-for-service basis, which is subsidized by the BBA. The association also made about $15,000 from timber harvest in 1996.[13]

New Land Trust for Future Acquisition

The trustees set up a new spin-off land trust, the Nichols Smith Conservation Land Trust, to accept gifts of land, easements, and conservation restrictions for BBA lands (many of which were donated or acquired without development restrictions) and other lands in the area. All the new land trust trustees are local people. Although the impetus for the new trust was the need to protect the association's lands, the trustees did not want to limit the land trust to association lands because other area conservation organizations also had the need for a vehicle to hold permanent development restrictions. Since 1998, the Nichols-Smith Land Trust has acquired easements or title to approximately four hundred acres of association lands while also acquiring a few acres of inholdings in land swaps from private landowners.

The Future of the BBA in the Merrimack Watershed

From 1993 to 1997, the composition of the BBA board changed by approximately 80 percent. Most of the founding members had died or moved out of direct involvement. Land acquisition efforts for the future are unclear, partly because of sharply increased land values in the area and staff efforts in other programs. Beaver Brook has identified abutting properties they are interested in acquiring or gaining conservation easements on. Andrews says,

> We'd like to acquire some [more] of the inholdings and have identified key parcels (trail crossings and Rocky Brook and Beaver Brook properties), but we don't want to get involved in picking up parcels. We're also quite conscious of the fact that we have 10 percent of the land in the town, and we don't want to be perceived as a land-hungry nonprofit taking property off the tax rolls—even though we all know that is beneficial.

The danger of the perception of a "land-hungry nonprofit" is particularly notable because of the structure and local impact of New Hampshire's tax system. New Hampshire is a lonely holdout in the modern age as a state without either broad-based sales or income tax. Consequently, government services, including public schools and all municipal services, are financed exclusively through local property taxes and numerous fees imposed by the state.

As a charitable organization, Beaver Brook is exempt from local property taxes, so the financial implications of adding private taxable lands to the exempted lands can be a critical local political issue with predictable financial impacts. Like many other private educational organizations in the state, the BBA continues a practice started by Hollis Nichols of making an unrequested "payment in lieu of taxes" to the towns of Hollis and Brookline. Though New Hampshire is without a broad-based sales tax, it does have many specific sales and use taxes, including a 10 percent timber harvest tax whose proceeds benefit the towns.

Mullin is more cautious than Andrews about future land acquisitions, stating that with the rise in value of the surrounding lands (in part because of the amenity of open space that Beaver Brook provides adjacent landowners), he does not foresee any major land acquisitions by Beaver Brook or its new Nichols-Smith Conservation Land Trust. Mullin may be reacting to his role as an executive director still catching up with the growth of educational programs and with years of deferred maintenance on buildings and trails prior to his arrival on staff. The organization had experienced great leaps in management and program delivery since Mullin's arrival in 1995.

One long-term management issue is the fact that many of the trails crossing private land are based on handshake agreements with Jeff Smith. According to Mullin, "For some of the inholders, I think the idea of giving the land to Beaver Brook galls them a little bit. So, they have been thinking about it for a while, even though they have no practical use or access and don't want to continue paying taxes on it." Andrews adds, "Some people have the idea that Beaver Brook is sitting on a big pile of money because Hollis Nichols at one time was our money source. They seem to think we could purchase their land at a big price. . . . I keep my fingers crossed and hope that the issue of trails going across private property doesn't become an issue in the future."

The BBA's effort is a microcosm of the challenges facing communities at the urban–rural interface. It deals with issues of class illustrated by the changes of the Roxbury Latin student body (and the transfer of the majority of the school-based programs to the now more influential urban area of Nashua) and the change of the local communities of Hollis and Brookline from working farm towns to commuter/bedroom communities with expensive new housing sprouting among the hay fields. It deals as well with the disconnection of children and adults from the natural environment and with the need for a different and smarter forestry management and restoration effort for the entire watershed. Beaver Brook, in the course of its education programs, is managing its forestlands to improve its condition, harvestable value, wildlife habitat, and recreational potential while consciously modeling an example for the region. Both the towns and the BBA have contributed to and benefited from the studies of the Environmental Protection Agency's Merrimack Watershed Initiative and are explicitly conscious of their role in the larger picture.

The BBA board's mission has been rewritten from "dedication to the advancement of knowledge and appreciation of the natural world among people of all ages" to "promote understanding of natural world interrelationships and encourage conservation of natural resources through education and stewardship." Its objectives include natural resource education, land protection, natural resource stewardship, land and water management, demonstration farms, outreach and community relations, and facilities management—links to the past and perhaps steps to a sustainable future for the watershed.

Mullin concluded that the BBA's

key challenges for the next ten years include maintaining the integrity of the natural resources in the face of growing population. Whether we expand our program or not, the population visiting Beaver Brook land is going to increase. We have more than half a dozen access points to our property, and the number of visitors is steadily increasing. I'm worried about the fact that the town of Hollis is changing from rural–suburban to suburban–urban and the changes that will come about as a result of the increased uses by the people who live next door.

New England Prospects

For Mark Lapping and other contributors to the 1982 book *New England Prospects,* the question posed by the evolution of a "working rural landscape" might be, Do the BBA lands make a difference in a landscape view of the ecology of the region, or are they solely a new kind of theme park for the ever-growing population of the region? Steve Blackmer, president of the Northern Forest Center[14] (a regional forest and cultural protection think tank based in Concord, New Hampshire) says that despite the encroaching population growth and sprawl, it is still an open question. "A piece of land like that can be critical if it is part of a broader landscape conservation effort. If, however, it becomes an island of 2,200 acres surrounded by housing developments, it is of limited value (unless it happens to contain some specific instance of an endangered species)." Blackmer continues, "For Beaver Brook, the question is whether there is the potential for enough other protected land around the reservation to make up a meaningful network of protected areas and corridors. I think the chance is still there, but it would be very easy to let the region go the way of so many nice forests."

Acknowledgments

Responsibility for any errors in fact or interpretation lie solely with the people on the following list (just kidding—of course, the author accepts full responsibility for any errors). Many individuals contributed to the research for this case study, including Dick Ober of the Society for the Protection of New Hampshire's Forests; Curt Laffin and Ralph Goodno of the Merrimack River Watershed Council; Trish Garrigan from the Environmental Protection Agency's Merrimack Watershed Initiative; Steve Blackmer, president of the Northern Forest Center; Kelly Short of the New Hampshire Rivers Council; Linda Kennedy of the New Hampshire Department of Revenue Administration; Dave Delaney, geographic information systems guru of the EPA's Merrimack Watershed Initiative; the staff of the New Hampshire Historical Society; Jonathan Nute, Hillsborough County Cooperative Extension agent; John Ferguson, consulting forester; Karen Bennett, University of New Hampshire Cooperative Extension Service; Lee Kantar, Beaver Brook Association; and Thomas Brendler of the New England Forest

Trust. This list would be incomplete without special thanks to Syd Lavigne, Jane Munson, Steve Blackmer, and Kelly Short, all of Concord New Hampshire; Darshan Brach of Boston; and Cassie Thomas of the National Park Service's Rivers Program for their friendship, advice and sustenance.

Special thanks are also especially due to Tom Mullin, BBA executive director, for his patience and time with multiple requests for materials, interviews, and tours of the BBA property; Ralph Andrews, BBA trustee, for his time, commitment, wit, and wisdom; and Jonathan Kusel of Forest Community Research and Nancy Parent for their inspiration, friendship, editing, and patience.

Notes

1. See, for example, John Berger, *Restoring the Earth* (New York: Knopf, 1985), and Lynne Cherry, *A River Ran Wild* (New York: Harcourt Brace, 1992).

2. See, for example, "Gordon Smith and the Piscataquog Watershed Association," *Forest Notes,* Summer 1997, 23.

3. Telephone interview with Linda Kennedy, New Hampshire Department of Revenue Administration, August 4, 1997.

4. Selectmen are the part-time chief elected officials in most small New England towns. Selectmen have powers somewhat analogous to county commissioners in the western United States or city councilors in cities without a strong mayoral system, with some crucial differences.

5. Population figures from 1990 to 1996 from the U.S. Bureau of the Census Annual Time Series found at www.census.gov/population/estimates/metro-city/sets96/sc96t-NH.txt. Population Projections to 2010 from the plotted map "Merrimack River Watershed Population Density and Projected Change," EPA Merrimack River Initiative, March 1996.

6. Population estimate from U.S. Bureau of the Census data of area ranging roughly from Buffalo, New York; to Montreal; to Portland, Maine; to Baltimore, Maryland.

7. Beaver Brook Timber Inventory, Summer of 1979 by Karen Bennett, BBA Files.

8. Contrast this with the 16,693 program participants in 1996.

9. Mark Lapping, "Toward a Working Rural Landscape," in *New England Prospects: Critical Choices in a Time of Change,* ed. Carl H. Reidel, Hanover, N.H.: University Press of New England, 1982, 59–84.

10. New Hampshire alone shows the trend clearly with a decline from a high of over 30,000 farms in 1880 to approximately 15,000 in 1940 to under 5,000 in 1970. Acres of farmland declined in similar proportion; Lapping, "Toward a Working Rural Landscape," 62. The dangers of population expansion in the Beaver Brook area along the Massachusetts border were clearly identified in the essay as well, with the population change map showing a growth of greater than 5.6 percent in Hillsborough County between 1970 and 1976; Lapping, "Toward a Working Rural Landscape," 81.

11. Lapping, "Toward a Working Rural Landscape," 81.

12. For a sampling of recent analysis on this topic, see, for example, Robert W. Adler, "Addressing Barriers to Watershed Protection," *Environmental Law* 25, no. 4 (Fall 1995): 973–1106, and Peter M. Lavigne, "Watershed Approaches: What Have We Learned?" *River Voices* 6, no. 3 (Fall/Winter 1995): 1.

13. The BBA, as a nonprofit educational institution, is not required to publish a public financial statement. These figures were obtained in interviews with the BBA executive director and from a cursory treasurer's report in the 1996 annual report.

14. Blackmer is an experienced policy advocate and forester with degrees from Dartmouth and the Yale University School of Forestry who over the past two decades has served as vice president for policy for the Society for the Protection of New Hampshire's Forests, conservation director of the Appalachian Mountain Club, founder of the Concord Community Land Trust, chair of the New Hampshire Rivers Campaign, and city councilor in Concord, New Hampshire, among other activities. He can be reached at The Northern Forest Center, P.O. Box 210, Concord, NH 03302-0210; e-mail: info@northernforest.org or at www.northernforest.org.

References

Adler, Robert W. "Addressing Barriers to Watershed Protection." *Environmental Law* 25, no. 4 (Fall 1995): 973–1106.

Beaver Brook Association Annual Report (1996).

Dobbs, David, and Richard Ober. *The Northern Forest.* Post Mills, Vt.: Chelsea Green, 1995.

"Gordon Russell and the Piscataquog Watershed Association." *Forest Notes,* Summer 1997, 23.

Interviews and site visits in June and August 1997 with Lee Kantar, Tom Mullin, and Ralph Andrews of the Beaver Brook Association; foresters Karen Bennett and John Ferguson; and Jonathan Nute of the Hillsborough County Cooperative Extension.

Interviews in 1997 with Dick Ober and Paul Doscher of the Society for the Protection of New Hampshire's Forests and Ralph Goodno and Curt Laffin of the Merrimack River Watershed Council.

Interviews and correspondence in 1998 with Ralph Andrews, Tom Mullin, and Lee Kantar of Beaver Brook Association; Steve Blackmer of the Northern Forest Center; and Ralph Goodno of the Merrimack River Watershed Council.

Merrimack River Watershed Council (56 Island St., P.O. Box 1377, Lawrence, MA 01842-2577).

Merrimack River Watershed Protection Initiative: Past, Present, Future. U.S. EPA Region 1 Water Management Division, November 1987.

New Hampshire Department of Revenue Administration. 1997. Current Use Report.

New Hampshire Forest Market Report 1996–1997, UNH Cooperative Extension.

Newsletters and miscellaneous publications of the Beaver Brook Association.

The Northern Forest Center (P.O. Box 210, Concord, NH 03302-0210).

Ober, Richard, ed. *At What Cost? Shaping the Land We Call New Hampshire.* Concord, N.H.: Society for the Protection of New Hampshire's Forests, 1992.

Reidel, Carl H., ed. *New England Prospects: Critical Choices in a Time of Change.* Hanover, N.H.: University Press of New England, 1982.

Society for the Protection of New Hampshire's Forests (54 Portsmouth St., Concord, N.H. 03301).

Steinberg, Theodore. *Nature Incorporated: Industrialization and the Waters of New England.* New York: Cambridge University Press, 1991.

U.S. Bureau of the Census. www.census.gov.

Secondary References

Berger, John J. *Restoring the Earth: How Americans Are Working to Renew Our Damaged Environment.* New York: Knopf, 1986.

Cherry, Lynne. *A River Ran Wild.* San Diego: Harcourt Brace, 1992.

Cronon, William. *Changes in the Land: Indians, Colonists and the Ecology of New England.* New York: Hill & Wang, 1983.

Diers, Ted. *The Merrimack River Initiative: A Watershed Approach to Natural Resource Planning.* Proceedings of the Seventh National Urban Forest Conference, New York, September 1995.

League of Women Voters of New Hampshire. *New Hampshire's Land.* Concord: League of Women Voters of New Hampshire, 1975.

Massachusetts Department of Environmental Management. *Massachusetts Outdoors! For Our Common Good 1988–1992.* Boston: Massachusetts Department of Environmental Management, 1988.

Northern Forest Lands Council. *Finding Common Ground: Conserving the Northern Forest.* Concord, N.H.: Northern Forest Lands Council, 1994.

"Watershed Approaches: What Have We Learned?" *River Voices* 6, no. 3 (Fall/Winter 1995): 1.

Conclusion

Jonathan Kusel

The twelve cases profiled in this volume highlight community involvement in the management of forest resources that are vital to community well-being. Case researchers explored the effectiveness of community-based work that linked ecosystem health and community well-being. They examined factors that prompted group action and asked whether groups were making a difference on the land and in their communities.

The very existence and the work of the community-based groups reflect less on the success of community-based approaches than on the continued failure of traditional resource management and the paralyzing gridlock associated with natural resource management. In so many of the cases, community members rolled up their sleeves and began to work together not because they wanted to but because they had to. Because most of the community-based groups in these case studies are relatively new, and because one of the lessons that we have learned is that achieving successes takes far more time than anyone imagines at the outset, the focus here is on some of the factors stimulating community-based group formation and work. It is these factors that will continue to challenge community-based groups and their ability to address them and will, at least in part, determine their success.

A primary reason community members came together was because their access to land or land management decision-making processes was constrained or because the terms of engagement were unacceptable. In simple terms, they wanted a voice, which is not to be confused with control. Over the past three decades, and particularly in the West with its vast tracts of government-administered land, public involvement in the management of that land has been treated more as a mandated activity and necessary evil than as part of an active process integral to successful resource management. Private land management, governed by federal, state, and local law, typically offered even fewer opportunities for meaningful participation. One reason the Applegate Partnership started was because members recognized that a coherent plan for the watershed required bringing multiple agencies and public and private ownerships together in ways that had not been done before. And in Lake Umbagog in New Hampshire, coming to grips with development around the lake meant that residents had to transcend administrative and organization boundaries pertaining to private land and public resources.

Another reason community members came together was because local knowledge and perspective had for too long been ignored, and this was not simply due to faulty public involvement processes. Gifford Pinchot got it wrong; sound forestry was not the province of only scientifically trained and dispassionate experts. Residents, like those in the Ponderosa Pine Partnership in Colorado and the Swan Valley of Montana, recognized that local perspective was needed because of the local variability of the forest conditions and because of the growing recognition that long-term engagement with the land and community meant something, not the least of which was a commitment to maintaining long-term health and productivity of the land and the people who rely on it. The Beaver Brook Association in the Merrimack River Watershed in New England and the Western Upper Peninsula Improvement District in Michigan recognized explicitly in their work that humans were part of the natural systems and that forest ecosystems needed to be managed with that in mind. From an urban orientation, the Baltimore case makes a similar point.

Increasing recognition of the value of local knowledge and perspective also grew with increasing disenchantment with the hegemony of the managerial and scientific elite that too often seem to exacerbate problems rather than solve them. The disenchantment with expert-led forestry was also stimulated by the spillover from community development practice in non-resource-focused disciplines in the United States and from resource management and community-based development outside the country. A new civic science responsive to local stewardship interests has been called for.

Like community-based work stimulated by community development practices in other fields and community-based forestry outside the country, the rise of community-based forestry in the United States is taking place during a renaissance of the advancement of the concept of community and democratic practice. Closely related to this point is that interest-based politics results in insiders and outsiders in decision process.

The rise of community-based work has been stimulated by the recognition of residents that their local communities were a Ping-Pong ball in a game played by distant interest groups. Scientists could be found on any side. Catron County is a potent example of where interest group battles led to debilitating internal community conflict. Decision processes that leave out communities and groups within communities not only are undemocratic but also result in practices that do not adequately articulate the issues or problems that community members feel need to be addressed. While interest groups regularly claim to hold the best interests of the community at heart, fierce battles have played out as communities were often fought *over* but rarely fought *for*.

Attempts to reverse long-term practices that impoverished the land or degrade communities led to community-based work such as that of the Hoopa Tribe in California. With access and control over their reservation land, the Hupa people offer an example of how making the connection between culture, community, and the forest can rebuild and restore both the people and the land. The City of New York realized that it would be cheaper to invest in upstream communities and their land management practices rather than pay for pollution control equipment. While the New York case can be seen simply as identification of a cheaper alternative for the city—and it may prove to be that—what is revolutionary is that New York City invested in people and the landscape of the upper Hudson watershed, a decision that carried with it a considerable amount of political risk and tremendous uncertainty. Reversing long-term impoverishment of people and landscapes, whether it is in Baltimore; in Aitken County, Minnesota; on the Hoopa Reservation in California; or in the Applegate Valley of Oregon, because of the institutional barriers is perhaps one of the greatest challenges of all for community-focused efforts. Including *all* the human and ecological costs of doing business is part of this work. It is not about finding someone to blame for past transgressions. Rather, it is about figuring out how to make future investments in people, communities, and the land.

While almost every study concludes with saying more research is needed, alas, this one is no different. Community-based involvement in natural resource management is a relatively new phenomenon, certainly with the increasing emergence across the country. More research is needed on community-based groups and their work to better understand the connection between community well-being and ecosystem health. Equally important, participatory research and learning and a civic science are needed to advance the work of existing groups and to identify how and where community-based approaches might be effectively utilized and advanced.

Though perhaps more sobered by their case study work, the case study researchers continue to believe in the value of community-based approaches. These cases reflect some of the many possibilities and hopes of residents across the country. For the researchers and members of the Seventh American Forest Congress Communities Committee, they reflect also the kinds of projects both groups hope to see a lot more of in the future.

Index

65–67, 91–92, 107–8, 109, 153–54, 196, 197–98, 218
"Toward a Working Rural Landscape," 266, 277nn10–11
Tree Farm Program, 265
Tree planting, 182
Tree Tribe, 182, 184
Tribal sovereignty, 52
Trinity River, 30, 34, 49–50
Tsemeta Forest Nursery, 41, 44–45
Turner, Frederick, 57–58

Umbagog, Lake: budgetary crisis for, 145–46; development of, 139–40, 147; history of, 135, 136–38
Umbagog National Wildlife Refuge: creation of, 141–43; local assessment of, 143–46
Unionization, 228–29
Unverzagt, Mark, 97
Upper Androscoggin Valley, New Hampshire, 146–47
Upper Swan Valley, Montana, 149–69: bull trout preservation in, 157; community well-being of, 158–61; ecological setting of, 149, 151–55; economic diversification plan for, 157; employment in, 152–53; land management of, 158–61; social setting of, 149–50, 151–55. See also Swan Citizens' Ad Hoc Committee
Urban forests: in Baltimore, Maryland, 173, 174, 180, 181–84; benefits of, 180; in New Hampshire, 258, 263–64; restoration of, 181–84, 260
Urban Resources Initiative, 174, 181
"Urban wilderness" parks, 173

Vallejos, Laura, 109
VETS (Victims of Environmental Terrorism and Subversion), 154

Wahkiakum County, Washington: ecosystem of, 224; grange movement in, 223; growth management non-

participation of, 248; income of, 225, 246–47, 247; land allotment of, 225; land ownership of, 224; population of, 225–26
Wait, Scott, 195
Washington: demographics of, 224, 246; Department of Natural Resources, 248; ecosystem of, 224; employment in, 225, 246–47, 247; forest restoration in, 250–51; Growth Management Act, 247, 248; history of, 222–23; income of, 225, 246–47, 247; land management of, 248; land ownership in, 224, 224–25, 225; salmon allocation in, 223, 224, 236–37, 247; watershed restoration in, 236, 237. See also Columbia-Pacific Resource Conservation and Development Council
Wastewater treatment, 230, 240, 252–53
Water: community well-being and, 3–24; enhancement programs, 17–20; filtration, 3–4; New York City, 5; pollution, 57, 81n2, 176, 178, 179, 262; quality, 3–24; rights, 34; waste, 230, 240, 252–53
Watershed(s): Applegate, 126–27; associations, 176–79; Baltimore, 173, 176–81; Catskill, 5–6; Chesapeake Bay, 171; communities, 6–7; Delaware, 5–6; education programs, 174, 179; forestland in, 5–6, 17–20, 257–58, 269–70; Gwynns Falls, 173, 176–77, 179–81, 182–83; Herring Run, 173, 179; Jones Falls, 173, 177–78; management, 267; Merrimack River, 257–79; Nashua River, 259, 262; pollution, 176, 178, 179, 262; restoration, 45–48, 126–27, 176–79, 236, 237, 259, 260, 262; Revitalizing Baltimore projects on, 176–81; in Washington, 236, 237. See also specific names of watersheds
Watershed Agreement: barriers to, 20–21; decision making under, 16–17;

About the Contributors

Elisa Adler worked as a research associate with Forest Community Research for this project. For many years she worked as an English instructor, editor, and translator. She lives in the northern Sierra Nevada.

Mark Baker is a program associate at Forest Community Research based in Arcata, California. He has studied community forestry and local irrigation management in India as well as the evolution of watershed institutions in California.

Jill Belsky is an associate professor of sociology at the University of Montana, Missoula, specializing in rural and development sociology, environmental sociology, and community-based resource management. She lives in Missoula.

Thomas Brendler is the executive director of the National Network of Forest Practitioners, a membership association of people working to create job and business opportunities around sustainable forestry and forest restoration. He lives in Providence, Rhode Island.

Sam Burns is professor of sociology and the director of research for the Office of Community Services at Fort Lewis College in Colorado. He has worked as a facilitator and coordinator on several projects with the U.S. Forest Service on the San Juan National Forest.

Barb Cestero is a research associate with the Sonoran Institute's Northwest Office in Bozeman, Montana. She works with communities and public land managers involved in community-based conservation projects and currently directs their Yellowstone to Yukon initiative.

Gerry Gray directs the Forest Policy Center at American Forests, where he is vice president, and serves on the Steering Committee of the Communities Committee. He lives in the Washington, D.C., area.

Jonathan Kusel is founder and director of Forest Community Research. He is rural sociologist who has conducted social assessments of large rural regions of the western United States and has worked with community groups throughout the U.S. He lives in the northern Sierra Nevada.

Jonathan Lange is professor of communication and director of training and organization development at Southern Oregon University. He conducts research on environmental conflict and is a consultant in mediation and conflict management. He lives in Ashland, Oregon.

Peter Lavigne is an attorney specializing in environmental and administrative law. He is director of the Watershed Management Professional Program at Portland State University and president of The Rivers Foundation of the Americas. He lives in Portland, Oregon.

Kimberly McDonald worked for ten years as a lawyer before becoming an instructor for the College of Forest Resources at the University of Washington, Seattle. She lives in Seattle.

Rebecca McLain is a principal with the Institute for Culture and Ecology. She is a sociologist who conducts research on nontimber forest products and mushroom harvesting and community development. She lives in Portland, Oregon.

Mary Mitsos is director of community conservation for the National Forests Foundation following many years as director of community-based forest stewardship at the Pinchot Institute. She is a member of the Steering Committee of the Communities Committee. She lives in Missoula, Montana.

Ann Moote is a research specialist with the Ecological Restoration Institute at Northern Arizona University. She is involved with numerous community-based partnerships in the Southwest and serves on the Steering Committee of the Communities Committee. She lives in Flagstaff, Arizona.

Tim Richard is a research associate with the Office of Community Services at Fort Lewis in Colorado. He lives in Durango, Colorado.

Ellen Stein moved from the Western Governors Association to her position of executive director of the Community Agriculture Alliance. She lives in Steamboat Springs, Colorado.

Victoria Sturtevant is professor of sociology at Southern Oregon University and is a consultant for the U.S. Forest Service and the Bureau of Land Management. She lives in Ashland, Oregon.